THE STATE AND ECONOMIC LIFE

EDITORS: Mel Watkins, University of Toronto; Leo Panitch, York University

13 MICHAEL M. ATKINSON and WILLIAM D. COLEMAN

The State, Business, and Industrial Change in Canada

The late twentieth century has seen profound changes in the character of the international economic order. According to the authors of this study, Canada has failed to come to terms with those changes. Our industrial policy is diffuse, ad hoc, and sectoral. Michael Atkinson and William Coleman argue that in order to analyse Canada's industrial policy effectively, particular attention must be given to industry organization, state structures, and systems of interest intermediation at the sectoral level.

To make such an analysis they introduce the concept of policy network, and apply it to three types of industrial sectors: the research-intensive sectors of telecommunications manufacturing and pharmaceuticals; the rapidly changing sectors of petrochemicals and meat processing; and the contracting and troubled sectors of textiles, clothing, and dairy processing.

Through the lens of these sectors Coleman and Atkinson shed considerable light on the intersection of political considerations and policy development, and offer a new base on which to move forward in planning for economic growth.

MICHAEL ATKINSON is Professor of Political Science, McMaster University. He is co-author of *The Canadian Legislative System* and co-editor of *The Politics of Canadian Public Policy*.

WILLIAM COLEMAN is also Professor of Political Science at McMaster University. He is the author of *The Independence Movement in Quebec, 1945–1980* and *Business and Politics: A Study in Collective Action*.

The State, Business, and Industrial Change in Canada

MICHAEL M. ATKINSON

WILLIAM D. COLEMAN

UNIVERSITY OF TORONTO PRESS
Toronto Buffalo London

© University of Toronto Press 1989
Toronto Buffalo London
Printed in Canada

ISBN 0-8020-5682-2 (cloth)
ISBN 0-8020-6615-1 (paper)

Printed on acid-free paper

Canadian Cataloguing in Publication Data

Atkinson, Michael M.
  The State, Business, and Industrial Change in Canada

  Includes bibliographical references and index.
  ISBN 0-8020-5682-2 (bound). – ISBN 0-8020-6615-1 (pbk.)

  1. Industry and state – Canada. I. Coleman,
  William D. (William Donald), 1950-   . II. Title.

  HD3616.C33A86 1989   338.971   C89-093710-9

Cover photo:
Artist's conception of MSAT (Mobile Satellite) in geostationary orbit (courtesy Department of Communications)

For Peter, Margaret, and Rosa

Contents

Preface

This project began as an innocent conversation. One of us (we can't remember who) asked what political conditions would be necessary for the Canadian state to intervene effectively on the side of industrial development. That seemed to be a straightforward question. The answer would probably require a little research. Nothing too taxing.

In 1982 we began to live with the consequences of our innocence. We advanced upon Ottawa in the fall of that year. Our object was to listen and to learn, and we have been listening and learning ever since. The fact that we were never forced into wholesale retreat is a testament to the patience of the men and women we interviewed. Almost all showed keen interest in our project and a remarkable willingness to co-operate. One by one they helped us to the point that we could begin to write this book. Peter McGuire extended his hospitality and offered us the benefit of years of political experience. We owe him a special debt of gratitude.

Since then we have relied heavily on the background information, coding assistance, and data analysis supplied by our research assistants, Shelley Gilmour, Ken Marley, Bob Nigol, and Richard Powers. They must have wondered at times if we knew what we were doing or if we would ever finish. Now that we have, it's possible to say something we knew all along: it couldn't have been done without them.

The painstaking job of transcribing interviews, so that we could pore over them, fell to a wonderful secretary, Yvonne Moss. The broader task of organizing our lives – taking our telephone calls, setting up our meetings, and managing our manuscript – was performed by three outstanding secretaries: Lori Hill, Mara Minini, and Lori Farrell.

Our colleagues at McMaster suffered quietly through this project, always expressing interest, but never asking too many sensitive questions (such as:

'When will this be finished?'). We would like to thank, in particular, Kim Richard Nossal, Henry Jacek, Bill Chandler, and Tom Lewis for offering their help so willingly. Simon McInnes arranged for us to present a preliminary version of some of the ideas in chapter four to a bracingly sceptical seminar at the Ministry of State for Science and Technology. Thanks also go to Jeanne Kirk Laux, Wyn Grant, G.A. Ferguson, Joel Lexchin, Marsha Chandler, Kenneth Woodside, Kenneth Woodrow, and J.B. Morrissey, all of whom read parts of this manuscript and offered expert advice.

At the University of Toronto Press, we extend our grateful thanks to Virgil Duff, the managing editor, and to Lydia Burton, whose expert copy editing introduced us to (and saved us from) the dangling demonstrative pronoun. We also owe a debt of gratitude, as they are well aware, to our colleagues at the University of Toronto, Marsha Chandler and Peter Russell.

This research would not have been possible without the generous assistance of the Social Sciences and Humanities Research Council. The council stuck with us for three years, and we take special pleasure in acknowledging its support. This book has been published with the help of a grant from the Social Science Federation of Canada, using funds provided by the council. We extend our sincere thanks to the federation.

We have published several articles based on the data collected in this project. One of these articles appeared in the *British Journal of Political Science* (vol. 19 [January 1989]: 48–67) and we gratefully acknowledge their permission to publish it, in revised form, as chapter four of this book. Chapter three was originally presented as a paper at a conference on German and Canadian federalism held at McMaster University in 1985. Part of this chapter appeared in William Chandler and Christian Zollner, eds, *Challenges to Federalism*, published by the Institute of Intergovernmental Relations at Queen's University (1989).

Our final thanks go to the two anonymous readers of our manuscript. This project has taught us a great deal, not the least of which is the value of constructive criticism. These readers were both demanding and constructive, and we made some important changes based on their comments.

Our families have been most understanding and supportive, but if we thank them too heartily they will grow suspicious. They already sense that this may not be the end.

Abbreviations

AIAC	Aerospace Industries Association of Canada
BCNI	Business Council on National Issues
CAMI	Canadian Apparel Manufacturers Institute
CATA	Canadian Advanced Technology Association
CCA	Department of Consumer and Corporate Affairs
CCPA	Canadian Chemical Producers Association
CDC	Canadian Dairy Commission
CDMA	Canadian Drug Manufacturers Association
CIRB	Canadian Industrial Renewal Board
CMA	Canadian Manufacturers' Association
CMC	Canadian Meat Council
CTI	Canadian Textiles Institute
DFC	Dairy Farmers of Canada
DOC	Department of Communications
DREE	Department of Regional Economic Expansion
DRIE	Department of Regional Industrial Expansion
EC	European Community
EEMAC	Electrical and Electronics Manufacturers Association of Canada
EMR	Department of Energy, Mines and Resources
GATT	General Agreement on Tariffs and Trade
GPMC	Grocery Products Manufacturers of Canada
HPB	Health Protection Branch
ITC	Department of Industry, Trade and Commerce
MFA	Multi-fibre Arrangement
MNC	multinational corporation
MSED	Ministry of State for Economic Development
NDC	National Dairy Council of Canada

NEP	National Energy Program
NIC	newly industrializing country
NRC	National Research Council
OCS	office communications systems
PCO	Privy Council Office
R&D	research and development
SPI	Society of the Plastics Industry of Canada
TCB	Textile and Clothing Board
TLC	Trades and Labour Congress

The State, Business, and
Industrial Change in Canada

Introduction:
Political Institutions and
Public Policy

The debate in Canada in the 1980s over a policy for Canadian industry had some striking similarities to the debate that took place exactly a century earlier. The big issues appeared to be the same. On one side, there were the proponents of free trade with the United States. These included industrialists dependent on American firms for intermediate goods, some sections of the farming community fearful of the costs associated with trade barriers, and resource firms already exporting heavily to the United States. Among the opponents of free trade were global traders and economic nationalists concerned about the political and economic integrity of Canada, workers fearful of losing their jobs, farmers concerned about retaining domestic markets, and businesses apprehensive about direct competition with American firms. But the party alignments and the majority position of the business community had changed. In the 1880s, most of the business community supported protectionist measures and the Conservative party of John A. Macdonald. In the 1980s, the business community stood virtually united behind a bilateral free-trade agreement that the Mulroney Conservatives had signed with the United States.

Despite this change in political alignments, the key characteristic of industrial policy in each era was the same: minimal intrusion by the state into the affairs of firms. In neither period did the state itself undertake any systematic industrial planning. Both the National Policy tariffs and the free-trade agreement respected the autonomy of the firm and the individualist ethic. Both allowed governments to pay some attention to the political consequences of individual business failures without compromising seriously overall policy objectives.

This market-oriented solution to the problems of industrial growth invited considerable criticism in the Canada of the 1980s. Opponents argued that developments in the international economy, particularly changes in the nature and intensity of international competition, demanded a national economic response. They pointed to a number of states that had stepped in to shape advantages for domestic firms. Of course, these industrial strategies placed heavy demands on both state bureaucracies and national business communities. Planning was necessary and it required regular consultation with business and occasional consultation with labour. Co-ordination of policies across a number of areas – research and development, plant modernization, employee training, and social welfare – was the result. Opponents of the free-trade option argued that Canada needed to adopt similar strategies if it was going to succeed in this new and difficult economic world.

This debate over Canada's economic future has been dominated by these arguments about the advisability of state intervention in the economy. There is no shortage of analysts dedicated to explaining what type of policy we should have. But it is not our intention to review these arguments or to evaluate economic critiques of state intervention. Our subject is the politics of industrial policy. Our major question is: What types of industrial policy, specifically policy for secondary manufacturing, are possible for a country with a small, open economy? We approach this question impressed by the need to specify political requirements. These requirements are not understood well nor have they been given the prominence they deserve in discussions of industrial policy. This book seeks to fill this gap by offering an assessment of the institutions of industrial policy making and the structure of state/society relations in key areas of secondary manufacturing. But an understanding of the political requirements of a realizable industrial policy begins with an appreciation of the role of institutions in general in the policy-making process.

An Institutional Approach

Theoretical work in modern economics and political science has increasingly assumed that policy outcomes are best understood, in the words of James March and Johan Olsen, 'as the aggregate consequences of behavior comprehensible at the individual or group level.'[1] This approach to the political process takes the rational individual as its principal unit of analysis and argues that collective behaviour should be understood as the product of individual choices. In this perspective, as Peter Hall notes,'policies are best explained as the outcome of a game-like contest in which power-seeking individuals, or institutions acting like individuals, compete for resources and the support of electors who are also seeking to maximize their personal resources.'[2] From utilitarian premises and information about decision situations, it becomes possible to deduce rational behaviour.

In this version of political life, institutions are little more than rules of the game. They are not a source of preferences for political actors. Tastes and preferences are generated by exogenous forces such as the economy, class interests, and technology. Institutions govern decision making in the sense that they influence which societal preferences are included or excluded from the process of social choice. This interpretation of institutions thus owes a great deal to economics. The realm of politics is subsumed in a competitive equilibrium model where politicians have stable, exogenously determined preferences, and public policy is treated as a residual category of the economic system.

Modern conventions in market theories of economics picture a proper political system as forgoing most issues concerning the allocation of scarce resources. Within such a conception, politics may properly be involved in decisions about the distribution of wealth (and other initial resources) and in setting the rules of the game, but it is not properly involved in allocative decisions except to correct imperfections in the functioning of the free market, particularly externality problems and problems of concentration. [3]

Consequently, only certain types of questions are asked of political institutions: How efficient are they? What are their relative resource endowments? What are the preference curves of individual actors? [4]

We find these kinds of questions too restrictive. They ask little or nothing about what political actors value and how they come to acquire these values. Yet for the study of industrial policy, indeed for the study of any policy area, these are vital questions. They are especially so where the fit between political institutions and policy objectives is at issue. In subsequent chapters we examine in some detail the political requirements for industrial policy. In doing so, we assess the appropriateness of existing institutions and the range of policy options that a given set of political institutions can support. This latter question is crucial because, as Stephen Krasner notes, the 'range of options available to policymakers at any given point in time is a function of institutional capabilities that were put in place at some earlier period, possibly in response to very different environmental pressures.'[5] These historical legacies make it necessary to examine not just the efficiency but also the competence and integrity of institutions: Do political and societal institutions, joined in policy networks over a period of time, develop and use genuine expertise of relevance to policy problems? To what extent does the policy process shaped by institutional arrangements transcend special interests to take account of a larger public good?[6]

These questions imply that political life in general, and the preferences of political actors in particular, are likely to be heavily influenced by institutional experience. In this interpretation, institutions are able to structure political discourse and offer independent interpretations of what constitutes rationality.[7] Institutions are no longer viewed as aggregations of individuals or as extensions of societal cleavages. They are, or at least can be, autonomous and coherent actors capable of defining problems and diffusing the ideas, perceptions, and ideologies upon which individuals act. As such, an institutionalist approach to policy 'gives preferences as endogenous political explanation: preferences are formed through opposing and supporting institutions.'[8] Rationality is no longer exogenously determined, but is endogenous to institutions themselves. In this way, institutions have an enduring impact on economic and political processes independent of a narrowly construed set of current conditions. They not only aggregate individual 'preferences,' they shape individuals' values, influence the definition of interests, and provide opportunities for developing these further.

Such a perspective on institutions and public policy has two immediate implications.[9] First, a particular set of political and economic institutions will provide a measure of regularity in the *form* of policy – that is, how policy is designed, and how it is eventually implemented. Thus we argue in this book that the similarities in the debate over industrial policy between the present day and a century ago result in part from the enduring consequences of Canadian political institutions. Second, because institutions have a decisive impact on the form of policy, new types of policies or reforms to existing policies are often not possible without basic changes in institutional arrangements. As Krasner points out, institutional changes are never easy to accomplish.[10] If new policies are introduced without accompanying institutional changes, they will either be abandoned or gradually reworked in order to remain consistent with institutional constraints.

An emphasis on institutions is not something particularly novel in political science or economics. In both disciplines, institutional studies have a long tradition, albeit one that fell into disfavour in the post-war period. But we are not simply recalling those traditions. First, we intend to combine our knowledge of micro, or individual, political behaviour with a consideration of institutions writ large. Thus, documentary materials and research on organizational procedures and objectives are combined with information on the behaviour and attitudes of individuals operating within organizations in order to inform our understanding of those institutions. There is no contradiction between examining the interpretations of individuals at a given moment in time and stressing the importance of institutional traditions.[11] Individual perspectives can only be understood within an institutional context, while a careful analysis of the ideals and values of individuals will clarify further the nature of institutions.

Second, the institutional analysis undertaken here is not confined to the standard structures of parliamentary government and federalism. We locate our analysis in both state and society.[12] This means that we consider the organization of markets as well as the organization of the state, the relationship between financial and industrial capital as well as between line departments and central agencies. Most important, our consideration of industrial policy leads us to an examination of policy networks, systems of relationships among state and societal organizations.[13] These networks have a looser structure than the organizations themselves, and are best thought of as a 'negotiated order,' within each issue area.[14] We argue that policy networks exist throughout the policy-making system and that an institutional analysis, such as the one proposed here, requires an examination of these networks, the core values they embody, and the division of labour they presume.

Objectives and Organization

The first purpose of this book, then, is to demonstrate the relevance of organizational factors for the development of industrial policy. It is our premise, defended in part one, that in the study of industrial policy in Canada, particular attention must be given to industry organization, state structures, and systems of interest intermediation at the sectoral level. It is not that national policy structures or horizontal policy instruments are irrelevant. Far from it. But these structures and instruments leave considerable room for decision makers to countenance a variety of options when it comes to specific problems in a given sector.

Chapter one sets the stage for this argument by situating Canada in the global economy. Two basic types of industrial policy – anticipatory and reactive – are introduced and applied to the Canadian case. We argue that Canada has pursued primarily the reactive policy option at the macro or economy-wide level. But, elsewhere, policy innovation has depended on institutional characteristics specific to a given industry.

Part of the explanation for this pattern rests on the specific institutional characteristics of Canadian industry, the political system, and the state administration. They are the subjects of chapters two and three. Chapter two begins with an analysis of the relationship between the financial system and industrial development. It argues that the capital markets-based system in Canada and the commercial character of Canadian banking have bound business interests to an interpretation of industrial development based on the sanctity of the autonomous firm and a minimal role for the state. This perspective has continued to dominate policy making in Canada for over a century, despite the objections of labour and agriculture. Chapter two traces the political dominance of business to particular characteristics of the party and interest intermediation systems.

These institutional patterns have reinforced an industry culture hostile to state intervention. Kenneth Dyson has defined industry culture as a set of beliefs and practices arising from the micro organization of the economy and the relationships between government and business.[15] Characteristic of the Anglo-Saxon liberal tradition are a scepticism about government's competence in industrial affairs, an unwillingness to act in advance of political pressures, and a belief in the self-sufficiency of the firm.[16] These values appear to be common in Canadian business and government circles and arise from the pattern of economic development outlined in chapter two.

Chapter three contains an examination of state institutions. Although there are numerous examples of state intervention on a large scale in Canada, these have been primarily in the areas of resource extraction and transportation. Where intervention has occurred, it has not been premised on the need for a *dirigiste* state, committed to planning economic development. Chapter three argues that Canada has a weak state tradition with no appreciation of the state as a separate legal or political entity and no administrative/bureaucratic élite committed to broad projects of industrial development.

The legacy of this tradition is the absence of a capacity for centralized and co-ordinated control over industrial policy making. Efforts to bring some order to the bureaucratic/political machinery responsible for economic policy have been marked by conspicuous failure. As a result, industrial policy is very much the preserve of the line departments, whose expertise in these matters significantly outweighs what has been assembled at the centre. Yet many programs delivered by these departments are dominated by the logic of 'garbage can' decision making in which the goals of the programs become apparent only after implementation has occurred.[17] A weak state tradition means that officials at the centre of the state apparatus are both unwilling and unable to spearhead any particular vision of industrial development.

None the less, a wide array of policies, some with significant state direction, have been tried at the sectoral level in Canada. Understanding the shape of these policies, including why they succeed or fail, requires a close analysis of the specific institutional arrangements governing behaviour in the given sector. Chapter four provides a conceptual framework for examining the political economy of a given industrial sector. Central to this framework is the concept of policy network that is operationalized by employing two organizational variables: state structure (as it bears upon the sector) and the mobilization of producer interests in the sector. We identify six types of networks and argue that the network in place is critical to the choice of industrial policy instruments and goals in a sector. Some networks are capable of sustaining rather elaborate anticipatory policies, others only reactive policies.

In part two we examine in depth four types of industrial sectors and the policy networks that govern their behaviour. Chapter five treats two rapidly expanding sectors – communications satellites and telecommunications equipment – and shows how the Canadian state has intervened systematically and deeply in the former but relatively little in the latter. The pharmaceuticals industry, a more mature and stable sector, is the subject of chapter six. Here industrial policy has been largely regulatory in character and has been aimed at balancing the interests of large foreign-owned industry with the demands of consumer groups and domestically owned generic-drug firms. Chapter seven examines two sectors – petrochemicals and red meats – in which the industrial policy goal has been to establish world-scale manufacturing facilities to expand export opportunities. We conclude in chapter eight with an examination of three industries threatened with decline: dairy processing, textiles, and clothing. We show that different policy networks in each sector have contributed to their relative capacity to manage decline.

The concluding chapter examines the implications of our findings for theories of the Canadian state and for future policy options. It argues for a disaggregated view of the Canadian state as the only feasible means of understanding Canadian industrial policy making. What takes place at the macro-political level, which includes the basic features of parliamentary government, federalism, the party and interest-group systems, and the state bureaucracy, constrains but does not determine outcomes at the sectoral or meso level. Policy outcomes at the sectoral level depend on the institutional arrangements relating state agencies, interest groups, and industry structures, that is, the policy networks in place in the sector. In some cases, these arrangements have encouraged policy innovations.

A Note on Sources

As the reader will quickly discern, we have made extensive use in this book of the work of other Canadian academics, particularly in the field of political economy. The research volumes published by the Royal Commission on the Economic Union and Development Prospects for Canada have been of special importance. In addition, recent work on the developed economies and their political underpinnings has given us the opportunity to make comparisons that would otherwise have been impossible.

Our own views and approach are the product of a decade-long interest in business, bureaucracy, and industrial policy. We have drawn heavily, in this analysis, on our knowledge of and research on business-interest associations. We refer here in particular to a series of exploratory interviews and follow-up discussions with associations whose officials have been kind enough to share their views. In some instances, we were also able to make comparisons with European associations studied in the Organization of Business Interests research project headed by Philippe Schmitter and Wolfgang Streeck.[18] We have also followed and commented upon the myriad of programmatic responses and organizational changes that have marked industrial policy at the federal level in recent years.

Finally, our own understanding of the industrial policy process in Canada has been deeply influenced by interviews conducted in 1982 and 1983 with officials in the federal government responsible for the development and implementation of industrial policy. Four industrial sectors were chosen for intensive analysis: food processing, chemicals including pharmaceuticals, textiles and clothing, and telecommunications equipment. As noted above, these sectors were chosen in order to provide us with a mix of expanding, mature and stable, and declining industries. Between September 1982 and March 1983, interviews averaging a little more than an hour in length were completed with 102 officials. Research began in the lower levels of the bureaucracy in the line departments responsible for the above sectors and finished at the senior levels of these departments and in central agencies such as the Department of Finance and the Ministry of State for Economic Development (abolished in June 1984). At the end of each interview, officials were given a written questionnaire that contained some questions on political attitudes, on bureaucratic and extrabureaucratic contacts, and on personal background.

The resulting sample of officials was drawn from seventeen departments and agencies at a range of different ranks. Slightly over 22 per cent of the group were at the deputy minister and assistant deputy minister level, a further 20 per cent at the director general level, 29 per cent at the director level, and the remaining 29 per cent below the director level. The sample varied, too, in background and experience. A little over one-half the sample (56 per cent) had worked both in the private sector and in government. The most common professional background was in economics (26 per cent), followed by engineering (19 per cent) and commerce (9.7 per cent). As expected, the officials in the sample were highly educated: 94 per cent of them had earned a university degree and 76.7 per cent had proceeded to post-graduate studies. Finally, the group was almost exclusively male. The snowball sampling technique we used led us to include only 2 women in our set of 102 officials. (See appendix for format of interviews.)

These interviews concentrated on what might be thought of as the enduring themes of industrial policy in Canada. We are convinced that, taken together, they offer a compelling picture of the organizational culture of state and society in the realm of industrial policy. We refer to these interviews specifically in many parts of this book, but their value extends well beyond these references. The discussions we had with officials stimulated much of our thinking and have had an impact on all parts of this study. Although in chapter three we discuss the strongest attitude patterns and use these data to buttress our major arguments about the character of the Canadian state, our purpose in this volume is not to make an extensive report on this data set. These data, and our other primary sources, have been used instead to assist us to refine our conceptual appreciation of the industrial policy process in Canada and to provide us with much-needed detail in the policy areas discussed in the latter half of this book.

PART ONE

State and Economy:
An Institutional Perspective

1 Industrial Policy Options in a Changing Global Context

Canadians are constantly reminded of their middle-power status in the inter-national economic system. Although a participant in the economic summit process, Canada is often excluded from direct participation in key decisions, particularly monetary decisions, taken by the finance ministers of the largest OECD (Organization for Economic Cooperation and Development) countries. Invited to some parties but not to others, Canada exists in something of a shadow world on the international economic stage.

This 'neither here nor there' status is responsible, in important respects, for the ambivalent and ambiguous nature of much of Canadian economic policy. Like most of her partners in the OECD, Canada's economic fortunes lie in the world trading system. In fact, Canada is particularly vulnerable to changes in this system and to changes in the international monetary order that underlies it. In the international arena Canada is a policy taker, subject to the pressures of a hegemonic power when one exists and to the instability of economic anarchy when one does not.

In spite of, or indeed because of, the small and open character of the Canadian economy, some form of industrial policy will always be necessary in Canada. The critical question is just what type of industrial policy Canada can be expected to have. The answer requires, in the first instance, a consideration of the major production patterns evident in the Canadian economy, the available industrial policy options, and the historical pattern of industrial policy making in Canada. We argue that radical changes in Canada's approach to industrial policy are unlikely, but that opportunities for creative intervention do exist provided the necessary political requirements are met.

The Politics of Production

Canadians are no longer surprised by economic downturns. The business cycle has long since been absorbed into the economic policy-making frameworks of the Department of Finance. What has changed is the nature of policy making, or at least our understanding of it. It is no longer plausible to argue that a creative application of the tools of demand management constitutes the beginning and the end of enlightened economic policy. It seems more and more reasonable to suggest that at least some of our economic problems are structural. They have to do with the manner in which the productive process is organized and with the performance of key actors, both corporate and state, in managing changes forced on them by the exigencies of international competition and the changing character of domestic demand. It is not that macro-economic issues and the political business cycle are less important than was once assumed, only that micro-economic conditions and the politics of industrial adjustment are probably more important.

The differences between the politics of production today and at the end of the Second World War are striking. The international economic regime established in the post-war period has broken down, with profound repercussions for all Western societies. The Canadian economy had performed admirably during the war and policy makers were determined to devise policies suited to maintaining the growth of exports. For this reason, they were committed to increased international collaboration and the removal of trade barriers. Such an approach made particular sense because of the peculiar triangular trade relationship Canada enjoyed with the United States and Britain.[1] Canada remained in a high-deficit position with the former but in a strong surplus relation with the latter. The Canadian government thus gave strong support to the establishment of a new international economic order that included the Bretton Woods system and a multilateral approach to the reduction of trade barriers. Hence, Canadians supported fixed exchange rates, an end to trade discrimination, a decrease in tariff levels, and the multilateral settlement of disputes. Domestically, these policies were complemented by an 'optimistic' use of Keynesian policies: the state would have a marginal and indirect role in producing a suitable business climate and would occasionally tinker with the tax system to manipulate demand.[2]

While Canada's approach to international matters remained unchanged until the early 1970s, domestically the bloom was off the Keynesian rose within a decade of the end of the Second World War. The triangular trade relationship changed as the British market declined in importance, increasing the significance of bilateral trade with the United States. The relationship with the United

States was scrutinized more and more closely as policy makers became concerned about the development of Canada's secondary manufacturing base, a point emphasized in the report of the Royal Commission on Canada's Economic Prospects in 1957. In the mid 1950s, the Conservative party released proposals calling for more planning with an emphasis on increasing the level of manufacturing in Canada, a departure from Canadian Keynesianism.[3] As the downturn in the business cycle hit in the late 1950s, the Conservatives gradually introduced a series of sectoral and micro policies on an ad hoc basis. The retreat had begun in earnest. Over the ensuing decade, Conservative and Liberal governments alike multiplied such policy thrusts and gradually reorganized government departments in order to deliver more efficiently programs of support for Canadian industry.

This search for alternative policy avenues was prompted by growing evidence that changes in the international economic regime were rendering macro-economic strategies insufficient for managing capitalist economies. The shift of production to new sites in the global economy had begun to threaten domestic industry. Developed countries still trade primarily with one another, but the share of manufacturing exports from developing countries increased from about 5 per cent in 1970 to 11 per cent by 1980. The penetration of manufactured goods from newly industrializing countries into the markets of developed economies constituted the most dynamic element in world trade by the 1970s.[4] Several prominent sectors in the developed economies faced intensifying competition. In Canada, clothing, textiles, consumer electronics, and shipbuilding, among others, were pushed to the brink of collapse by these changes.

The product-cycle effects of technological innovation are only partly responsible for these developments. It is undoubtedly true that products initially developed in the home markets of OECD countries were gradually shifted to low-cost producers as the technology became standardized and accessible. But the product cycle itself has been superceded by multinational corporations (MNCs) that are prepared to conduct global searches for the most appropriate site on which to manufacture a wide variety of products. These global scanners are not simply transferring standardized technology and they are not committed to ensuring that developed countries continue to enjoy the advantage of technological leadership.[5] Moreover, the goods being exported are not limited to traditional sectors such as textiles and consumer electronics. No product is immune from this strategic behaviour unless it enjoys an unassailable comparative advantage, an increasingly unique situation.

These changes in production sites were one signal that the international economic regime was undergoing a significant transformation. A second feature of this regime, the Bretton Woods system, collapsed in the early 1970s. In this system, the American dollar had served as the international reserve currency and all participant countries were obliged to buy their own currencies, with American dollars, at a fixed rate of exchange. The system could work as long as participants were sufficiently satisfied with the performance of the American economy to risk holding their assets in American dollars, which were convertible to gold at a fixed rate. By the 1970s this confidence had eroded. Domestic inflation caused by President Johnson's response to the Vietnam War, combined with a drastic decline in the merchandise trade balance, invited international speculation on the future of the dollar as a reserve currency. The American response was to abandon its commitment to convert foreign currencies at a fixed rate of exchange and to usher in the system of floating rates.

This move destabilized patterns of international trade even further, creating a potentially serious problem for Canada, a trading nation with an open economy. Their elegant simplicity notwithstanding, floating rates have placed additional pressure on the traded-goods sector of economies. The price for running a deficit is no longer simply an adjustment in the level of domestic prices. It now includes the prospect of a fluctuating exchange rate, one that responds not only to trade results, but also to currency speculation. And a shift in the demand for a currency, prompted by changing views about its safety as a store of value, has an independent effect on the value of a country's tradables.[6]

The crisis in the international economy that began in the 1970s was not only a crisis of production but also one of theory. Increasing scepticism about the soundness of economic theory created a series of disputes best illustrated by the evident lack of consensus on just which economic developments should be considered 'problems.' For some observers, the decline of traditional industries does not constitute a policy problem; the latter arises only when politicians and bureaucrats attempt to reverse the process.[7] For others, structural changes in the economy produce patterns of employment and a distribution of income that are decidedly public matters.[8] Just as governments once assumed responsibility for stabilizing the economy, so they must now recognize, it is argued, that the structure of the economy – what goods are produced, by whom, and where – is a public policy concern.

With debate firmly engaged on the subject of what are the real economic problems, opportunities abound for further disagreements on the forces underlying economic change. Developments such as the global rationalization of production by multinational corporations, the saturation of OECD markets by standardized products, and the fall in productivity among advanced capitalist countries have all been mentioned as illustrative of, or causes of, current dislocations. Their relative importance, as well as their connection to one another, has by no means been resolved.

In Canada, analysts openly disagree about the policy implications of the changes in the international economic order. There are some who argue that a continued reliance on fiscal policy coupled with attention to monetary aggregates has served Canada well in the past decade and will continue to do so in the future. If the goal of policy is to create the highest possible aggregate rate of growth in the economy (the standard neoclassical policy goal) then, if anything, less rather than more state intervention and planning are required.[9] From this perspective, concern about the future of Canada's secondary manufacturing sector is simply misplaced. If any initiative is required, it is toward an enlightened trade policy. For these observers, a multilateral trade agreement would be ideal but a bilateral trade agreement with the United States is preferable to any form of structural intervention. After all, they argue, Canada's comparative advantage in primary products has brought Canadians an enviable standard of living.[10]

Indicators of macro-economic performance offer some support for this interpretation. In the period from 1960 to 1980, the period during which problems with the international economic regime were beginning to develop, Canada's economy grew at a rate that compared favourably to most other countries. In the early part of the period, Canada's experience with inflation was similarly envious, although more recently the Canadian pattern is almost indistinguishable from that of other OECD countries. What does distinguish Canada is its rate of unemployment. During the twenty-year period from 1960 to 1980, Canada experienced the worst record in the OECD, with an average level of unemployment of 6 per cent. Only the United States came close to this mark with a rate of 5.5 per cent. At the same time improvements in productivity in Canada did not match those of the smaller European countries or of Japan and Germany. That Canadian manufacturing remained competitive in the 1960–80 period is a testament to the exchange rate and the ability of firms to compensate for slow productivity by keeping labour costs down. An over-supply on the labour market presumably assisted in this regard.

With respect to the performance of Canadian manufacturing over the past two decades, the overall impression is one of neither spectacular progress nor disturbing decline.[11] In essence, Canada has held its own in a period in which its level of protection, as measured by tariffs, has fallen. During the two decades from 1960 to 1980, the penetration of the Canadian market by imports rose from 20 to close to 30 per cent, but this was counterbalanced by a similar rise in the export of manufactured goods. Compared with the performance of other OECD countries, Canada's record is enviable. In 1960, Canadian manufactures captured 3.3 per cent of the total manufactured goods exported by developed market economies; twenty years later, this share had risen to 4.2 per cent.

While others experienced spectacular increases (Japan) or decreases (United Kingdom), Canada's performance was relatively stable. Some analysts were alarmed that the deficit on manufactured goods trade, which stood at $812 million in 1960, had risen to $2.5 billion by 1980, but even here there are soothing interpretations. Roy Matthews, for example, argues that, allowing for substantial cyclical fluctuations, trade deficits have remained roughly proportional to the corresponding increase in trade generally: 'Thus, although these deficits have increased over the twenty years when measured in dollar amounts, they have, if anything, declined when set against the country's total trade and output.'[12]

None the less, this performance profile leaves many policy analysts in Canada uneasy. The concern is that, as the terms of trade change, Canada will be poorly placed to maintain its existing markets or claim a share of new ones. Canada is as dependent on exports of primary resources in the 1980s as it was a century earlier. Although there are exceptional sectors in Canadian secondary manufacturing, such as automobiles in the 1980s, it is trade in resources that consistently makes the largest positive contribution to Canada's trade balance. Unfortunately, some of these resources are non-renewable, and will be exhausted in the next half-century. Others are renewable in theory more than in practice. Poor planning and environmental pollution threaten the continued viability of the forest industries and the fisheries on both coasts.[13] Moreover, unemployment is disturbingly high in the regions dependent on these resources and (notwithstanding bilateral free trade) persistent trade frictions threaten access to the major market for these products, namely the United States.

These are not the only reasons offered for pessimism. Critics of Canadian policy have drawn attention to Canada's relative isolation from the world's major trading blocks,[14] to the mature and slow growth character of its industrial structure,[15] and to the deleterious effects of continued high levels of direct foreign investment.[16] Even those with little faith in the capacity of governments to pick winners concede that without active, albeit cautious, support to particular industries, the level of investment in high-growth, but high-risk, sectors may be less than is socially optimal.[17] The need for intervention appears to be particularly true in the so-called 'Schumpeterian sectors,' where the pattern of competition is such that early leaders obtain an unassailable advantage over would-be competitors. Nations without Schumpeterian firms (firms with technological innovations and capital to bring these to market) are relegated, then, to producing low-technology goods and eventually to receiving a lower national income.[18] There is a strong incentive, therefore, to find some means of subsidizing these firms, although there is no consensus that targeting favourites is the most suitable way of doing so.

In short, concern has mounted over the future consequence of a strategy based on fiscal policy, monetary aggregates, free trade, and generally muddling through. Two major alternatives have been proposed. The first of these, loosely termed monetarism, has been tried in the United States, the United Kingdom, and the Netherlands. In this view, Keynesian demand stabilization supported by a relatively comprehensive welfare policy net creates unfortunate expectations and harmful vested interests. Such a policy strategy introduces too many rigidities into the economy, preventing flexible adjustment. In particular, the Keynesian formula has muted the message of the market by providing institutional protection against wage loss. By vesting workers with the right to an income whether or not they are participating in the production process, and by providing a generous social wage, the Keynesian welfare state has not only undermined the linkage between wages and unemployment, but has also created massive public debt.[19] Unlike the deficit spending of the post-war years, monetarists claim that this round of growing indebtedness cannot be justified as a necessary stimulant to production. Government borrowing has had the effect of increasing demand in financial markets and driving up interest rates. Moreover, many analysts allege that in feeding the 'unproductive' public sector the state has robbed the private, or marketable-goods, sector of the investment necessary to ensure increased production.[20]

Governments wedded to this policy direction reject the idea of concertation with social groups, especially labour, in longer-term policy making. They interpret any agreement based on consultation as merely protective of special interests and hence likely to reinforce the market rigidities created by Keynesian demand management. Instead, they seek to join tight control over the money supply with significant cuts in public spending, especially in the area of social policy. In addition, monetarists have urged the removal of rigidities in markets whether these be trade-union privileges in the labour market, quality control in product markets, or traditional barriers between banks and other financial institutions in capital markets. Pursuit of this policy strategy invariably occasions confrontation between the state and various socio-economic groups, in particular labour and representatives of the disadvantaged.

Canadian policy makers have shown little taste for the confrontation promised by the monetarist alternative. Indeed, the general direction of thinking on these matters since the mid 1970s – thinking summarized at length and with some passion in the report of the Macdonald commission – has stressed the need for more consultation. The commission reflected upon the need for structures that would encourage negotiation among social partners and concurred with the widespread sentiment that as much as possible of the welfare state should be preserved. The rather limited success (some would say failure) of the monetarist 'experiments' in the United States and Britain has undoubtedly influenced this line of thinking.

Unimpressed with monetarism, unwilling to trust in the continued efficacy of fiscal policy, and unconvinced by the advocates of free trade, some policy analysts have turned to consider more seriously a second alternative, namely industrial policy. This interest in industrial policy has been sparked, in part, by the efforts of such countries as Japan, France, and several of the newly industrialized states. One major assumption underlies their approach to industrial policy. In the words of Paul Whiteley, they believe 'that new industries do not spring spontaneously into existence; they have to be identified or created by public or private action. There is a great payoff to countries which invest time and resources in identifying future markets and products.'[21] To be sure, such intervention is often *marktkonform*, that is, designed to maximize the efficiency of market forces, not to create monopolies or excessive, destructive competition. The industrial policy option recognizes that all industries go through life cycles from birth, to maturity, and finally decline. It is the task of the state to assist in these transitions, especially in the early stages when critical new industries are often most in need of support.

The implication of this analysis is that, in the wake of the experience of the 1960s and 1970s, governments must intensify their level of intervention. Those that have followed this prescription, rather than retreating from the marketplace, have consciously adopted activist strategies emphasizing long-term economic development, particularly strategies of export-led growth. Instead of waiting for markets to develop, they have sought to create makets.[22] Co-production agreements and local content requirements are among the standard tactics that the governments of Japan, France, and those of the newly industrializing countries have been prepared to employ.[23] Identifying their strengths in the global economy – strengths that vary from a special technological capacity to a low-wage labour force – these states have worked closely with their business communities, and occasionally labour, to create and then capitalize on their comparative advantage.

The political requirements of this strategy are substantial.[24] Above all, it is necessary to develop relationships between producer groups and the state that are premised on collaboration and consultation. In this respect, relations with business are particularly important. Much of the power of capital is structural. It is independent of the specific decisions of business and based instead on the fact that in capitalist economies the fate of individual workers and the members of other social classes, to say nothing of politicians, is in the hands of business. In an important sense, the private investment decisions of business are necessarily public matters.[25] The state must come to terms with the fact that 'this confers an unusual degree of systemic power on capital.'[26] In formulating industrial policy, the state must explicitly invite business to share in the policy-making process in exchange for compliance and co-operation in the matter of long-term investment decisions.

Canadians have by no means embraced this type of economic strategy. As we will see below, industrial 'policy' in Canada consists of a rather confused and uneven amalgam of initiatives. Chapters two and three will suggest why the political requirements of industrial policy are difficult to meet in Canada. It would be wrong, however, to conclude that Canada has rejected the industrial policy option. But to appreciate the pattern of Canadian industrial policy and the reasons that lie behind it, it is necessary to consider industrial policy options in more general comparative terms.

Industrial Policy Options

The demand for industrial policies is, in general, the demand for measures that will assist industries to manage the risks associated with exogenous shocks, risks that have been borne disproportionately by mass-goods producers and by labour. It is, in particular, the demand for a set of selective measures, to be adopted by the state, that will alter the structure of industrial organization to the long-term advantage of both workers and the owners of capital.[27] Industrial policy advocates want creative intervention by the state both to assist those whose jobs and livelihoods are threatened by changes in the international econ-omy, and to offer the necessary economic and political assistance to firms that are poised to capture world markets with innovative products and processes.

All industrialized countries have industrial policies. All seek to influence, to some degree, the investment decisions of private capital. But not all countries have the same policy; indeed, there exist different *types* of policy premised on different assessments of what is needed, what can be accomplished, and what constitutes an appropriate role for the state in the market-place.[28] Two major alternatives have emerged as ideal-types: *anticipatory* industrial policy with its emphasis on intrusive policy instruments that are integrated with one another and aimed at structural transformation; and *reactive* industrial policy, which is organized around the immediate needs of specific firms (often for distress financing) and is devoted to creating a climate attractive to investment.

The essential characteristics of these types are captured in an examination of three dimensions of industrial policy. First, industrial policies vary in their objectives. The goal of industrial policy may be either rapid adjustment to economic change or defensive protectionism. If the former, the stress will be on improving labour markets, modernizing plants, and facilitating the development and transfer of technological innovations; if the latter, emphasis will be laid on relieving the excessive social costs that accompany rapid contraction, often by employing quotas and other barriers to trade.

It may be convenient to define industrial policy in terms of either one or the other of these objectives,[29] but industrial policy can involve both. After all, the overriding objective is to manage the changes forced upon industry and to allow for orderly adjustment consistent with the need for industrial renewal. The premise of industrial policy is that such a process cannot be left to markets alone because capital, labour, and product markets are often defective.[30] The key question is which set of objectives is stressed. In the case of anticipatory policy, adjustment objectives take precedence; protectionist objectives dominate in the reactive case.

The second important dimension of industrial policy is its intrusiveness, the degree to which the industrial policy initiatives of the state require it to participate in, or even direct, the investment decisions of individual firms. At the heart of reactive policy lies the strategy of 'environmental intervention.'[31] A series of broad measures, provided through the tax system, general schemes of industrial subsidy, or programs of trade protectionism, create what policy-makers hope will be an appropriate climate for investment. The decision to use the investment opportunities created by such intervention is left in the hands of individual firms. The rationale for environmental intervention is usually that of market failure. Although sweeping in scope, these policy instruments are introduced only where policy-makers believe that 'distortions or imperfections in the market mechanism prevent industry from optimizing its performance.'[32] It should be added, however, that reactive policies are also congruent with a political rationality based on maximizing votes by maintaining jobs. Such a rationality predisposes policy makers to favour instruments that hide the costs of job preservation: domestic-content regulations, government procurement policies, direct subsidies, and tax expenditures.[33] This creates a rather complex and amorphous system of political favouritism.

The anticipatory alternative is 'structural intervention.' It is distinguished by a set of programs targeted to specific sectors or firms and based on an assessment of appropriate industrial structure. The rationale for intervention is founded on more than an appreciation of market failure. The working assumption is that for many purposes market signals will not be in accord with overriding national policy goals, especially the preservation and nurturing of what are considered strategically important industries. By the same token, structural intervention does not assume that the investment decisions of particular firms are, in every sense of the word, private. In fact, it is precisely their public character, their impact upon both workers and the owners of capital, that draws them within the ambit of public authorities. Because of this public character, industrial development is not envisaged as company-led. It must be either a state-led or a tripartite negotiated phenomenon.[34] In either case, structural intervention presumes a considerable degree of technical expertise and a set of political institutions capable of engineering the necessary degree of consensus.

The final dimension of industrial policy is its degree of integration. Typically, reactive policy is not characterized by a high level of policy integration. It often gives the appearance of a series of ad hoc measures applied to firms and sectors as the need arises. In some circumstances, such support is highly appropriate. Reactive policy is driven by market considerations, either traditional forms of market failure or the politically charged elimination of weak firms. Hence, industrial assistance is spread unevenly across industrial sectors and, once provided, may remain in place indefinitely, whether or not the justification for assistance has been removed.

Alternatively, anticipatory policy takes a comprehensive approach in which all firms and all sectors are evaluated against a set of criteria engineered at the political/bureaucratic centre. An intensive information-gathering effort undergirds the comprehensive approach and, whether justified or not, the state operates as if it possesses the skill and the legitimacy to conduct industrial policy on a broad scale. All departments and agencies are industrial bureaus in one way or another, but the strategic element of industrial policy is directed from the centre. Intervention by governments in this instance is not based upon widely varying criteria. Strong efforts are made to achieve a measure of complementarity, with special attention being paid to backward and forward linkages among industrial sectors.

It should be evident from this discussion that what we have outlined are industrial policy ideal-types. Nowhere do they exist entirely on their own. Instead, elements of both anticipatory and reactive policy types are to be found in most countries and sometimes in the same policy area. The task, therefore, is to sift and sort through a government's initiatives to construct a synthesis representing the core policy response. This task is made easier by differentiating levels of industrial policy making that correspond to the scope of policy objectives. At the *macro* level are policies conceived at the highest degree of generality. They are directed at the industrial system taken as a whole and are formulated with minimal attention to the specific needs of sectors or individual firms. These are the classic horizontal policy instruments – including subsidies and tax expenditures – where the recipients are those who meet the criteria, with no special preference shown for sectors or specific firms. The sectoral level itself can be thought of as the *meso* level of policy making. Here policies are sector-specific, tailored to the common needs of a set of producers. Finally, at the *micro* level are those policy measures designed for particular firms. They range from bail-outs to the promotion of national champions and include negotiated planning agreements, where firms agree to investment and employment strategies in exchange for state assistance.[35]

The idea that several levels of analysis coexist in the conduct of policy is only weakly developed in comparative political economy. The most explicit recognition of levels of policy analysis has been introduced through debates on interest intermediation and neo-corporatism. Alan Cawson, for example, has argued that 'macro-corporatism is on the wane' and that attention must now be turned to meso-corporatism, where a more restricted set of issues is addressed by a wider range of participants.[36] Others, such as Arthur Wassenberg, have drawn attention to what they call the 'interorganizational logic' of corporatism in which the macro level serves as a stage for symbolic polarization between capital and labour, the micro level provides the setting for direct class confrontation, and the meso level serves as the arena in which concrete and pragmatic negotiations are carried out.[37] Finally, and in a similar vein, Gerhard Lehmbruch has directed attention to a variety of 'policy-mixes combining macro-economic management with micro-economic and supply-side interventions.'[38] What these authors seem to be saying, in the context of comparative institutions, is that an appreciation of something as complex as the management of the economy requires not only a recognition of levels of policy but also an understanding of the interactions among them.

Anticipatory and reactive industrial policies place a different emphasis on each of these levels. Reactive policies are usually conceived at the macro level and targeted at individual firms. The economy is viewed in terms of healthy and ailing firms rather than of promising and declining sectors. Firms rather than sectoral organizations are the primary agents of policy implementation. Anticipatory policy, in contrast, takes systematic account of all three levels. Policies are developed at a global or macro plane, drawing on a comprehensive assessment of sectors and individual firms. They are implemented using a combination of instruments, some environmental or macro in character, others directed at whole sectors, and still others that are firm-specific. Anticipatory policies give considerable priority to sectoral planning and consider firms in the context of this broader sectoral perspective.

Anticipatory and reactive policies also differ in the degree of co-ordination demanded. Anticipatory policy in its ideal-typical form is co-ordinated across all three levels. The emphasis on sectoral planning dictates a simultaneous consideration of macro and micro policy instruments. It is also co-ordinated across time. François Duchêne notes that industrial policies can produce changes only at the margins. To have a lasting effect, they must be 'steady and cumulative,' with steps being taken in some sort of coherent progression.[39] Re-active policy, however, is formed in response to electorally relevant market signals and tends to be uncoordinated. Environmental instruments such as tax expenditures for research and development or capital costs designed to en-courage rationalization or modernization may be countermanded by higher tariffs for a given sector or bail-outs of individual firms. Contradictions across levels are not necessary but, in the absence of any priorizing on a macro plane, they become much more likely.

The issue of co-ordination across these three levels points again to the im-portance of political institutions. The co-ordination associated with anticipatory policy is possible only under particular circumstances. The first requirement is a centralized, highly autonomous state bureaucracy that can plan on a global plane, priorize sectors, and choose particular firms for special encouragement. Highly diffused bureaucracies or those that have been penetrated by interest associations are much less capable of performing in this way.

The second requirement is an integrated and representative interest asso-ciational system that is able to provide business and labour with the means to engage in concertation on the general framework for industrial policy. Nor-mally, anticipatory policy relies on what Richard Samuels calls the 'politics of reciprocal consent' between business firms and the state.[40] The implementation of anticipatory policy is made easier when the state can draw on sectoral and regional affiliates of peak associations that negotiate the co-operation of indi-vidual firms. When interest associational systems are neither inclusive nor hierarchical, they tend to be characterized by differentiated, independent action among competing groups whose primary interest lies in intensive lobbying rather than policy planning and negotiation. Chapters two and three take up these institutional issues in the Canadian context.

Industrial Policy in Canada

There can be no doubt that the Canadian state, particularly at the federal level, has always been active in the industrial policy field. In the nineteenth century, tariffs were the centre-piece of industrial policy and their impact on the eco-nomic development of Canada has been profound. But industrial policies did not stop with high tariffs. The subsidization of transportation systems, the creation of crown corporations to generate and deliver hydroelectricity, the establishment of a 'manufacturing condition' to accompany grants of crown resources, and the provision of an infrastructure necessary for agriculture and forestry were among many industrial policy initiatives of the nineteenth century. Canadian politicians, as Michael Bliss has pointed out, 'were not adverse to using government powers and resources in the cause of supporting Canadian industries.'[41]

It is tempting to see these developments as part of a grand strategy that included a clearly articulated role for the state and a theory of industrial development. In fact, statist nostrums were seldom employed to justify intervention. The Canadian state reacted to circumstance and opportunity.[42] Its theory of industrial development was that of import substitution industrialization, and it was designed as a supplement to a resource-extractive economy. It was expected that high tariffs would produce a quick return on investment without challenging the accepted notion of development within the British Empire.[43] As for a relationship between the National Policy of protective tariffs and other development policies, none can be clearly discerned.[44] In fact, to refer to the National Policy as a strategy is to ignore the evidence that politicians were responding in an ad hoc manner to the demands of old and emerging constituencies. Not until the 1920s was a conscious attempt made to use some policies to compensate for the effects of others, and not until the 1930s, in response to unprecedented crisis, did the Canadian state begin to contemplate radical responses to the industrial economy.[45]

In the post–Second World War period, the long-range objectives of industrial policies were given relatively less attention as policy makers turned to the macro economy and the management of cyclical fluctuations with Keynesian policy instruments.[46] Industrial development was premised on foreign investment and utilization of wartime crown corporations in such rapidly evolving industries as nuclear energy, petrochemicals, and aerospace. But oscillation and confusion on these matters was not over. In some sectors, such as automobiles and defence, production was rationalized on a continental basis, with Canadian-based manufacturers enjoying a negotiated entry into the American market. In others, industries such as textiles and footwear, manufacturers lobbied successfully for protective tariffs and quotas. Since then, many sectors of industry have been forced to face the rigours of international competition, while others, such as dairy, are shielded by a highly effective price-support system. Foreign investment itself has been alternatively welcomed and discouraged, sometimes by the same government. The entire relationship between trade and industrial policy is clouded in confusion.

Uncertainty with respect to the objectives of industrial policy is well illustrated in the area of research and development (R&D). Science policy in general, and research and development in particular, have enjoyed a special place in the Canadian state's panorama of industrial-support programs. But this status was fading in the late 1980s as these programs were increasingly obliged to meet the demand for regional economic development. Programs of industrial subsidy were gradually expanded to become omnibus in nature and a great many activities associated with industrial development were made eligible for support via the most general and regionally sensitive of these programs, the Industrial Regional Development Program (IRDP). Tax assistance in the field of research and development was so undisciplined that a wide variety of investments, many only loosely associated with R&D, were the beneficiaries of tax credits.

This mega-program and tax-expenditure strategy reflects a crisis of confidence in both the objectives and the instruments of R&D policy. There is no longer any consensus that establishing targets for R&D spending is the best way to conceptualize objectives.[47] Nor is there a ground swell of support for direct participation in the volatile technologies in the aftermath of such high-tech disasters as Consolidated Computers.[48] Thus, in the one area in which a policy of consistent support might be detected, recent governments appear to have lost their appetite for active intervention. The rhetoric of 'industrial strategy,' which echoed in bureaucratic offices and cabinet committee rooms in the early 1970s, has since been replaced by a piecemeal rationalization of particular projects. The technical, administrative, and political demands of 'across-the-board' anticipatory policy were simply too great.[49]

The same cannot be said for bail-outs. The Canadian state has felt compelled to spend vast sums on weak firms employing large numbers of workers. Observers of this process have been unable to divine any logic to this type of intervention, save that of a simple electoral calculus.[50] But even here, efforts have been made to establish agencies at arm's length from incumbent politicians. Their purpose has been to manage the disposition of marginal assets absorbed into the public sector (the Canada Investment Development Corporation) or to direct funds in declining sectors toward promising firms (the Canadian Industrial Renewal Board). In neither case have politicians expressed an intense interest in directing the affairs of private or even public enterprises. There is a strong predilection to allow markets full rein with a minimum of political interference, except where electoral considerations make intervention unavoidable.

To complete this picture of uneven intervention, it should be noted that at both the federal and provincial levels the Canadian state has limited its industrial policy initiatives to a restricted range of policy instruments. Taxes, subsidies, and tariffs have been the main weapons, and in each case they have been used to change the price of factor inputs. The major exception to this pattern has been the occasional, but inconsistent, employment of public corporations.[51] The result has been an ad hoc, piecemeal response and a very confusing combination of horizontal and vertical adjustment policies whose impact on the economy goes largely unmonitored. Other policy instruments, in particular competition policy and labour-adjustment measures, have seldom been utilized for industrial policy purposes in spite of their proved potential.[52]

In light of this brief overview, it may seem reasonable to conclude that Canadian industrial policy corresponds almost entirely to the reactive model. It appears to be primarily negative in its objectives, environmental and firm-specific in its scope, and poorly integrated in its delivery. The reality is more complicated. There can be little doubt that there is a serious absence of integration. No attempt has been made to draw together the programs of even a single level of government in the industrial policy arena, and there can be no assurance that the efforts of one ministry will not be offset by those of another. Moreover, industrial policy in Canada operates at all three levels – macro, meso, and micro – and there is no indication that policies are even vaguely co-ordinated. Even in the case of the National Energy Program, which the Liberal government of Pierre Trudeau launched in the early 1980s, policy was developed in isolation from the provinces and the industry. When the policy failed and was aborted, succeeding governments returned to an approach based on politically salient mega-projects, ignoring longer-term proposals such as those offered in the Kierans Report.[53]

With respect to objectives, Canadian industrial policy includes both adjustment and defensive elements. At the macro level, adjustment objectives appear to dominate, with R&D policies offering the best example. At the micro level, celebrated bail-out cases suggest the predominance of defensive objectives, although both federal and provincial governments have experimented with 'picking winners' and the federal government, at least, has offered some innovative adjustment policies. At the meso (or sectoral) level, objectives differ from industry to industry. Here the political requirements of industrial policy cut the deepest. The political organization of each sector – including responsible bureaucratic agencies and the representatives of producer groups – varies widely with the result that each sector has its own set of objectives, which sometimes include a combination of protectionism and adjustment.

Finally, it is clear that at the macro level Canadian industrial policy is far from intrusive. The programs offered by both federal and provincial governments are, with few exceptions, demand driven: it is up to firms to seize the opportunities afforded by governments. But at the meso and micro levels the picture is much less clear. As the chapters in part two will show, in some cases the state has taken a very strong interest in the future of particular firms and the direction assumed by particular sectors. In others, officials have been much more circumspect, seeking to avoid any responsibility for industrial development.

It seems best to describe Canadian industrial policy as consistently coloured by the reactive model, but containing the elements of anticipatory policy making in selected industrial sectors. In the remainder of this volume we show why this is so: why it is that reactive policy is so dominant, and how it can happen that anticipatory policies will none the less emerge. The key to the former question lies in the historical pattern of industrial policy formation in Canada and in the institutional character of the Canadian state. Each has fostered beliefs about the capabilities of firms, markets, and the state, and these continue to exert a profound influence on the conduct of industrial policy. Anticipatory policies do emerge, nevertheless, but mainly at the meso or sectoral level. It is here that the burdens of national politics can occasionally be thrown off and policy innovations can emerge.

2 Industry Structure, Business Dominance, and Industrial Policy

The character of industrial policy in developed capitalist systems is a function of the organization of society and the organization of the state. In this chapter we explore the structure of Canadian society and those interests whose organization has been critical to the formation of industrial policy. As we have already suggested, the most important of these is business. Although, as the subsequent discussion will show, the role played by other social classes has had a formative effect on the expression of business interests in the industrial-policy arena, none of these social classes has been capable of dislodging business from a position in which its claims and needs are the most heavily indulged.

In modern political systems there are two realms in which interests are mobilized and expressed: the realm of interest intermediation, often referred to as interest-group politics; and the realm of the party system. In what follows we will argue that Canadian business interests have succeeded in dominating both these realms. Success has been achieved not by virtue of superior organization, however, but by capitalizing on the weakness of class rivals, particularly agrarians and labour. Success against class opponents has made it possible for business to ensure that industrial policy respects the autonomy of the firm and the pre-eminence of markets. Yet dominance of pressure-group politics and the party system has discouraged business from developing the organizational capability necessary for engaging in a more intrusive, anticipatory industrial policy. In fact, this chapter concludes by discussing the consequences of business fragmentation at the national level for the definition of industrial policy options.

Underlying this fragmentation is a particular type of industry culture. Industry culture refers to attitudes and beliefs, shared by societal and state actors, concerning the proper structure, functioning, and behaviour of firms, the content of rights that apply in the workplace, and the understanding of the role of the market mechanism.[1] In the Canadian case, the business-community's dominance of the party and interest-intermediation systems has fostered within the state a firm-centred industry culture. This culture, which is also dominant in Britain, emphasizes the self-sufficiency of the firm, the independence of management in making decisions on investment and workplace organization, and the reliance, whenever possible, on markets for the allocation of capital and labour. Such an industry culture treats examples of state intervention as anomalies and insists that economic development continue to be premised on company-led growth. This view implies that a firm line must be drawn between the economy and the polity and that ordinarily the intrusion of politics into the realm of economics should be stoutly resisted.

How Canadian business came to assume both its dominance and its firm-centred culture is the subject of the first part of this chapter. It is argued here that the organization of business interests arises from the pattern of Canadian economic development and, in particular, the relationship between financial and industrial capital. This relationship set the stage for a particular form of business domination, one which has been accomplished not by achieving conspicuous national organization, but by establishing a commanding position in the party system, beginning with the National Policy. The final section of this chapter suggests that the legacy of weak interest-intermediation systems leaves the business community divided and struggling to maintain its preferred approach to industrial policy making.

Patterns of Industrial Development

Of the models employed to capture the distinctive features of Canadian industrial development, the most influential have emphasized the subordinate position of the Canadian economy, whether as a satellite of Britain or the United States.[2] There can be no doubt of the importance of Canada's relationship to imperial powers for an appreciation of the structure of Canadian industry. However, we seek in this chapter to augment these interpretations with one that lays greater emphasis on domestic Canadian factors and on the particular path Canada has followed toward industrial development. It is this path, we will argue, that has created significant barriers to the state intervention associated with anticipatory industrial policy and has encouraged the growth of a firm-centred industry culture in the Canadian business community.

In seeking to understand Canada's particular form of industrial capitalism, we employ a model proposed by Alexander Gerschenkron that compares paths of development laying stress on the connection between finance and industry.[3] This model is explicitly comparative and draws on a coincident consideration of industrial development, financial systems, and state structures. However, Gerschenkron's model serves only as a heuristic starting point. Many of its predictions have failed to materialize, in particular the expectation that in a country like Canada a structural link would develop between financial institutions and industrial corporations. But the Gerschenkron approach does stress precisely those institutional arrangements that are likely to have the greatest effect on the long-term character of business organization in Canada.

Gerschenkron begins by distinguishing between early industrializing states, such as Britain, and 'later industrializers' such as Germany and Russia. Fundamental to his argument is the proposition that late industrializers possess two major liabilities when it comes to entering the industrial age and competing with more advanced states. First, they lack a skilled industrial labour force – a group of workers that is stable, reliable, and disciplined and that has cut the umbilical cord to the land. The absence of such a labour force, according to Gerschenkron, predisposes the late industrializer to enter sectors where technological advances have made modern and efficient labour-saving techniques available. Ironically, then, delayed industrializers are drawn toward competition in the most advanced sectors of their time. Their second problem follows from the first. Moving into technologically advanced sectors requires a large infusion of capital. Yet, investment capital tends to be both scarce and diffused in most late industrializing countries. In short, the scope of the industrialization movement, the need for more technologically advanced plants, and the preference for sectors with a high capital-to-labour ratio place heavy strains on the financial system.

According to Gerschenkron, these pressures encouraged policies of forced savings and the development of industrial banking systems. Unlike the commercial banks prevalent in England, which served as a source of short-term capital, countries that began to industrialize later than England and the United States looked to industrial banks in order to finance the long-run investment needs of the economy. Rather than financing industrial development through a series of short-term loans and the purchase of bond issues on capital markets, industrial banks make longer-term loans and sometimes take an equity position in chosen firms. As such, they become the virtual motors of industrial development and private planning organizations attuned to longer-term industrial policy concerns. In certain cases, where a country lacks even the rudiments of a capitalist financial system (the case cited by Gerschenkron is that of Russia), the state substitutes for the banks by working through the tax system to mobilize the capital needed to finance longer-term investments.

Generally speaking, scholars have found Gerschenkron's argument to be quite persuasive when applied to the cases he studies in greatest depth, Germany and Russia.[4] The theory is of potential interest to Canadian scholars as well, because Canada, like Germany and Russia, began intensive industrialization somewhat later than Britain and the United States. Although Canada's economic development is seldom treated in an expanded comparative context, it is instructive to consider it alongside Japan, Sweden, and the Netherlands, which, like Canada, began their industrialization drives in the last three decades of the nineteenth century.

Kuznets provides a first indication of Canada's relative position in his estimates of the distribution of the labour force among agriculture, industry, and services between 1890 and 1900.[5] His data show that 33 per cent of the Canadian labour force was engaged in industry in 1901 compared to 28 per cent in Sweden, 36 per cent in the Netherlands, 35 per cent in Italy, and about 20 per cent in Japan. Even if those engaged in logging, fishing, hunting and trapping, and mining and quarrying are removed, Canada still had 20.5 per cent of its labour force occupied in manufacturing in 1901.[6] In 1913, Canada's share of world manufacturing production was 2.3 per cent compared to 2.7 per cent for Italy, 1.2 per cent for Japan, and 1.0 per cent for Sweden and the Netherlands respectively.[7] Moreover, Canada's manufactured goods were not simply of the semi-processed variety.[8] In short, the evidence supports the conclusion that Canada was holding its own with other late follower countries at the turn of this century.

Despite its status as a late industrializer, Canada did not face the type of difficulties anticipated by Gerschenkron. For example, Canada did not experience the labour shortage of some other industrializing countries. Historians remain divided over how a capitalist labour market evolved out of the pre-capitalist agricultural practices dominant at the beginning of the nineteenth century.[9] There is little doubt, however, that from the middle of the nineteenth century, Canada possessed a considerable pool of 'free wage labour.'[10] The relatively high skill levels of many of these workers and the relatively wealthy domestic market (provided by the staple economy) permitted this labour pool to develop quickly into a high-wage proletariat.[11] Faced with higher labour costs, capitalists sought to enter the same sectors predicted by the Gerschenkron model, those that were capital intensive and relatively advanced technologically. Thus, a second problem anticipated by the model remained: How could the large amounts of capital needed for entering these sectors be accumulated?

The answer is found in Canada's complex set of financial ties to Britain and in its own system of commercial banks. The Canadian financial system originated with the founding of banks for the promotion of commerce early in the nineteenth century. Hence, the chartered banks began their lives as commercial banks, adapted to the financing of the primarily extractive production of the pioneer economy.[12] In the words of R.M. McIvor, 'the history of the early banks in Canada shows that the chief reason for their existence was the service they performed by exchanging their own credit obligation in the form of bank-notes for the credit obligations of their customers which, however good they might be, were prevented by their very form from passing current as money.'[13] By the period of intensive industrialization at the end of the century, several of these early banks had grown relatively large on the basis of the staples trade. Overseas trade was quite significant relative to the national income and bankable securities passed to a restricted number of countries. According to Ian Drummond, both these factors fostered a relatively centralized banking system with strong connections in London financial markets.[14] As a British colony, Canada also had developed ties to British commercial banks and used foreign borrowings to expand its transportation and communications infrastructure.

There were other sources of capital that also set the stage for the development of a relatively efficient capital market in Canada. In addition to imperial banks, which continued to maintain a presence, life insurance companies were expanding rapidly, with Canada Life and Sun Life being the dominant companies.[15] Also present were trust companies, mortgage institutions, savings banks, and stock exchanges. The two principal exchanges in Montreal and Toronto had been incorporated in 1874 and 1878 respectively, but had been active since before Confederation. Prior to the turn of the century, there were relatively few bond dealers, but their numbers were to grow quickly over the next two decades as capital markets developed.[16]

Thus, an industrial banking system, such as that found in Germany, did not develop in Canada. The German banks dominated the whole system of corporate finance: they mobilized capital, invested it by taking an equity position in industrial firms, and maintained substantial control over capital markets.[17] In contrast, Canada's financial system adhered more to the British pattern. Much of industry was sufficiently profitable that it could finance expansion through retained assets.[18] When it came to the external financing of manufacturing in Canada, the larger indigenous commercial banks continued to provide short-term financing, using accumulated assets from investments in the primary sectors.[19] They also encouraged their clients to meet their additional, longer-term requirements in capital markets. The larger chartered banks gradually absorbed or edged out of the market-place numerous 'unit banks' in New Brunswick, Nova Scotia, and small towns in Quebec. These banks had been willing to make longer-term investments than the commercial chartered banks, but by 1895 branch banking had become the norm.[20]

In the two decades prior to the First World War, the Canadian chartered banks and the other financial institutions responded to the growing demand for capital and, in so doing, created efficient capital markets. In this period, the chief sources of demand included the federal government, the provincial governments, municipalities, railways, public utilities (including tram and power companies), and industrial firms. The federal government and to a lesser extent the provincial governments, raised capital primarily by issuing securities on the London market. The Bank of Montreal had established an office in London in 1870 and had been appointed the federal government's fiscal agent in London in 1893, replacing two English merchant banking houses.[21] By this time, the Bank of Montreal had already developed an expertise in underwriting in both the London and New York markets. The Canadian Bank of Commerce opened a London office in 1901, with the other banks following closely behind.[22] By the beginning of the war in 1914, the larger bond houses also had offices in London. The railways employed the same financing strategy as the federal government. The Canadian Pacific and the Grand Trunk Pacific were largely British-owned and raised capital in London by issuing bonds and shares on their own or through their British bankers. The Canadian Northern, which was Canadian-owned, also looked to the London market but through the Canadian Bank of Commerce.[23]

Where, then, did indigenous industrial firms find their capital? Three sources were employed during this period. The first of these was the bond market. Municipalities and public utilities had already begun to raise capital by issuing securities through the small number of Canadian bond houses. As these issues succeeded, the practice became more and more common and the bond market in Canada expanded.[24] With this market increasingly available, the Canadian banks could adopt the British attitude and push those clients interested in long-term financing into the securities market. Drummond notes that many firms serving the expanding agricultural market issued bonds; they included milling companies, meat packers, and dairies. The practice was also used by shipping companies working the Great Lakes and by numerous small companies in other sectors.[25] The second option, self-financing, was available to more established companies that sought to raise capital through the private sale of privileged shares and the public sale of common shares on the stock exchanges.

The third option, and the most controversial in retrospect, was foreign equity investment. Canada's status as a 'late industrializer' meant that the primary source of this kind of capital was foreign (especially United States) industrial firms. US direct foreign investment began to increase significantly at the turn of the century and accelerated even further after the First World War. In many cases, Canadian manufacturing firms lacked the accumulated capital and technical expertise to found new plants or expand and modernize older ones. Neufeld sees this lack of maturity of Canadian industry, compared to industry in the

United States, as a crucial factor in the predominance of US firms as suppliers of equity capital. In capital markets, in contrast, Canadian institutions dominated. 'A possible explanation is that the emergence of efficient bond buying intermediaries in Canada came about as quickly as it did in the United States, so that Canada did not suffer a comparative disadvantage in supplying funds to the bond market; but Canada may have had a comparative disadvantage in supplying equity capital, in part because of the close association between the provision of such capital and the provision of managerial and other technology.'[26] In short, there was indeed equity investment in Canada, but it did not come from indigenous banks. It came instead from retained earnings and from foreign industrial firms. As in the case of industrial banks, which gain a powerful voice in the affairs of their 'clients,' the foreign firms involved acquired significant control over the process of industrial development in Canada. Many of their branch-plant operations, having accepted equity capital and technology from abroad, were content simply to secure the domestic market, an ambition that corresponded to the wishes of parent firms.[27]

On the financial side, a very different pattern was emerging. By 1914, Canada possessed developed capital markets. Chartered banks had been joined in these markets, first by life insurance companies and later by trust companies, trusteed pension plans, and bond dealers. Concentration and centralization also increased rapidly in both the financial industries and the railways. Gradually, leading banks coalesced with the railways into powerful economic groups, with the strongest centred around the Bank of Montreal and the Canadian Pacific Railway.[28] At the same time, manufacturing firms were becoming larger. They were opting increasingly for incorporation and had begun to issue shares. Canadian financial intermediaries acted as financial advisers and sources of short-term capital for these firms, and they created corporate communities through the sharing of directors. The banks, however, continued to favour bond-issue investments when it came to longer-term capital and were active purchasers of issues sponsored by the railways and governments.[29] In the meantime, foreign firms, particularly from the United States, moved heavily into those sectors of Canadian manufacturing – machinery, transportation equipment, and electrical equipment – that constituted the most advanced industries of the day.

In the system we have described, financial institutions and industrial corporations meet as autonomous entities across what Zysman has called 'the divide of competitive markets.'[30] This system, in place by the First World War, continues to the present day. The chartered banks devote themselves primarily to short-term personal and corporate lending, while long-term capital is raised by industrial corporation in securities markets. Until 1987, banks were restricted from acting as direct intermediaries in these markets, a function reserved for accredited investment dealers.[31] The chartered banks have been prohibited by law from owning more than 10 per cent of the shares of non-financial companies. Similarly, non-financial corporations have not been allowed to gain significant control over chartered, or Schedule A, banks.[32]

None of this means that the banks and industry operate in entirely autonomous spheres. But the banks maintain their ties to industrial firms through interlocks on boards of directors. Changes in the financial system, including the internationalization of banking and the introduction of huge holding companies, such as Power Corporation, Argus, and Edper, have made the overall system more complex. What has not changed is the unwillingness of banks and other financial intermediaries to undertake long-term and equity investment in industrial firms. The pattern predicted by the Gerschenkron model did not materialize in Canada.

The financial system that has emerged in Canada places financial institutions, industrial corporations, and governments in distinct spheres. As such, it has had two major consequences for the Canadian business community. First, the relative autonomy of finance and industry from the state creates a significant barrier for the kinds of state interventions associated with anticipatory industrial policy.[33] The state has little ability to influence the investment decisions of firms, save on those few occasions where it acts as a lender of last resort. The vast majority of critical investment decisions are taken principally by the managers and owners of industrial firms, perhaps in consultation with their financial advisers – the banks and investment dealers. Governments can influence capital markets only indirectly through their own bond issues and through interest rates based on the price of treasury bills they sell through their agent, the Bank of Canada.[34] They have been loath to dictate how investment capital is to be allocated. Any attempt to do so will bring the state into conflict with financial institutions that are ardent defenders of free capital markets and, it must be added, important purchasers of government bonds. Governments need these institutions to manage their own long-term financing, a fact that makes them even more reluctant to intervene in relationships the banks hold sacrosanct.

Second, Canada's capital market system has contributed to a firm-centred industry culture. The early reliance on capital markets or retained earnings as the sources of long-term investment enabled firms to remain autonomous from both banks and the state. Branch plants endorsed this image of the self-sufficient firm as they internalized a similar philosophy from their us parent companies.[35] As we shall see, the weakness of labour gave free rein to the idea that management controlled the workplace. In short, without the experience of direct intervention by banks or the state in the internal affairs of business, firms have been free to celebrate the virtues of independent management and to be sceptical about the competence of governments in industrial matters. For Canadian business, the principle of competitive markets is enshrined to the point that the internal decisions of firms are not considered legitimate targets of political action. Under these circumstances, the prospect of a concertative relationship, in which business and government collaborate in making longer-term investment decisions, is greeted with hostility. As a result, this firm-centred culture inhibits an anticipatory approach to industrial policy. Owners and managers are unwilling to surrender prerogatives acquired in the economic system to pursue collective endeavours in politics.

Establishing Business Dominance

The absence of an ideological predisposition on the part of the state to intervene in the affairs of industry, and the presence of a firm-centred business culture, established the conditions under which business became involved in politics.[36] The insertion of a business perspective on industrial policy comes, as we have noted, in two realms: the system of interest intermediation and the party system. What is most striking about business participation in these realms is the extent to which, as a class, its views have prevailed over alternatives offered by labour and farmers.

In the formative years after Confederation, business championed an approach to industrial policy centred on the National Policy tariff. It succeeded in having this policy adopted not because of the overwhelming strength of its own instruments of collective action, but because of the remarkable organizational weaknesses of its class opponents. In fact, business realized its victory even though it developed only a weak system of interest groups and relied on ad hoc front organizations for specific political campaigns. In the process of achieving this victory in the interest-group sphere, business also came to dominate the party system. Closely tied to business interests, the leaders of the two major parties supported an approach to industrial policy that showed considerable respect for the autonomy of the firm and the independence of financial markets.

Business and the Tariff

A coalition among the financial, industrial, and transportation sectors of business dominated the politics of industrial policy for sixty-five years after Confederation. The key to its dominance was what has come to be called the National Policy. In the face of spasmodic opposition from farmers and labour, business pressed for a set of tariffs that eventually entered political rhetoric as part of a national development strategy. In the words of Paul Craven and Tom Traves, 'the tariff question ... was one among the very small number of persisting causes that served to define the visible centre of Canadian politics, and it did so because, like the schools question or conscription, it reflected a fundamental source of tension in society. In federal politics, the tariff question stood for class conflict.'[37] The centrality of the tariff reflected the strength of this business coalition and its ability to go it alone in politics without working out an accommodation with farmers or labour. Industrial policy was largely limited to the tariff and on matters of industrial development, the state heard business above all. It responded in ways to which the financial system predisposed it, with a policy that required little systematic intervention into the internal affairs of industrial firms.

The industrial structure of Canada in the years immediately after the Confederation settlement already contained a number of sectors, such as boots and shoes, agricultural implements, and carriage manufacturers, that were capable of meeting domestic demand.[38] Complementing these sectors were a number of others, such as cottons, earthenware, and paints, with lower capacity but potential for growth. Together they represented a sufficiently large portion of manufactures to suggest the possibility of a broadly based protectionist coalition. In addition to these firms, French-Canadian élites favoured protection as a means to stem the tide of emigration to the factories of New England.[39] This potential coalition was gradually actualized in the midst of the depression that overtook Canada in the 1870s.

Supporters of protection pursued their objective on two fronts. They looked first to collective action through interest associations, forming the Ontario Manufacturers' Association in 1874, the parent organization of the present-day Canadian Manufacturers' Association (CMA). This permanent association played a decisive role in mobilizing industrialists in Ontario behind the idea of protective tariffs in the run up to the 1878 election.[40] Interest associations representing the other elements of the business coalition were too weak and too regionally based to succeed without further support. The Conservative party played a crucial role here by fashioning a protectionist coalition of associations and firms that assisted it in winning the 1878 election. Free-trade supporters, firms dependent on exports – timber, dairy, mining – as well as those requiring the importation of partially manufactured items, engaged only in party politics. They relied on the Liberal party, in power between 1873 and 1878, to act on their interests. When that party was defeated, free-traders were left in disarray, lacking the independent associational base possessed by the protectionists.[41]

After 1879, fissures in the business community on the protection issue became less pronounced. Debate within business circles largely died out: the National

Policy had become business policy.[42] The business community maintained the policy over successive elections through 1911, successfully arguing that it was, in fact, for the interests of all. Michael Bliss has observed that 'on no other issue did businessmen present such elaborate and persistent and successful justifications of their position. On no other issue did they so completely and successfully manage to identify their own interests with those of the Canadian nation.'[43]

For labour, however, the tariff issue presented serious difficulties. The material interests of workers pushed them to support the policy. After all, protection of Canadian industry meant further security in the workplace. However, to the extent that the policy meant the redistribution of wealth away from labour to capital on the broader plane, labour was opposed.[44] Until the turn of the century, labour's support for increased protection was lukewarm and by no means unanimous. By that time, agrarians had significantly increased their opposition to the tariff and industrialists were obliged to put additional pressure on labour to openly join supporters of the National Policy.

The campaign began in 1901 and continued unabated through the 1911 election. With the gradual expansion of the franchise and the growth of the farming community in western Canada, the Canadian Manufacturers' Association looked to labour for additional support. However, the times were not auspicious for co-operation. Just as the CMA began its campaign, there were renewed attempts by manufacturers in central Canada, not to mention resource firms in the west and the east, to rid the workplace of trade unions, specifically the international unions in the Trades and Labour Congress of Canada (TLC). The CMA straddled the issue of trade-union recognition, making it clear that it had little love for the unions. Yet it was reluctant to lead the charge against unions for fear of alienating labour from its tariff campaign.[45] In the absence of concrete support from the CMA, industrialists formed local employer associations that were designed explicitly to fight the unions.[46] The veiled opposition of the CMA to unionism, when coupled with these bitter struggles taking place in local workplaces, created serious obstacles to co-operation between business and labour on the tariff.

The other issue that divided labour and capital at this time was immigration. For obvious reasons, the TLC had consistently opposed unrestricted immigration. It linked this issue to the tariff, asking why there should be protection for capitalists in the form of the tariff while there were few restrictions on the inflow of labour.[47] The CMA was hardly sympathetic and had even established its own employment recruiting agency in London in 1904.[48] When the association simultaneously created a front organization, the Canadian Industrial

League, to agitate for wider popular support for protection, labour refused to become involved.

The inability of the CMA to recruit labour to the side of the industrialists did not in the end prove especially harmful to its cause. The TLC was not a serious political force. It fit the pattern of labour organization still present in Canada today: it was a rather loose confederation of unions with no capacity to aggregate the interests involved or to enforce a particular policy stance. Accordingly, the congress saw many of its members make common cause with industrialists in the ensuing years and it was never strong enough to offer any concerted opposition to business on the tariff issue. It did not even take a position in the 1911 election.[49] Thus, the tariff approach to industrial policy, the approach preferred by business, dominated, in the first instance, because of a lack of effective opposition from labour.

Although the players were different, the same pattern held for the agrarian class. As the farming population, particularly in Ontario, was drawn more and more into production for export markets during the last quarter of the nineteenth century, its opposition to the tariff increased significantly. But, until after the First World War, it was unable to translate the intensity of its feelings on this issue into a serious challenge to the business alliance. As in the case of labour, agrarians were plagued by organizational problems. As Gordon Laxer points out, these difficulties began in the 1830s, with the defeat of farmers in the rebellions in Lower and Upper Canada.[50] Collective action by farmers in the Canadas was inhibited by the language barrier between French and English and the religio-cultural barrier between Catholics and Protestants. These same obstacles to organization persisted during the post-Confederation period. For example, the Patrons of Industry, an association that played an important role in representing farmers in Ontario in the last two decades of the century, criticized the tariff and the development of monopolies. But this association was also tied to the Protestant Protective Association, thus limiting its political effectiveness and continuing the tradition of overlaying farmers' politics with sectarianism.[51] Laxer concludes: 'Internal national and regional conflicts and the undemocratic ethos associated with the Canadian interpretation of "Britishness" transformed farmers politics into sectionalism, with leadership from other classes.'[52]

It was only when farmers were able to break out of their regional and sectional differences to form the National Progressive Party of Canada that they were able to have an impact on policy. The Progressives won sixty-five seats in the 1921 election, drawing support from the prairies and rural Ontario. Gradually, Mackenzie King succeeded in wooing the Progressives to the Liberal party and, in the process, tariffs were reduced on a variety of products.[53] Consequently, farmer discontent diminished and disorganization outside the party arena followed. The Canadian Council of Agriculture, a peak organization with members from all provinces except Quebec, succumbed to internal struggles and folded. With the gradual disappearence of farmer party governments at the provincial level, the challenge to business receded.

The victory of business over labour and farmers in the field of pressure-group politics left it relatively free to build a system of narrowly based interest associations attuned to the needs of member firms and committed to a firm-centred industry culture, highly resistant to state intervention. The Canadian Manufacturers' Association remained an organization with a surprisingly narrow domain compared to analogous business associations in Europe. It excluded resource extraction, transportation, and financial firms. A direct membership association rather than a peak association on the European model, the CMA fell into the role of providing selective services for its members after the First World War.[54] Rather than vertically integrated peak associations, business in Canada has relied on narrowly based sectoral associations for lobbying on routine matters. When faced with broader issues, especially those involving class conflict, ad hoc temporary organizations have been the usual instruments employed. Such an approach was already followed during the tariff debate with the creation of the Canadian Industrial League. The same strategy was used in the 1911 election, when business founded the Canadian Home Market Association to fight the free-traders and the Liberals.[55] A version of this organization was resurrected at the end of the First World War, given a new coat of paint as the Canadian Reconstruction Association (CRA), and charged once again with convincing labour of the utility of tariffs, among other things.[56] The recent free-trade coalition, the Canadian Alliance for Trade and Job Opportunities, headed by Donald Macdonald and Peter Lougheed, was a worthy successor in this tradition of ad hoc organizations.

In summary, business succeeded in promoting its particular version of industrial policy by dominating the arena of pressure-group politics. The Canadian Manufacturers' Association practised the art of pressure politics more effectively than either the Trades and Labour Congress or the various agrarian organizations ranging from the Dominion Grange, the Patrons of Industry, the Canadian Council of Agriculture, to the various provincial farmers' organizations. Under these circumstances, business lacked any incentive to develop strong peak associations. Its ability to rely on sectoral associations and more broadly based ad hoc front organizations was reinforced by developments in the party system. Business consolidated its pre-eminent position by working through the old-line parties to ensure that its preferred approach to industrial policy was sustained.

Business and the Party System

The play of party politics occupies a crucial place in the definition and elaboration of industrial policy. When party conflict takes place on the basis of class issues, party leaders are forced to address the concerns of labour and farmers as well as those of business. The subject of state intervention in the affairs of firms is forced onto the political agenda and bourgeois parties experience a pressing need to find some means of achieving collaboration among opposing social classes. Consultative approaches to policy making are suddenly much more attractive than confrontation. Under these circumstances, there is a serious prospect that a tradition of concertation will develop in the field of industrial policy, but it has not happened in Canada. Party politics in the formative years after Confederation did not centre heavily on class differences. The party system contained two bourgeois parties, both of which were content to collaborate with business and no one else in the development of the national economy.

The party system has reinforced business hegemony in the determination of industrial policy in two interrelated ways. First, it has defined the issues and terms of debate in a manner that has served to unite business on the one hand but divide classes opposed to business on the other. Second, both major parties, but the Liberal party in particular, have been successful in co-opting labour and agrarian discontent, thereby deflecting the formation of powerful class-based opposition parties.

The two major parties do more than aggregate voter preferences. They actually define, with varying degrees of success, the criteria on the basis of which preferences are formed. Janine Brodie and Jane Jenson claim that parties 'identify which among a broad range of social differences and tensions will be raised and debated in elections, and ... nurture and sustain the criteria by which an electorate will divide against itself in a more or less stable system of partisan alignments.'[57] Especially favoured among these divisions has been that of bicultural politics, the need to reconcile the two largest ethnic groupings in Canada, the French and the English. In many election campaigns, this issue has been permitted to dominate all others. Related to it is the broader question of national unity. Both parties have appealed to disaffected regions arguing that the monumental task of nation building requires co-operation and consensus. The major parties have embraced the view that regional discontent is an obstacle to national development that a country like Canada, with its immense geography and its heterogeneous demography, can ill afford. Brodie and Jenson conclude that the stress on these themes has hindered the development of class-based politics in Canada.[58] The two major parties have been content to act as brokers among ethnic groups and regions, seeking voters from all social classes.

Appeals to national unity are consistent with the interests of large corporations in Canada. The country began as a union among three British colonies, each with its own particular ties to the mother country and its own social structure. The development of capitalism involved the centralization of the various business élites from these colonies and the gradual incorporation and integration of outlying regions into a national economy. This process of centralization has been complemented by a stress on homogeneity. The formation of a national capitalist economy encourages the suppression of ethno-cultural differences and regional tastes and peculiarities.

Fierce local resistance to these trends has occurred throughout Canadian history, as the Maritime Rights Movement, the Progressives, Social Credit, and Quebec nationalist movements all illustrate. To the extent that political parties have capitalized on this discontent by co-opting regionally based leaders in a politics of national integration, the party system has worked to advance the interests of big business. We have already noted that, after the 1921 election, the Liberals used the lowering of freight rates, some selective reductions in tariffs on farm machinery, and a spate of railway building to woo into the fold a wing of the Progressive party. Similarly, in 1943 and 1944, when the CCF (Co-operative Commonwealth Federation) appeared poised for a major break-through at the federal level, the Liberals undermined CCF support with the introduction of family allowances, the first of what was to become a series of universal social programs. Since that time, most workers and farmers have voted consistently for the two bourgeois parties without demanding any reduction in the support these parties show for the interests of business. Business continues to be a major source of funds for the two major parties. Even in 1984, they received almost half their monies from the corporate sector.[59]

The only serious challenges to the hegemony of business in the party system have come at the provincial level of government. As Boismenu and Jalbert have argued, each of the numerous regionalist movements that have surfaced throughout Canadian history has represented a challenge to the dominant business coalition.[60] Generally, they have involved groups and classes somewhat at the margin of capitalist development that are threatened by the expansion and concentration of large central-Canadian corporations. 'Conscious that the orientation of change is away from them and that their social status is threatened, the traditional *petite* bourgeoisie, and particularly agrarians, plus certain fractions of non-monopoly capitalists, have been able to constitute the core of a class alliance carrying a regional orientation.'[61] Several of these movements have enjoyed a degree of electoral success at the provincial level, but all have failed abysmally when they have transferred their energies to the federal plane. Those that have actually captured power in a province have had to contend with significant federal powers over the economy and occasionally the use of reservation and disallowance.[62]

Canadian parties have not been simply the instruments of corporations. They have an organizational life of their own and, from time to time, have drifted some distance from the preferences of major business interests. When this has occurred, business has shown no compunction in transferring its loyalty from one major party to the other. When the Liberal party sought to champion reciprocity in the 1911 election, big business deserted the party in droves. In the 1930s, the CPR, still the dominant corporation in the Canadian economy, remained alienated from the Conservatives over the nationalization of private lines into the CNR in 1917. It moved to support the Liberals in the 1935 election and was followed by the large retailers, Eaton's and Simpsons, which resented the Stevens inquiries into pricing and mass buying.[63] Stanbury's analysis of corporate donations in the 1984 election campaign suggests a similar phenomenon.[64] Apparently disenchanted with the Liberals' energy and foreign-investment policies, the corporate sector gave disproportionate support to the Conservatives at the expense of the Liberals.[65]

With the opportunity to shift its support between the two governing parties, business in Canada has not been compelled to organize itself as a class to confront a socialist alternative. Where necessary, various fractions of business have been able to align themselves with one of the two major parties without posing a threat to their collective interests. Nor, as we have seen, were the incentives for collective action particularly pronounced outside the party arena. To put it simply, business organizations were never driven to expand their authority within the business community. Thus, although Canadian business dominates the party system, it is none the less weakly organized. Its associational system lacks the integration and the organizational capacity to aggregate business interests in a manner that transcends narrow, short-term concerns. In short, it is not capable of defining the interests of business as a whole.

As long as business remains unchallenged in the party system and relatively united on matters of economic policy, this system of associations is not a serious liability. However, if other political parties come to challenge the Liberals and Progressive Conservatives, or if serious rifts develop among fractions of the business class over appropriate economic policy, this weak associational system will become a distinct liability as a line of defence against a different version of industrial policy.

Business Organization and Industrial Policy

In organizational terms, business in Canada is divided. There are over 500 business associations and most of these represent very specialized product interests. There are no comprehensive peak associations, that is, broadly based associations whose members are other associations. Canada is quite distinctive in this regard. In all other capitalist democracies, except the United States, these peak associations exist to gather together more specialized groups and enhance business's capacity to define common interests. As such, they are capable of not only creating a longer-term view on policy but also participating in concertation arrangements for both the formulation and implementation of macro-policy. By contrast, the most comprehensive Canadian associations – the Business Council on National Issues, the Canadian Chamber of Commerce, the Canadian Federation of Independent Business, and the Canadian Manufacturers' Association – all enrol firms directly as members. Each is a champion of the autonomy of the individual firm and each treats with suspicion the idea of concertation with state officials on economic policy.

From the perspective of collective action, business in Canada is organized into three somewhat distinct components: the staples fraction, branch-plant manufacturing, and the nationalist coalition. The staples fraction is the strongest of these and traces its roots to the earliest days of Canadian capitalism. Many of the institutions discussed in the first section of this chapter, including transportation interests and the chartered banks, play leading roles in this grouping. These institutions are at the head of networks composed of investment or holding companies, affiliated financial intermediaries, and resource and related manufacturing companies. In identifying these networks, Carroll notes the important co-ordinating role assumed by the chartered banks and suggests that 'dense ties to common banks present opportunities for behind-the-scenes co-ordination and conflict resolution and for the development of a unified corporate orientation toward government policy.'[66]

The representative par excellence of the staples fraction is the Business Council on National Issues (BCNI). Analysis of the membership of this association shows four elements of the Canadian business class strongly represented:[67] (1) the resource-staples sectors, (2) the financial sector (all six leading chartered banks are members as are eight of the leading ten life insurance companies), (3) manufacturing sectors with linkages to staples production (steel, construction, pulp and paper), and (4) US-owned manufacturing sectors producing consumer goods. The very existence of this comprehensive association is a recent phenomenon. It indicates that the long-standing staple-merchant and industrial coalition is feeling a serious challenge to its pre-eminent status. The BCNI is the response. Consciously excluded from the association based on its constitution are all publicly owned corporations such as PetroCanada; less consciously and more informally excluded are the large co-operative enterprises in the agri-food sectors and prominent firms in what is described below as the nationalist coalition.

The second component of the business community consists of manufacturers oriented to the domestic market, but operating as branch plants of primarily US firms. This group finds its home in the Canadian Manufacturers' Association. Although providing some support for firms interested in export, the CMA's services are primarily directed toward helping members maintain their market share in the domestic economy. A reading of recent annual reports of the association reveals its concern for problems of productivity, management/labour relations, employment legislation, taxing policy, environmental and transport regulation. Only a small part of the association's energies is directed toward expanding exports.

Some of the members of this group have chosen to establish links with the BCNI as well. They have chosen to do so in part because of the transformation of the staples fraction. By reclaiming a larger share of the home market for manufactures, the staples fraction has diversified to the point that it is not as heavily dominated by the transportation, communications, and utilities sectors as it was prior to the Second World War.[68] With a more even distribution of assets across major sectors of the economy and an expressed interest in continental markets, the staples fraction has come to articulate political demands centred on free trade. This kind of posture is of particular interest to those US firms that have acquired a considerable degree of autonomy from their parent corporations. By joining the BCNI, this group has made common cause with the staples fraction and has weakened the CMA.

Since the 1950s, a third set of industries, which could eventually challenge the traditional dominance of the staples fraction, has developed. We refer to it as the nationalist coalition. It consists of two parts. First are the firms that are oriented to export markets and often heavily dependent on government procurement. These are primarily Canadian-owned enterprises that hope to use the procurement base as a springboard to markets abroad. They include increasing numbers of new French-Canadian firms, which developed rapidly with the assistance of the Quebec government's Quiet Revolution reforms. Typical in this regard are Bombardier in transportation equipment, Lavalin in construction, Agropur in food processing, La Laurentienne and the Mouvement Desjardins in finance, and, of course, Hydro Québec. Fundamental to their orientation appears to be what Niosi has termed an ideology of continental nationalism.[69] Proponents favour increased Canadian control over major sectors of production and a greater measure of international expansion, especially into the United States.

The second part of the nationalist coalition is more inward-looking in orientation. Among the businesses in this grouping are the new cultural industries that have received state support since the 1950s, following publication and subsequent implementation of many of the recommendations of the Massey commission. These, plus many firms in the agri-food industries, were highly critical of free-trade overtures.

The political importance of this nationalist fraction of the business class is evidenced by the numerous concessions made to it by the Liberal party. The Walter Gordon budget of 1963, the establishment of the Canada Development Corporation, the Gray Report and subsequent creation of the Foreign Investment Review Agency, and the creation of PetroCanada all represent indications of the influence, albeit spasmodic, of this section of the business class. Stephen Clarkson has observed that the striking turnabout in the Liberal party between May 1979 and February 1980 – when the party shifted toward a much stronger nationalist position – is partially explained by the influence of this nationalistic group of Canadian-owned firms.[70] In particular, he identifies Robert Blair of NOVA Corporation, John Shepherd of Leigh Instruments, Jack Gallagher of Dome, and Raymond Royer of Bombardier. All have had direct connections either with the energy industry or with markets heavily dependent on government procurement.

Firms in the nationalist coalition are inclined to work through specialized, sectoral associations. Some of these sectoral-level associations have been founded out of frustration with, or in opposition to, older associations dominated by firms from the staples and branch-plant fractions. Prominent examples include the Canadian Advanced Technology Association, created to counter the diffuse and branch-plant orientation of the Electrical and Electronic Manufacturers Association of Canada, and the Independent Petroleum Association of Canada, a nationalist response to the domination of the Canadian Petroleum Association by foreign multinationals. Other associations in the nationalist coalition, such as the National Dairy Council and the Canadian Conference of the Arts, have been created to sustain preferential treatment for Canadian firms. Few of the members of the nationalist coalition would feel comfortable with membership in the BCNI. Instead, these associations have shown themselves to be adept at forging coalitions with labour, farmers, and artists – coalitions not normally countenanced by the other two fractions of business.

The simple fact that fractions of the business class in Canada have been forced to participate increasingly in pressure-group politics indicates that the private understanding and consensus between the business community and the two bourgeois parties on industrial policy has been seriously eroded.[71] The debate over free trade with the United States that emerged to dominate industrial policy discussions in the 1980s illustrates well the onset of dissensus. The decision to begin negotiating a free-trade agreement was the culmination of four decades of liberalization of trade policy with the United States. A free-trade strategy implies a preference for firm-based decision making and an aversion to selective government intervention consistent with anticipatory industrial policy. In this respect, at least, it is very similar to the National Policy. Yet even with these properties, the policy divided the business community.

Free trade enjoyed the support of the resource-extraction firms, the financial community, and manufacturing sectors tied to the staples industries, in short, the staples fraction. Long dominant in the business community in Canada, these are the sectors in which Canada has a comparative advantage and that enjoy large export markets in the United States. Also supportive of free trade were those sectors producing consumer goods through branch-plant arrangements. Firms in these sectors have spoken out in favour of free trade through their association, the Canadian Manufacturers' Association. They expected that free trade would ease inter-border transfers and remove some of the political obstacles encountered in the moving or closing of plants.

In contrast, the government of Ontario expressed grave concern about the impact of free trade on the future development of these sectors. Export-oriented firms in the nationalist coalition spoke with more ambivalence about free trade because they wished governments in Canada to retain the option to use policy instruments such as procurement, research and development subsidies, and export financing used by other trading nations. Those firms oriented to the domestic market – Canadian-owned cultural industries, agri-food sectors, and others in the nationalist coalition – were strongly opposed to free trade.

From the perspective of the state, free trade has always been the least-demanding industrial policy option. One reason is that state officials have been able to draw on business associations and firms for advice. But business participation was, none the less, limited to those who were supportive of this particular macro-strategy. Were industrial policy to take a different form – if it were comprehensive in scope, sectoral in design, and anticipatory in character – it is unlikely that business could engage in the intensive and demanding discussions required for its successful implementation. Although business may not lose its political allies in the party system, its legacy of weak associations has left it unprepared for a different type of state initiative.

The history of business organization in Canada has placed some serious limits on the scope for state intervention and on the role that business can play in the formation of industrial policy. The relationship between finance and industrial capital occasioned by the development of a capital-market-based financial system has erected barriers to state involvement in business enterprise and has fostered in business a firm-centred industry culture antagonistic to business/ state concertation. The results are evident in both the party system and the system of interest intermediation. Although business has succeeded in conquering the party system, this firm-centred industry culture has restricted its capacity to participate in the interest-intermediation system. In fact, success in one system has bred weakness in the other.

In part because of the proclivities of business, the interest-intermediation system and the party system in Canada are quite autonomous. Business-interest associations are explicitly non-partisan: they identify with neither of the two bourgeois parties and rarely donate funds. They are capable of articulating the interests of their members, but not of aggregating these in a fashion that would assist politicians and state officials to define and to attend to the long-term interests of business. Neither politicians nor business leaders are encouraged to turn their attention from short-term political problems to longer-term systemic questions. This type of relationship means that the state cannot count on the support of major socio-economic producer groups for the purpose of orchestrating anticipatory industrial policy.

This is one of the reasons that, at the macro level, industrial policy in Canada has been reactive in nature. Beginning with the National Policy in Canada's first half-century, and continuing with the policies of market Keynesianism and, most recently, free trade, successive governments have shown an interest in pursuing industrial policy only via the stategy of company-led growth. Within these broad frameworks, decisions on the direction of industrial development rest largely with individual firms rather than with the state. The past century of industrial policy making in Canada has left behind a politico-institutional structure incapable of supporting an anticipatory industrial policy at the macro level. In the following chapter we shall see why the Canadian state has been unable to compensate for these deficiencies.

3 State Tradition, Bureaucratic Culture, and Industrial Policy

The object of this chapter is to suggest how the structure of the Canadian state has contributed to the evolution of industrial policy in Canada. Both the architecture of Canadian institutions and the beliefs of bureaucratic officials are the focus of this analysis. This chapter identifies and discusses both the critical organizational properties of the Canadian state and the beliefs of bureaucrats about the appropriateness and feasibility of state intervention.

We argue that Canada has only a weak state tradition; that is, the idea of 'the state' is only rudimentally appreciated. This circumstance is the product, in part, of Canada's institutional structure, and it is reflected in the attitudes displayed by key bureaucratic officials responsible for industrial policy. Ultimately, a state tradition presumes the presence of a large and influential coterie of what have been called 'developmental bureaucrats': people who assume they have superior knowledge and insight into public affairs and who are inclined to couch solutions to developmental problems in universalistic terms.[1] With some exceptions, Canadian officials do not fit this mould. We outline how they interpret and pronounce upon projects of industrial policy, the organization of the bureaucracy itself, and the Canadian federal system. On the whole, their beliefs are consistent with a weak state tradition, reflect sympathy for a firm-centred industry culture, and support a reactive rather than anticipatory approach to industrial policy. We begin with state structure itself, outlining what is meant by a state tradition and identifying the key features of the Canadian state.

The Statist Tradition

There have been two approaches to the study of the state advanced capitalist societies. In the first of these, emphasis is laid on the characteristics common to any capitalist state. In the functionalist neo-Marxist paradigm, for example, it is argued that all states seek to maintain social cohesion and ensure the persistence of capital accumulation.[2] Precisely how these functions are to be performed in a country like Canada is a question of some interest, but neo-Marxists are in no doubt that what compels the state in Canada does so in other capitalist societies as well. In this respect, the state comes, as Przeworski and Wallerstein put it, 'ready to wear.'[3] Its functions are already determined and its particular form is of limited interest.

This same ready-to-wear quality can be found outside of the neo-Marxist tradition. Some liberal theorists assume that the state has a considerable degree of autonomy from society and that state officials are free to give expression either to private visions of the public interest or to personal ambitions.[4] Their ability to do so is a given and there is no particular need, in this formulation, to take into consideration either the precise beliefs of these officials or the character of state institutions.[5] Indeed, both of these theoretical approaches assume that the organization of the state does not make a decisive contribution either to the performance of its functions on behalf of capital or to the exercise of its autonomy.

A second approach treats the state as a variable: whatever convergence economic and political forces have created among states in capitalist systems, there remain important differences in state structure. These differences are often evoked by expressions such as 'strong state' and 'weak state.' In this formulation, strong states are able to realize their goals in the face of opposition from society's strongest elements; weak states are more easily penetrated by social groups and find it difficult to resist their demands.[6] State strength is a function of bureaucratic centralization, the quality of bureaucratic élites, and the degree of control exercised by the state over financial resources. Of these, the most important is centralization. Strong states are sufficiently centralized that they can organize and sustain a 'stable settlement' for distributing the costs and benefits of economic growth.[7] From this Weberian perspective, centralization is sometimes seen as an inexorable product of bureaucratization. The emergence of multiple centres of authority, in contrast, is the quintessence of state weakness and may presage the ultimate destruction of state authority.[8]

In recent years, students of comparative political economy have been hesitant to characterize entire states as 'strong' or 'weak.' They have observed that, depending on a host of contingencies, so-called strong states may yield to societal pressures and weak states may succeed in imposing policy initiatives.[9] As well, political systems may be distinguished by the very *idea* of the state itself. In some societies (Kenneth Dyson calls them 'state societies'), the state is recognized as an abstract, impersonal entity:[10] the state embodies a sense of the public interest that is more than the sum of private interests in society.

Dyson puts it this way: 'The state is seen as a unique collectivity whose dignity and value reside in its embodiment of an impersonal and comprehensive set of moral ideas that have an existence apart from the conflicts and fluctuations of social and political life.'[11] Such states are autonomous in the sense that state institutions have their own culture and their own methods of conflict resolution. The core of the state is its administrative-bureaucratic apparatus, which is characterized by élite training and by an insistence on the distinctions between government and administration and between public and private law.[12] The impersonal quality of state action is underlined by the preference for legalistic and formal responses to petitions. The administrative culture is steeped in tradition and responsibility, a responsibility that officials discharge in concert with, not as servants of, elected personnel.[13] By assuming responsibility for the public interest, such a state possesses a built-in rationale for intervention and a predisposition toward anticipatory industrial policy.

France has often been cited as a good example of a 'state society.' The problems of political integration in France, associated with its feudal heritage and with the timing of the French Revolution, combined to propel France toward the development of elaborate state institutions. France has experienced a steady trend toward centralization from the Ancien Régime to the present.[14] It is true that the central authorities met resistance, but by using départements to establish the presence of central authorities in the peripheries they eventually succeeded in breaking down local allegiances. Notwithstanding the vicissitudes of French history, the French state, armed with an elaborate system of administrative law, has consistently pursued a strategy of intervention and control in the economy. This culminated, in the post-war period, with the Gaullist state and its embrace of the wonders of economic planning.[15] The development and execution of these plans were exercises in which elected representatives, drawn together in the National Assembly, played a very limited role. Executive power in France has been exercised through the administrative apparatus of the state and not through the institution of the National Assembly. The latter's task has been to petition officialdom on behalf of local concerns; and its own autonomy has been undermined by the presence of civil servants in its ranks.

For Dyson, Britain typifies societies that lack a state tradition. Britain is widely viewed either as a society without a state[16] or one in which both state institutions and idea of the state as a political and legal concept are underdeveloped.[17] Britain is governed through Parliament, not through autonomous administrative institutions. Political and bureaucratic careers are kept apart, reflecting the highly suspect idea that it is possible to separate politics and administration. The permanent public service remains faceless (and, in that sense at least, impersonal), but such autonomy as it enjoys does not arise because it is an emanation of the state. The civil service in Britain constitutes what J.P. Nettl has called a 'self-sufficient caste.' It is separate, certainly, but it has been 'content to regard administration as an unspecific and highly pragmatic form of problem-solving.'[18] It has pioneered no administrative techniques nor offered any indication that it subscribes to the view that the problems of political administration are unique. Ministers in this system have acquired a larger-than-life quality in part because of the doctrine of ministerial responsibility, and in part because statute law frequently confers power either on individual ministers or the ministry as a whole rather than on impersonal state corporations.[19]

Canada, like Britain, is not a state society. The study of political institutions in Canada begins, not with the bureaucracy, but with the set of working assumptions that constitute the Westminster model of parliamentary government.[20] According to this model, a strong and united cabinet governs the country by commanding a working majority in the House of Commons. The Crown in Canada, which might be considered a symbol of constitutional unity, possesses no serious instrumental powers that would give expression to a transcendent authority. It is Parliament that is the political centre, the institution that links the public to the executive. Parliament is, first and foremost, a representative institution; its members are drawn from civil society and owe their loyalty to the party leadership and the constituency that elected them. Neither on their own, nor in combination with other elements in the constitutional balance, can they be said to encourage a state tradition.

As a result, Canadians see the state as essentially a complex set of institutions delivering a bundle of services. The key features of the Canadian state are its federal structure and its parliamentary form, but neither have contributed to the development of a statist tradition in Canada. The former had designated a variety of decision-making centres with independent authority; the latter has required that political power be exercised through party government premised on single-member constituencies. In both cases, the representation of geographically defined areas has been the dominant form and legislatures the dominant vehicle. In short, no grand theoretical argument has been made that the state in Canada embodies an authority that is separate from, or in some manner superior to, the authority exercised by the duly constituted government of the day.

It is hard to over-emphasize the importance of state tradition for the conduct of industrial policy. Where state tradition is weak, state institutions often reflect the interests of the strongest organizational forces in society. Much of the state's apparatus is devoted to transmitting and responding to these demands. And because these demands are conflicting, and state structure under these circumstances is generally inchoate, industrial policy is typically a rather confusing amalgam of reactive policy initiatives. Policy innovation is inhibited by the absence of political and bureaucratic leadership.

Of course, bureaucratic initiatives, made possible by flexible organizational responses, can occur in spite of a weak state tradition. But these will seldom be evident at the macro level. Here state tradition is reinforced by state structure, and anticipatory industrial policy has very little legitimacy. In what follows we indicate the contribution made by principal institutional features of the Canadian state – parliamentary government and federalism – to this policy legacy and how these features affect the attitudes of the industrial policy bureaucracy.

The Westminster Model of Parliamentary Government

The first organizational principle of the Canadian state is that of the Westminster model of parliamentary government. According to this principle, parliament is the central political institution through which the executive must work and to which it is attached by virtue of membership. The constitution requires the executive to organize and mobilize Parliament to meet the demands of modern governance. It therefore must command the confidence of the House of Commons in more than just the formal sense of the term. This confidence is achieved through a system of cohesive political parties that provide the forces animating parliamentary deliberation, namely the government and the opposition. Members of Parliament are expected to confine their expressions of independent opinion to those few forums set aside expressly for this purpose.

Given the penchant of parliamentary scholars to decry the decline of parliament, it may seem somewhat ironic to insist on the centrality of parliament as a critical principle. But parliament is important because, whatever its deficiencies, it is a representative institution. As such it gives expression to the principle of complaint.[21] Individual members, on behalf of their constituents, use the proceedings of the House of Commons to petition the government for attention and redress. And it is a representative institution in a second sense, namely that it aspires to incorporate within it the fundamental political divisions of the day. It does so by virtue of containing an institutionalized opposition and the tradition of seeking public virtue via public debate. The idea that a public contest, within the confines of parliament, between two or more political parties might produce enlightened opinion on matters of public policy may appear hopelessly outmoded and eccentric, but this does not gainsay the fact that an enormous amount of political energy is consumed in precisely this endeavour.[22]

One of the conditions for comprehensive anticipatory industrial policy is the relative isolation of policy formation from partisan conflict. Adversary politics conducted in a broadly representative institution does not provide much scope for developing a political consensus on macro-industrial policy. The Westminster model does not countenance the possibility that parliament might profitably be considered as an institution that is more than just a forum for the government and opposition. After all, to conceive of Parliament as a distinct corporate entity would raise the spectre of the State, the idea that it is possible to have an institutional embodiment of the idea of the public interest.[23] In the Westminster model, parliamentary accomplishments are normally partisan in character and there is precious little opportunity for the expression of political differences that have not been filtered through the lens of partisan advantage.

It must be added that cabinet, the efficient centre of the Westminster model, has proved most resistant to any reform that would remove or restrict the expression of partisan political impulses in its deliberations. Cabinet has achieved some important organizational innovations,[24] but none of these, including the advent of an elaborate division of labour, has been without detractors, often ministers themselves. Organizational innovations cannot disguise the fact that cabinet is an important representative institution.[25] Not only has cabinet been employed to balance regional and linguistic interests, but it is fundamentally a political, not a managerial or planning, body. As an emanation of parliament, it cannot afford to develop its decision technology to the point that it is out of touch with the political sensitivities of members of parliament.

The tension between management and politics is manifested in the lack of a consensus on what constitutes an appropriate relationship between the realms of politics and administration. The apparent need to rotate ministers (and now their deputies) has done nothing to dislodge the model of the politician as gifted amateur. More important, the Westminster model does not make it clear to what extent and for what purposes bureaucrats, let alone ouside producer groups, should participate in the formation of public policy. As Hall has demonstrated, in discussing the rendering of policy advice in France, these questions do not represent serious intellectual obstacles in state-centred societies.[26] It is only where the state tradition is weak that the matter of bureaucratic authority is an unsettled question.

The weak state tradition in Canada provides minimal encouragement to the development of the autonomous bureaucracy necessary for macro anticipatory industrial policy making. The fact that patronage was the issue that dominated the public bureaucracy in Canada until about the end of the Second World War illustrates this point well. R.M. Dawson was probably not exaggerating when he wrote, in 1929, that 'review of the history and present organization of the

Canadian service shows that its life has been dominated throughout by one, it might be said by only one, thing, viz., political patronage.'[27] Even in the late 1940s critics warned that downgrading the role of the civil service commission, as proposed by the Gordon Report of 1947, risked opening the door, albeit ever so slightly, to those who would use the public service for partisan purposes.[28] And while it must be said that the merit principle is now so firmly established that the threat of overt manipulation is remote, the political neutrality of the public service remains a pressing issue in Canada, with two main themes dominating. First, how far should public servants be permitted to exercise their rights to political activity? Second, can a coterie of senior officials who have rendered policy advice to one political party for a number of years serve its successor with equanimity?

What is remarkable about this constant concern for political neutrality is that neither of these problems poses a serious threat to the status of public officials in Canada. The battles that they recall have largely been won. While ministerial staffs have grown, patronage has been restricted to the fringes of the public service and the wholesale dismissal of senior officials has simply not occurred. Yet winning has had its price. Although most public servants in Canada have been elevated beyond the reach of partisan political machinations, this status has been at the expense of autonomy in other spheres. In particular, the Canadian public service is almost entirely innocent of the training systems employed in European states to build a core of state officials capable of exercising technical as well as political judgment independent of outside assistance. To be sure, Canada has not followed Britain in adopting the cult of the gifted amateur or the ideal of an administrative class. But, by the same token, it has not partaken of French methods of public-service training, including the creation of a homogeneous élite, ostensibly trained in technical subjects at the Ecole Polytechnique and the Ecole Nationale d'Administration. Instead, bureaucrats in Canada, even those at the senior levels, endorse the view that they are merely the servants of elected officials and as such have no business articulating policy positions independent of what they understand to be the agenda of the governing party.[29]

As a result, the autonomy that public servants in Canada enjoy is little more than the freedom from partisan political interference. It is explicitly not the freedom to engage in planning with producer groups or in public discussions of the broad elements of economic and social policy. Bureaucrats in Canada do not make a habit of seeking public office, as is increasingly the case in France and Germany, nor are they to be heard on matters of public policy unless the issue is sufficiently technical as to render their participation unavoidable. The integration of political and administrative roles in the upper reaches of the Canadian state continues apace,[30] but it is not clear that it enhances the prestige or the autonomy of senior officials. In the meantime, the remainder of the public service, where ideas and technical skills are combined, is cut off from the political centre and normally lacks the resources of a state tradition to distinguish its own interests from those of its clients in the community of interest associations.

Very little central direction and co-ordination can be expected under these circumstances. The merits of centralization, like those of anticipatory industrial policy, are, of course, much debated. However, the issue here is not the advisability of centralized decision making, a precondition for anticipatory policy, but the capacity to engage in it. Where that capacity does not exist, critics are deeply sceptical of the ability of states to conduct policies of state-led growth or to negotiate plans of development with major producer groups.[31] The decentralized state, populated by a host of autonomous sub-units, 'is in danger of dissipating its own special contribution, which must lie in its ability to operate on the basis of a more general and inclusive vision than is feasible for private actors embedded in the market.'[32] Such dissipation has characterized the United States and Britain, where major developmental and co-ordinative challenges, such as the building of railroads and mobilization for the First World War, were met with a strong reluctance to intervene on the part of public officials.[33] In summing up her indictment of the US administration at the onset of the New Deal, Theda Skocpol observed that in a polity based on divided sovereignty, 'no centrally coordinated, executive-dominated national bureaucratic state could emerge, not even during World War 1.'[34]

The problem in such cases does not lie merely in an incapacity or unwillingness to act, but in the evident dissipation of public authority that occurs once action is unavoidable. In societies with weak state traditions, bureaucratic units are in no position to maintain their autonomy against well-organized interest groups. The best they can hope for is some type of pluralist equilibrium. Groups and legislatures make demands that are used by bureaucrats to ensure that their utility functions are not entirely forgotten in the rush to use public authority for private purposes.[35] These bureaus pursue narrow, short-term goals that often draw them into conflict with other bureaus engaged in similar strategies. Their inclination to treat problems sequentially sets the stage for what Lindberg calls 'sectoral decomposition,' the tendency to break large decisions into simpler, more manageable ones.[36] Thus the large picture is sacrificed for the immediate convenience, nay necessity, of striking bargains with organized clientele groups. The type of government offered under these circumstances is 'nonconsensual and incoherent' with 'no integrating ideology or philosophy, only a set of specific ideologies about specific problems.'[37]

The Canadian Bureaucracy and the Westminster Model

Does this portrait of bureaucracy in non-statist societies capture the Canadian public service, or is there a discernible 'centerpoint from which to shift the direction and priorities expressed in the routine accumulation of particular bargains'?[38] At first glance, the recent history of bureaucratic developments in Canada might be interpreted as an effort to define just such a centre-point. The commitment of one prime minister, Pierre Trudeau, to developing the machinery of government capable of rendering rational policy decisions meant that until the mid 1980s the most immediate response to economic crises was the development of central agencies. This is what Colin Campbell has in mind when he speaks of 'the Canadian fascination with coordinative machinery.'[39] It began with the institution of a thorough division of labour among ministers and an elaborate cabinet-committee system organized around the principle of collegiality. In the sphere of economic policy, the Board of Economic Development Ministers was the first of these institutional innovations, followed by the Ministry of State for Economic Development (MSED).

From the perspective of the political-administrative centre, the need for co-ordinative mechanisms was obvious. During the 1960s and early 1970s, new centres of economic policy advice had developed in a relatively unrestrained atmosphere. In such departments as Industry, Trade and Commerce, Communications, Agriculture, and Consumer and Corporate Affairs, bureaus had been created to introduce medium and long-term policy advice into the system. Often this advice was based on intimate knowledge of particular sectors of the economy. Although the Department of Finance was afforded the opportunity to oversee these developments, and thus enter into the spirit of co-ordination pioneered by officials in the Privy Council Office (PCO), Finance officials preferred to confine themselves to their traditional task of setting the levers of macro-economic policy.[40] The creation of new central agencies became the only real alternative.

Unfortunately, these efforts to co-ordinate and streamline policy advice at the centre proved increasingly unsatisfactory. Not only were politicians unimpressed by the proliferation of central agencies, but they also met spirited resistance from line departments. Further reorganizations followed, some of which were aimed at central agencies themselves. The Ministry of State for Economic and Regional Development (the successor to MSED) and its sister agency, the Ministry of State for Social Development, were abolished in 1984, with some of their responsibilities reverting to the PCO and the Department of Finance. The Cabinet committees remained, but no department or agency has emerged to co-ordinate the variety of industrial policy instruments now in play in Canada. The government embarked instead on wide-ranging reorganizations of departments with economic-development responsibilities. Central agencies watched as 'power ... was diffused throughout the institutions of government, finding a resting place wherever the congruence of role and structure provided a welcome.'[41]

Nowhere was the confusion about overall responsibility and co-ordination more evident than in the attempts by successive governments to create a forward-looking department responsible for industrial development. From its founding in 1963, the Department of Industry has lurched from one reorganization to another. This pattern began with the creation of a new department, Industry, Trade and Commerce (ITC), which combined industrial development with government expertise in export trade. Criticized for, among other things, being insensitive to regional needs, ITC was combined, in 1982, with the Department of Regional Economic Expansion (DREE), itself under attack as a political patronage machine.[42] Six years later, the cycle continued with the resurrection of DREE under the guise of region-specific development agencies and the reconstitution of a new industry department depleted of much of its sector-specific expertise, but containing responsibility for science and technology.

The results of this organizational upheaval are still the subject of dispute, but it is safe to say that its existence underlines our central point: the Westminster model of parliamentary government cannot be expected to facilitate the development of consensus on appropriate macro-level industrial policy. Perpetual reorganization cannot compensate for the divisiveness inherent in the party-political battle that characterizes the Westminster model. Constant stress on co-ordination simply compels politicians to engage in endless compromises with cabinet colleagues, often settling on decisions that embody only the lowest common denominator.[43] Inevitably, bureaucrats in line departments come to consider themselves divorced from the centre of decision making. Officials in central agencies, in contrast, appear preoccupied with reorganization as a means of solving political problems and isolated from the day-to-day challenges of managing programs with shrinking resources.

It is not surprising, therefore, that the reform of central policy institutions has done nothing to arrest the decline of the executive in Canada. As Pross puts it, 'power and influence, rather than being retained at the centre, have leached down into the middle levels of the bureaucracy,' rendering the concept of central dominance 'nothing more than a myth.'[44] Where the state tradition is weak, centralized authority cannot call on a store of legitimacy. And when adjustments to the machinery of government fail to produce anticipated improvements in the quality of advice and decision making, there is nothing to prevent line agencies from trumpeting the virtues of bureaucratic pluralism.

They are free then to return to the tasks of defining the public interest in their own particular fashion, which often entails tending to the needs of their clientele.

There is little doubt that the problems of a fragmented bureaucracy weigh heavily on the minds of officials charged with responsibility for industrial policy. When asked if the presence of a number of bureaucratic agencies and the potential for bureaucratic conflict constituted an obstacle in achieving declared goals, fully one-quarter of our respondents considered it the most serious problem they faced, the central obstacle. A further 22 per cent were prepared to consider it an important problem, if not the central one, leaving just over one-half our sample who saw bureaucratic conflict as either a minor irritant (29 per cent) or as no problem at all (24 per cent).

Without comparative data, it is difficult to know if the sentiments expressed here are in keeping with bureaucracies everywhere, or constitute a rather serious critique, by bureaucrats themselves, of the structure of the Canadian state. A closer look at the responses gives some indication. In the first place, bureaucrats are not pointing fingers at one another. If any subscribe to the view that public officials are lazy, irresponsible, or prone to binges of rent seeking, they are not inclined to venture these opinions publicly. Individuals are not the problem: it is, rather, the overall structure of bureaucratic arrangements, including the framework of cabinet organization. Common complaints include the proliferation of semi-autonomous agencies, a lack of direction in policy, and an atmosphere of policy confusion. From below the director level in the Department of Finance, an official makes this blunt assessment: 'If I were an outsider, looking at the federal government, I would be totally disgusted with what is going on inside. It's ridiculous ... Every government department has people that have their little fingers in the policy end ... You have all these different agencies floating off in this big netherland, going off in different directions without any sort of co-ordination.' And there is not much patience, among such critics, for bureaucratic reorganization as a means of solving policy problems. Once again from below the director level, this time in the Department of Regional Industrial Expansion (DRIE), an official registers a strong dissent:

The biggest obstacle? Uncertainty, lack of direction, great gulfs in communication. And all of this is caused fundamentally by the way in which government is organized ... For the past ten years every time the government has had a problem, rather than trying to address the problem, they've created new organizations to deal with it. And you've got organizations overlapping organizations, overlapping organizations. It just simply means that responsibility is so diffused that nobody is responsible. I defy you to find one person in government who is responsible for one thing. It just doesn't exist anymore. It's just a chaotic mess.

This line of criticism is by no means confined to the lower echelons of the public service. The same sentiments are expressed at senior levels, particularly in those departments that have clearly defined programmatic responsibilities. In short, these views are very widespread.

There is, however, one exception. State managers – that is, officials in central agencies who have co-ordinative or specific policy responsibilities,[45] – are not particularly concerned about bureaucratic pluralism. Although they compose only 22 per cent of our sample, 70 per cent of state managers do not see bureaucratic conflict as a problem, while only 47 per cent of other officials are equally sanguine ($p = 0.05$). This Privy Council Office official sums up the other point of view:

Maybe it would be a lot simpler [if bureaucratic competition were eliminated], but I think the decisions would be a hell of a lot worse. Simply because I don't mind proliferations of organizations as long as they reflect different objectives of society. I hate to see conflicts buried ... Maybe it poses a terrible problem for the people down at the operating level. I'm sure they just go crazy down there because you go way down the line and suddenly you discover that this department over here has got a completely different line and the thing gets destroyed. Maybe that's terribly frustrating. Well tough!

Not all state managers were as vociferous, but most either shared this point of view or else felt that the necessary degree of policy integration was already being supplied.

When it came time to suggest changes, once again a wide variety of opinion was expressed, but criticism did not translate easily into reform suggestions. Almost 40 per cent of our respondents were prepared to argue that, conflict or not, the present balance of bureaucratic force makes for good policy. A further 29 per cent were amenable to some minor changes, while the remaining 31 per cent argued for fundamental changes in authority relationships, a wholesale shake-up of the bureaucracy. But even among these 'reformers' no clear program of change emerged. Instead, anecdotal reflection on previous bureaucratic battles formed the core of their analysis, with only a handful of bureaucrats offering carefully reasoned positions on matters of centralization and decentralization or on general issues of managerial reform.

We have described an industrial policy élite that sees in itself a considerable degree of bureaucratic conflict, is divided on the matter of the importance of this conflict, and is unable and, to some extent, unwilling to suggest fundamental change. To that extent, these responses offer broad confirmation for the power-diffusion line of argument. No organizational home exists in the executive institutions of Canadian government that might provide a base for an anticipatory approach to industrial policy. There are lines of division in the federal bureaucracy, but there are very few clearly articulated points of view, and no recognizable schools of thought. If anything unites the industrial policy bureaucracy in Canada it is a rather broad-based animosity toward reorganization directed entirely from the centre. Considerable suspicion and resentment have been generated by reorganization for dimly perceived purposes. Thus it is easier to describe what does not exist in the front lines of this bureaucracy. What cannot be found is an organizational centre of gravity from which consistent political and bureaucratic instructions can be expected to flow. If cabinet is providing this overall direction in matters of industrial development, it has escaped the notice of most, if not all, of these officials.

Federalism and the Westminster Model

The second organizational principle of the Canadian state is that of federalism. The association of federalism with 'weak government' is an old and worthy idea. Since Dicey, countless observers of federal systems have argued that divided sovereignty cripples government action.[46] In Canada, the principle of divided sovereignty has featured prominently in assessments of economic policy making. Scholarship on the subject has rallied in recent years around the concept of 'province building' as a way of describing what many see as an unprecedented decentralization in the Canadian federation. Province building implies the development of strong, wilful provincial states bent on pursuing provincially defined economic strategies.[47] Whatever its source (and there are many interpretations of province building) these observers argue that the results are clear: provincial efforts to build diversified economies inevitably detract from national economic integration, thus imposing significant welfare losses on society as a whole.[48] Efforts by the federal government to intrude into the competition for investment are deeply resented and labelled either as brazen acts of favouritism or as ill-concealed attempts to impose an Ottawa-centred vision of industrial development on the rest of the country. Recalling the role played by the tariff in structuring the present pattern and character of industrial development, any claim by the federal government to represent regional economic aspirations suffers from a shortage of credibility.

There can be little doubt that the array of policy instruments unleashed by both federal and provincial governments is uncoordinated. In the words of Donald Smiley: 'To the extent that effective government requires the rationalization of public policy, federalism stands squarely in the way of this goal.'[49] In that case, industrial policy in a federal system will always threaten to deteriorate into a quagmire of competing programs. In support of this perspective, observers have pointed to the panoply of provincial programs of industrial assistance to illustrate how the provinces are committed to pursuing independent, and often counter-productive, industrial policies.[50] According to many economists, these programs will ultimately reduce the national income of Canadians and retard the growth of firms by limiting the size of the domestic market.

These observations appear to support the presumption that federalism constitutes an independent impediment to coherent industrial policy. It is unwise, however, to endorse this position whole-heartedly. There is little evidence to support the view that, on its own, a federal form can frustrate the wishes of public officials possessed of a consensus on appropriate policy direction. Federalism in the Federal Republic of Germany has not been a serious obstacle to policy development, and there are too many examples of federal/provincial cooperation in the Canadian case to sustain the proposition that federalism is everywhere an impediment to industrial policy making.

In Canada, the underlying problem is that no consensus exists on the need for an industrial policy that is designed and executed at the macro level. Federalism plays a role in discouraging this consensus, but primarily because it provides no nourishment for a state tradition. The very idea of divided sovereignty, the notion that either federal or provincial governments might embody and encompass the public interest, is antithetical to the idea of the state. In Nettl's words, 'the necessary overall superordination or sovereignty does not ... exist.'[51]

In this respect, federalism reinforces parliamentary government. The oft-remarked incompatibility of Canada's two constitutional premises – federal and parliamentary – arises because the federal form compromises parliamentary supremacy.[52] Beyond that, federalism and Canada's form of parliamentary government are more than compatible, they are mutually reinforcing. Both federalism and parliamentarism embody the ideal of territorial representation and have made it the primary organizing principle of the Canadian state. The single-member plurality electoral system, a critical feature of the Westminster model, is organized around provincial boundaries, further emphasizing the importance of the provinces as distinct units for purposes of national representation.[53] The political parties that animate parliamentary government in Canada act essentially as institutionalized adversaries and electoral machines, not as vehicles for devising alternative economic and social futures. None has been able to integrate the national and provincial electoral arenas. In each province, autonomous party systems yield provincial legislatures whose membership is preoccupied with the need to respond to local concerns. Without an institutional counterweight, federalism permits local priorities to emerge full-blown.

This is one of the reasons why, in each province, the object of province-led development is generally the same: to reduce dependence on external capital and to control the costs of labour. Ordinarily, and especially in those provinces dependent on staple exports, this objective is accomplished by an increasing diversification of the economy and the subjugation of labour.[54] All provinces have sought, with some success, to improve their technical and political capacities to attract capital, and all are committed to the use of tax expenditures, subsidies, and public enterprise as policy instruments. But in the absence of a strong state tradition, this diffusion of political authority has not resulted in widespread policy experimentation. None of the provinces has run off in a policy direction clearly at odds with the federal government because both the provincial and the federal states are a product of the same tradition. As a result, provincial programs are conventional and typically unintrusive; like federal industrial policies, they embody reactive principles.

The political requirements for reactive industrial policy are less demanding than those for anticipatory policy. Reactive industrial policy is delivered through a set of sector-neutral horizontal policies and ad hoc responses to the demands of particular firms.[55] In the Canadian division of powers, these horizontal policies have been designed and implemented by the federal government with little effective opposition from the provinces. Westminster-based systems are highly responsive to the employment impact of individual firms on local constituencies. Accordingly, each level of government organizes its programs of industrial assistance to meet the needs of individual firms. Under these circumstances, province building and nation building are not inherently contradictory strategies.[56]

Perhaps because of their reactive character, the impact of federal and provincial programs on the interprovincial flow of goods and services has not been particularly dramatic. Examples of internal barriers to trade are legion. They have included federal transportation and energy pricing policies, provincial agricultural marketing boards, licensing requirements and regulations, and industrial incentives of the provinces.[57] Yet when it comes to assessing their overall impact, researchers are reluctant to claim that the costs are high. In part, scepticism about high costs exists because interprovincial trade makes up only about 20 per cent of the activity of the Canadian economy, and these particular products and services do not appear to be seriously threatened by trade barriers.[58] Thus the Macdonald commission was led to the conclusion that 'the direct costs of existing interprovincial trade barriers appear to be small.'[59]

Turning to the federal level, few observers will quarrel with the observation that 'federalism places important constraints on Ottawa's capacity to make industrial policy independent of the provinces.'[60] Yet federal powers to intervene remain formidable, especially on those occasions when executive-centred parliamentarism produces political consensus.[61] And these powers, especially the federal government's spending power, have been used in recent years to address both industrial- and regional-development problems.[62] The result has been a parade of federal programs.[63] These programs, and international trading rules, have placed some limits on provincial policy making.[64] Some provincial initiatives make no sense without federal co-operation, while others cannot be contemplated without running afoul of GATT provisions. Thus, federal and provincial officials have been prepared to co-operate, and the effects of federalism on co-ordination have not been entirely deleterious.[65] The Canadian experience seems to suggest that in the place of categorical judgments about federalism, it is more useful to consider federalism in the context of particular projects and the likelihood that these might disturb the existing federal/provincial consensus on reactive industrial policy.

Federal Bureaucrats and the Federal Principle

Federal officials responsible for the conduct of industrial policy do not consider federalism to be a serious obstacle to the achievement of policy objectives. Only 5 per cent of those interviewed argued that it was the central obstacle they faced. A further 20 per cent claimed that it was an important obstacle, but not the central one. The remaining 75 per cent described provincial policies and practices either as minor irritants or – and this applies to 45 per cent of the total sample – as constituting no obstacle whatsoever.

When officials saw the provinces as problematic it was generally for two reasons, the first of which might be described as concrete program difficulties. Some federal officials have been embarrassed and annoyed by the aggressive marketing practices of the provinces or by blatant protectionist policies. The lack of co-ordination evident in a number of these provincial initiatives has, in their opinion, incurred some unnecessary costs. This particular problem has occurred in areas such as agriculture, where jurisdictional overlaps demand that care be taken in establishing co-operative arrangements. In such instances, the following type of complaint was not uncommon: 'We've had instances of Alberta, Ontario, and Quebec fighting for pork markets overseas, using their departments of Agriculture to do it for them. In other words what we are doing on a national scale is being done on a provincial scale without any thought as to whether or not it harms Canada.'

The second objection to provincial policies was a broad-based, principled one: the presence of a number of governments, all seeking to change the conditions of competition and the relative prices of commodities, interferes with the smooth operation of the market. In the words of one official:

If you want to put your finger on the biggest constraint to an effective industrial policy it is the problem of the industrial policies of the provinces and the Canadian structure which really gives the provinces much more power than is the case in other countries ... hell, you may get too many industrial complexes set up because the provinces are competitively bidding to get facilities. And then you end up with excess capacity, which is a disaster for everybody, or you end up with firms that are too small to get economies of scale, and that's bad too.

These comments notwithstanding, serious complaints against the provinces were offered only by a small minority. In sensitive policy areas such as com-munications, textiles and clothing, and pharmaceuticals, the level of co-op-eration described by officials was remarkably high. When asked if the provinces constituted a problem, a Communications department official replied: 'Not at all. Not in the field of Communications. On the contrary, we were very glad to see our government's thrust in high tech complemented by the provincial government's sensitivity to it ... The attitude we take is that as officials, civil servants, we do not have a mandate to discuss jurisdiction and the constitution. That has to be left to elected representatives. We are there to co-operate, technically speaking, and the more we co-operate the better it is.' Even allowing for halo effects, the essence of this response was repeated across the public service. Only one other position was as popular, namely that the provinces are not very important. A number of officials have little knowledge of, let alone animosity towards, the initiatives of provincial governments. An official in DRIE summed up this perspective in the following manner: 'The provinces are not a problem. We just ignore them. Much of what they want to do complements what we want to do anyway. There is a good working relationship and exchange of information at the junior levels, and that paves the way for agreement higher up. But really, the provinces aren't a factor. If we are being very attentive we will call up a province, maybe the deputy minister, and tell him what we are going to announce the next day and [we] call that consultation.'

Not everyone can afford this rather cavalier attitude, especially those whose work involves constant interaction with provincial bureaucracies. But it must be remembered that not all federal officials whose jobs bear on matters of industrial policy are in this position. Many approach the question of federalism in a blissful manner, not only because they do not feel the provinces constitute a threat, but also because they cannot imagine that federal initiatives are so intrusive as to be offensive to provincial sensibilities.

Attitudes toward the provinces are dependent neither on rank (senior executive or junior official) nor on structural location (agency or department) in the bureaucracy. The absence of systematic variation arises from the fact that consensus characterizes these attitudes. The most striking finding is the absence of serious division on the matter of the significance of the provinces. Beyond that, neither animosity, nor even impatience, characterizes bureaucratic relationships. If the centre is not embarking on broad-gauged schemes of industrial renewal, the occasion for conflict is much reduced, leaving principled objections to provincial initiatives as the most common form of complaint offered by federal officials.

State Intervention

These observations on the beliefs of public officials, the organizational traumas of the federal bureaucracy, and the policy impact of federalism are consistent, we believe, with the weakness of the state tradition in Canada. It is difficult to be precise about the consequences, but it would appear, at the very least, that the structure of the Canadian government and the quality and character of the Canadian bureaucracy limit the options of economic policy makers. The fragmented nature of the economic bureaucracy and the broad diffusion of political power place severe limits on the possibility of a national capitalist response to industrial policy dilemmas. There is only a thin tradition of technocratic expertise on which to erect consensus-building institutions, and the subject of state intervention itself is highly politicized. Achieving consensus is made even more difficult because there exist very few organizational linkages between unions and business on the one hand, and the parties of labour and the bourgeoisie on the other.[66]

Notwithstanding these institutional deficiencies, suspicions remain that the Canadian state still possesses the wherewithal to launch state-directed projects of development. Some organizational innovations within the Canadian state are consistent with developments in highly statist societies.[67] In addition, several academic observers believe that, state tradition or not, 'many government advisers have limited faith in the private sector in terms of achieving public policy goals such as employment.'[68] Champions of this perspective point to such initiatives as the National Energy Program to illustrate just how far a small, but committed, band of politicians and bureaucrats can go in substituting political outcomes for those that would have been fashioned by the 'free play' of market forces. By portraying public officials as rent seekers, this type of analysis severely downplays the significance of either institutional or constitutional factors and substitutes the image of a homogeneous and essentially predatory bureaucrat.

As these arguments illustrate, the weakness of the statist tradition in Canada remains a rather contested notion. Moreover, it is likely to remain so unless incidents of autonomous state action are put in some perspective. As we have suggested throughout, an understanding of the context for state intervention can be achieved only by drawing on the attitudes and experiences of officials themselves. The hallmark of a political system with a state tradition is the willingness of the bureaucratic élite in charge of industrial development to countenance, nay to promote, state intervention for economic growth. Many observers are prepared to credit bureaucratic officials with spectacular industrial policy successes.[69] Do Canadian bureaucrats see themselves as uniquely situated to offer leadership in matters of industrial development, or, as befits those whose careers have been formed with a non-statist tradition, do they eschew interventionist strategies and emphasize the limits of state direction? Do bureaucrats have their own culture of state intervention or do they share the firm-centred industry culture that prevails in the business community?

We inquired of our officials whether they would approve of the increased use of two instruments of industrial policy: sector strategies, which require selection and promotion of key industrial sectors at the expense of others; and chosen firm strategies, which imply similar choices at the level of the firm.[70] A small, but significant group (16 per cent) were judged 'very favourable' toward state intervention, while another 41 per cent offered some support for one or both of the strategies outlined. A large minority, 43 per cent, were not persuaded of the need for any increase in state intervention and about one-third of these vigorously denounced all intervention strategies. Without comparative data, it is difficult to draw firm conclusions from this pattern of responses, but it appears that at least some of the industrial policy élite yearn for more discretion and a wider public role in directing industrial development. A closer examination of these 'supporters' indicates, however, that their enthusiasm and support is rather qualified.

First, no single department or agency among the ones we studied can be described as a 'hotbed' of interventionism. In virtually every bureau there was a wide range of opinion. Similarly, it cannot be said that either junior or senior officials have a particular affection for a strategic approach to industrial policy. Efforts to isolate coteries of officials disposed one way or another toward state intervention proved impossible using these types of variables.

But a closer examination indicates that those who might profit bureaucratically from a more anticipatory approach to industrial policy are solidly behind it, irrespective of department. Thus we find, for example, that officials whose primary concern lies with industrial-development programs for the telecommunications equipment industry, whether they reside at DRIE, the Department of Communications (DOC), or the National Research Council, (NRC), are strong supporters of either sector strategies, chosen firms, or both. This consensus exists despite the fact that DRIE and DOC have been locked in bureaucratic warfare for several years. These officials may prefer particular instrumentalities, but few shy away entirely from the prospect of making choices.

Second, many supporters of state intervention are willing to approve of an increased emphasis on selective assistance to industry because they believe that this is already an established policy. 'For years we have had articles in the press saying that the government is not up to picking winners. Yet we do it nevertheless. We have done it in space, we have done it in remote sensing and in some defence equipment.' These remarks are echoed by officials responsible for textiles and clothing. 'I very strongly believe in sector strategies. You are probably aware that there are other circles in government that don't believe in them, that it's too "interventionist." But I happen to believe that government has to give some direction ... And we do have a sector strategy in textiles and clothing, unlike most sectors, and I think the situation would be worse without the sector strategy than it would be with it.' Thus, approval or disapproval is contingent to some degree on interpretations of existing policy. For some, these examples constitute necessary evils that do not alter existing commitments to market mechanisms; but for the officials cited above, they signal the possibility of greater reliance on sectoral instruments.

The final observation that must be made about the supporters of increased intervention concerns their overall level of commitment. As the figures cited earlier indicate, the largest group of officials were those whose support for intervention was in some fashion qualified. This often meant that while they supported one instrument, they did not support another. Support for a sectoral approach, for example, was often as much interference in the market-place as officials were prepared to endorse. 'Government leadership has to be exercised in presenting a plan for sectoral development. Particular firms have to find their own way to develop within that plan. Government initiatives will lead us nowhere ... I don't think we can be in that business. We can't go that far.' But others objected that sectoral choices ignore the potentially strong firms that exist in every sector. 'I think that the government should, in developing an industrial strategy, identify the best firms in every sector and involve itself actively in the development of those. In other words, to say that Canada should become of world importance in one sector and totally abandon the rest is not right.'

Still others, while acknowledging the necessity for sectoral and intra-sectoral choices, declared their preference for the broad macro-economic and infra-structural policies that have characterized state intervention in the past. This sentiment found expression even at senior levels in DRIE: 'If somebody gave me a choice between another half-billion dollars in grant funds and a macro-economic policy that would get us back to 3 or 4 per cent real growth and would reduce unemployment, I'd have no problem making a choice.' We are left, then, with an industrial policy élite divided not only on the advisability of intrusive state intervention but also on the most appropriate instruments for accomplishing it.

Ambivalence toward the instruments of anticipatory industrial policy is rooted in some measure in the relationships that state officials maintain with business. We have emphasized throughout that industrial policy is aimed at directing, or at least influencing, the investment decisions of business. Many officials are pleased to countenance such interference, but only if it is broadly supportive of the intentions of the firm's management. These officials partake generously of the firm-centred industry culture predominant in the business community. Reluctant to interfere with the autonomy of the firm any more than is absolutely necessary, they see their activities as promoting individual firms, the central players in the economy.

Nowhere is this firm-centred attitude more entrenched than among those officials charged with deploying distributive policy instruments, those such as tariffs, subsidies, and procurement that can be offered on a disaggregated basis to particular firms or groups of firms. These officials, who composed about one-half our sample, are found in a host of bureaus in line departments. They have strong lines of communication with individual firms, often at the most senior levels. They view sectors or 'industries' as something of an abstraction; and associations are somewhat suspect as representatives of sectoral interests.

A senior official in the Department of Regional Industrial Expansion de-scribed his feelings this way: 'I think that it's very important to know the people in the firms because the associations are getting an amalagm, the lowest common denominator of interests ... The aerospace industry association is governed very much by the five or six big firms and if you listen to them, you're inclined to forget that there are another hundred and ninety firms out there.' These officials expressed the opinion that in mediating between the bureaucracy and the industry, associations often prevent officials from learning what is really important. In the opinion of a director-general in the Department of Agriculture, 'They don't always let you get face to face with their principals, and I think sometimes we'd be better off to get into good down and out discussions with the real people in the real world who have a bottom line at the end of every month. And those are the people that know the kinds of decisions that have to be made in the food business to be successful.' Distributive officials identify with entrepreneurs and managers. They present themselves primarily as policy makers who are devoted to promoting or defending the interests of a specific and restricted clientele group of firms.

State managers, those charged with interpreting and organizing the process of industrial policy making, have a different view of business/state relations. They are promoters of neither firms nor associations. Indeed, as a group, they are the least dependent on business for information and are no more trusting than are distributive officials of associations as mediators in the policy process. To the extent that this group of officials is interested in endorsing state intervention, and they are not particularly enthusiastic, they have no intention of cultivating relations with business in order to achieve their objectives. What distinguishes state managers is their autonomy from business.[71] Their contacts with business are more symbolic than substantive. They are more interested in obtaining a share of the power exercised by their political masters than in sharing what power they have with outsiders. They are decidedly unwilling to champion the type of consultative process on which anticipatory industrial policy initiatives depend.

The only officials whose contacts could conceivably lay the groundwork for industry-wide co-operation are those responsible for the management of regulatory instruments. Like state managers, these officials composed about one-quarter of our sample. Unlike either of the other groups of officials, however, they rely heavily on associations in their day-to-day activities. For these officials, industry consensus is a precious commodity and associations hold out the promise that co-operation will provide a measure of legitimacy for policy initiatives. 'In most associations, you know the people get together and you do get some kind of a semblance of a general opinion that you can construe as being the real opinion of that particular sector ... You want to have, either in fact or in appearance, a feeling that what you are doing is condoned by a very broad spectrum of the people involved.'

This type of business/government relationship serves regulatory officials well in their technical task of iterative regulation-making and revision. But it is not the type of relationship around which longer-term or broader-based industrial policy making can be organized. Regulatory officials present themselves as technical experts applying specialized knowledge in the public interest. As such, they are policy professionals interacting in turn with professional colleagues in industry. Their tasks give these officials a measure of autonomy, but this is not easily expanded into other realms. Specifically, regulatory officials show no particular interest in using their industry contacts as a means of directing industrial development.

It would be wrong to conclude that officials responsible for industrial policy in Canada have rejected state intervention as a means of steering and accelerating economic growth. In the midst of a serious recession, and at a time when all government programs, but particularly programs of selective assistance to business, were coming under strenuous attack, a large proportion of officials persisted in the view that the Canadian state had some responsibility for providing policy direction. Yet these officials did not agree on the most appropriate policy instruments. Most worried openly about the risks involved, even in the strategies they supported. Structurally, there is no centre-point for anticipatory industrial policy, no single department whose members are strongly committed to state intervention. The most enthusiastic interventionists were officials who believed that the sectors with which *they* were involved had the most to gain. Central agents preferred sector-neutral policy instruments and passive relations with business. They were among those least supportive of any further industrial policy experimentation. Other officials have cultivated a pattern of relationships with business that actively reinforces the firm-centred industry culture that dominates within industry itself.

Some years ago Robert Presthus described Canadian support for state intervention as 'pragmatic.'[72] Those who support it now are inclined to argue that Canada has no choice, that a global restructuring of industrial production has already begun.[73] A number of officials agree. Their advocacy of state intervention (where it occurs) is based on an unflattering assessment of the market as a means of responding to this challenge, not on an abiding faith in state direction. There is certainly none of the bravado and self-assurance that one might anticipate in a bureaucracy tutored in economic management, possessed of self-confidence, and poised to launch far-reaching projects of industrial renewal.

Two conclusions emerge from this analysis. First, while the Canadian state is sufficiently differentiated to give expression to the wide range of interests affected by shifts in domestic and global economies, it is not sufficiently integrated to claim control over the process of change. Some societies, such as France, Germany, and Japan, inherited a state tradition from the absolutist regimes that dissolved in the transition from feudal to capitalist modes of production. The Canadian state, in contrast, was formed in the developing capitalist environment of British imperialism. The need for state intervention in these circumstances was clear, but it did not result in the state-building

exercise that characterized the European experience. The early political struggles in Canada were over responsible government, not the top-down extension
of state authority over autonomous political units.[74] Like Britain, the state in
Canada developed around the institution of Parliament, and as such it was
permeated from the outset by society's representatives. As Tom Traves notes,
all classes and interest groups sought, with some success, 'to embed their
interests within the state apparatus itself.'[75] As a result, the Canadian state is
not particularly autonomous.

Second, it is the combined institutional legacy of the Westminster model of
parliamentary government and federalism that fosters a weak state tradition
and discourages anticipatory policy making. In making this argument, we do
not attribute to federalism or parliamentary government a unique and invariable
weight in the policy process.[76] Both make a contribution to a much larger
pattern of policy making, one in which Canada's weak state tradition figures
prominently. It is this weak state tradition that has encouraged the broad diffusion of political power and provided only the thinnest of bases on which to
erect consensus-building institutions. It has led Canadian politicians and bureaucrats away from projects based on state intervention and toward the liberal,
continentalist option in industrial policy making. Given that the present pattern
of industrial policy is rooted in this tradition – that is, in the structures of
Canadian government and in the belief systems of bureaucrats – changing the
direction and content of policy will be an exceptionally long and difficult chore.

4 Policy Networks and Sector Strategies

The preceding chapters have identified global, or macro, constraints on the development of industrial policy in Canada. Chapter two argued that although many business associations exist in Canada, business is dominated by a firm-centred industry culture that has discouraged the development of vertically integrated encompassing organizations that are able to represent the collective interests of business. In chapter three, Canada was described as a country with a weak state tradition. There have been numerous examples of state intervention, but no understanding of the state as a separate entity, and no administrative-bureaucratic élite committed to broad projects of industrial development.

This chapter extends our analysis to the meso (or sectoral) level and outlines the political conditions that give rise to particular versions of industrial policy in different industrial sectors. At the macro level, industrial policy in Canada has been dominated by a set of horizontal, sector-neutral programs highly reactive in their conception and constrained only by the need to appear committed to market-based solutions to the problems of economic development. At the meso level, the picture is much more complicated. Within each sector, much greater attention must be paid to specific bureaucratic arrangements and to the relationships that the officials involved maintain with key societal actors.[1] Similarly, greater attention must be paid to the specific organizational properties of associational systems and individual firms. Such societal actors, in company with bureaucratic agencies, form the core of what we call 'policy networks' at the sectoral level. In this chapter we describe, in general terms, several policy networks – any one or more of which might conceivably obtain in a particular industrial sector. These networks, which are a function of both state and business organizations, have very different consequences for the development of industrial policy, for its stability, and for its success.

Before we begin, however, it must be emphasized that the macro and meso levels, although remarkably autonomous in the Canadian case, are not entirely isolated from one another. Programs designed at the macro level may inadvertently favour firms in some sectors more than others. By the same token, developments at the sectoral level do not go unnoticed by those charged with the macro instruments of industrial policy. Most important, both levels share a predilection for conflictual and competitive politics where a host of opportunities exist for narrowly defined interests to petition successfully for special favours and dispensations. In fact, the organizational features of state and society described in the last two chapters lay the groundwork for a pluralistic style of policy making.

Although there have been a number of interpretations of pluralism, in the context of policy making, most observers have identified three distinguishing features. The first of these is a fragmentation of state authority. A number of government departments and agencies share responsibility for the development and implementation of policy. These agencies are in open competition, influence is widely diffused, and politicians attend assiduously to constituency demands. Second, there is a rich assortment of interest groups, none of which is entirely dominant. Interests are organized in a haphazard fashion and group competition is considered a virtue, a satisfactory means of realizing common concerns. Finally, the policy style of the state is one of disjointed incrementalism. A great diversity of partisan opinions are fed into the policy process and officials attend to these demands by adhering closely to established routines and forging agreements based on minimal adjustments by all parties.[2]

The policy-making environment associated with pluralism dominates at the macro level in Canada and represents an equilibrium to which state/society relations are drawn. None the less, these characteristics of policy making need not be present under all circumstances. In particular, significant variations in the policy-making environment may exist at the sectoral level. In what follows, we outline some of these alternative relationships and explore their policy implications. Of particular concern in this regard is the manner in which these relationships change as industrial sectors evolve. The argument made here (and extended in succeeding chapters) is that, despite the dominance of pluralist arrangements, other policy networks may be more appropriate for the circumstances of particular sectors and the policy instruments in play.

Conditions for Policy Networks

Peter Katzenstein introduced the concept of 'policy network' to bring some order to the variety of relations that prevail between public- and private-sector actors in advanced capitalist systems. He argued that the amount of centralization in society and in the state, and the degree of differentiation between the two, were the critical variables in the establishment of policy networks. Once these were determined, the policy network could be described, and the range and type of policy instruments likely to be associated with such a network could be established. For example, in the United States, the decentralized state, fragmented business and labour organizations (the decentralization of society), and a low level of differentiation between state and society ('in practice a symbiosis between public and private actors') have served to limit the number of policy instruments available in the realm of foreign economic policy.[3] In Japan, by contrast, a centralized state bureaucracy and an integrated, hierarchically organized business community combine to make feasible the use of a wide range of policy instruments and, according to Katzenstein, 'successful sectoral policy.'[4]

Provocative as it is, this formulation is not without its problems. Determining just what constitutes centralization and differentiation is difficult in the abstract and is rendered only slightly more tractable by comparing nations. And because Katzenstein's formulations are intended to refer to entire nations, more complicated patterns of centralization and differentiation may emerge on closer examination of particular sectors.[5] Our own assessment of public- and private-sector relations at the macro level is contained in preceding chapters. This chapter elaborates the concept of policy networks for the characterization of state/society relations at the sectoral level in Canada. The elaboration of this concept requires some modification and expansion of the Katzenstein formulation, beginning with the concepts of state and society centralization.

It may be possible at the macro level to characterize an entire state apparatus as centralized or decentralized, but at the sectoral level the concept of centralization must have more nuance. In an important sense, industrial policy is seldom completely centralized. Ordinarily, a number of departments and agencies can lay claim to one or another instrument in a particular policy area. In pursuing their mandates, they will often make decisions that impinge on the prospects of individuals, firms, and sectors. Industrial policy decisions are seldom the exclusive prerogative of departments of industry.[6] Under these circumstances, policy making can become exceptionally diffuse.

Peter Hall emphasizes that the degree to which ultimate decision-making power is concentrated in the hands of a relatively small number of officials is critical,[7] as is the degree to which these officials are able to act autonomously. The first criterion, the concentration of power, will most likely be met when a single agency or bureau (of the several that are active) is able to dominate relations in a given sector. Such a bureau would have the capacity to aggregate authority from regional instances of government and draw information from sectoral actors, whether firms or interest associations. In contrast, then, the state is weak in a given sector when authority is dispersed and no one group of officials can take the lead in formulating policy for the industry. Under these circumstances, authority is typically diffused among the several bureaus and between levels of government, resulting in overlapping jurisdictions and bureaucratic competition.

The concentration of power is significantly enhanced when arrangements are in place that encourage the formation of informal alliances between members of the political executive and civil servants.[8] In sectors with strong state characteristics, task forces, co-ordinating committees, or working liaison groups encourage the independent thinking and broader perspectives required for longer-term policy planning. By contrast, in sectors with weak state structures, a wide range of politicians and bureaucrats can claim some jurisdiction, no institutions exist to link their activities, and a more traditional division of labour prevails. Such 'bureaucratic pluralism' encourages incremental, short-term decision making that is based on lowest-common-denominator criteria and always vulnerable to the introduction of a partisan political calculus.

The second criterion, following Katzenstein, is the degree to which state organizations are distinct from societal organizations or, put another way, the degree to which the state bureaucracy is autonomous. Concentration of authority and bureaucratic autonomy are not unrelated. John Zysman combines them with the system of civil-service recruitment to offer an estimate of the state's capacity for intervention. The more centralized, autonomous, and élitist a state's bureaucratic-administrative core, the greater is this capacity.[9] In a similar vein, Hall writes that policy innovation is easier when the actors holding a preponderant share of power are relatively free of vested interests.[10] Sulieman, in contrast, notes that a strongly centralized state on the macro level may limit the capacity of state bureaucracies at the sectoral level to achieve autonomy from special interests.[11]

What, then, are the conditions for state autonomy at the sectoral level? No exhaustive list can be supplied, but the following would appear to be particularly important:[12]

1. The bureaus involved should have a clear conception of their role and a value system consistent with and supportive of that mandate. Strong political support for the bureau's role is critical: bureaucrats and ministers should co-operate easily.

2. Where bureaucrats are charged with conveying and interpreting the demands of clientele groups, they should possess a professional ethos distinct from that prevailing among professionals in industry. Autonomy will always

be more difficult to maintain for those bureaus with a clientele rather than a functional mandate.[13]

3. Individual bureaus will be more autonomous when they administer a corpus of law and regulation that define their responsibilities and those of the industry. These rules will not be subject to negotiation, either in their interpretation or in their implementation.

4. Bureaus will be more autonomous when they themselves generate the information, technical or otherwise, required for the pursuit of their mandate.[14] Information may still be collected from firms and associations, but the autonomous bureau will require an in-house capacity to evaluate and employ this information.

When the state is penetrated by sectoral interest groups, bureaus have little autonomy. Officials see the sectoral groups as their clients and, accordingly, attend to their needs rather than to any broader public interest. A weak state organization disperses critical information among a large number of officials or leaves that information in the hands of firms and associations in the sector. The result is a dependency relationship.

If the autonomy of the state bureaucracy is a critical variable in establishing policy networks at the sectoral level, what is the sectoral parallel to Katzenstein's 'centralization of society'? The answer lies in the organization of relevant socio-economic producer groups, particularly business. We suggested at the outset that business is the state's critical partner in all matters of industrial policy. How business is organized at the sectoral level will help to determine whether and in what way major socio-economic producer groups can make a contribution to the development and implementation of industrial policies. There is, as we shall see, great variety in the sectoral organization of business in Canada. At bottom, however, the critical issue is mobilization. To what extent is the business community in a particular industrial sector mobilized to assume a role in the making and implementing of industrial policy?

A highly mobilized sector is characterized by the following:[15]

1. A horizontal division of labour will mark the associational system with separate associations or divisions representing different products, service groups, or territories. Such a division of labour implies the absence of overlapping organizations on the one hand, and of gaps in the associational system on the other. There will be no competition for members.

2. One and (normally) only one association will speak for the sector as a whole. Either sub-sectoral organizations will belong to this sector-wide association (so that a simple vertical division of labour is sustained), or individual firms will associate directly.

3. Both sectoral and sub-sectoral associations will have a high density, that is, a high proportion of the firms (or of the production) in a given sector will be represented by the association.

4. In oligopolistic sectors, where major firms enjoy the option of direct contact with the state, these firms will retain a high profile of activity in the association, thereby employing both direct and indirect means of securing influence.

5. Firms and associations will possess considerable in-house capacity for the generation of information, both technical and political.

6. In a highly mobilized sector, associations will have the capacity to bind member firms to agreements negotiated with the state and to offer assurances of individual firm compliance with policy decisions.

In Table 4.1 we combine the dimensions of bureaucratic autonomy, concentration of authority, and business-interest mobilization to create six categories of policy networks. It is important to make two observations at the outset. First, what is being described here are necessary, but not always sufficient, conditions for these policy networks. Developments at both the micro and macro levels will also be particularly important. Thus, although corporatism at the sectoral level requires a high degree of state autonomy and a highly mobilized business community, it may also require high levels of industrial concentration, low levels of foreign ownership, and a political commitment to negotiation with producer groups that can be secured only at the highest political levels. What can be said is that each category contains that policy network most likely to arise in the absence of a serious political or economic obstacle.

A second cautionary note: rarely can systems of business representation be expected to possess all the qualities outlined above. Similarly, very few bureaucratic systems at the sectoral level will possess all the attributes of concentration and a fully autonomous bureaucracy. In short, the policy networks defined below represent ideal types. They are not to be found pristine in the real political world. For that reason, there may be some ambiguity with respect to which network dominates in any particular industrial sector, and there will occasionally be evidence of more than one network.

Types of Policy Networks

Let us turn, then, to a brief discussion of the salient features of each network, beginning with pressure pluralism. In the pressure pluralist network, the particular circumstances of economic development and the organizational evolution of the bureaucracy in a sector combine to deny the state both autonomy and concentration of decision-making power. Business interests cannot be accommodated to one another, either because the organization of business is hopelessly rudimentary, or because there exist diametrically opposed interests in the same industry. As a result, these interests are fragmented, with groups operating on their own in narrow, specialized, and overlapping domains. No one is discouraged from organizing and no group possesses a monopoly of power. But groups are confined to the task of policy advocacy, and no power sharing is countenanced.[16] The objectives of state officials emerge in the process of competition among contending interests.[17]

The organization of the state in the pressure pluralist network resembles the organization of interests in society. Departments and agencies, each intent on organizational survival, pursue narrow short-term goals that bring them into conflict with other departments and agencies doing precisely the same thing. The phenomenon of bureaucratic politics, identified by Graham Allison and others,[18] amounts to applying the logic of pluralism to internal governmental processes.[19] Any clear distinction between state and society dissolves under these circumstances. Business interests cannot take over the state because no single interest in a sector has achieved a status of primacy and, besides, there is not much to take over. The state is little more than the distillation of societal conflicts and is, in any event, so torn by internal dissension that business would accomplish little by capturing a single part.

In the case of clientele pluralism, the state actually relinquishes some of its authority to private-sector actors who, in turn, pursue objectives with which officials are in broad agreement. Ostensibly, it is the details over which these 'private interest governments' have control.[20] Situations in which business associations (typically the instruments of clientele pluralist arrangements) undertake these responsibilities include those in which insufficient resources are available within state agencies, or where there are no objectives the state wishes to see achieved short of the prosperity of the sector itself. Because prosperity is precisely what the business community has in mind for itself, there is no better custodian of sectoral interests than the representatives of business.

Of course, business must be in a position to capitalize on the state's need to off-load responsibilities. The associational system that undergirds clientele pluralism must have at least some of the qualities that typify a highly mobilized sector. In particular, the representative agencies of business must have the capacity to obtain information on the practices and prospects of individual firms and to aggregate this information in a manner that makes self-policing and self-administration a relatively easy task. But because associations are not bargaining with state agencies, they need not have the capacity to bind members to negotiated solutions to common problems. Unlike in other networks, where several interests may be involved, in the clientele pluralist network one interest dominates and mediation is replaced by delegation. Similarly, the associational system need not be as hierarchical or as vertically integrated as the system required in a corporatist network, for example. That said, by bestowing the authority of the state on business associations, a large measure of order and symmetry will soon characterize interest intermediation. A system of privilege is created in which competition among groups is discouraged and participants are urged to accommodate themselves to the dominant system of clientelism.[21]

It is not uncommon for observers of state/society relations to stretch the term 'corporatism' to include what we have called clientele pluralism. Alan Cawson, for example, defines corporatism as a 'specific socio-political process in which organizations representing monopolistic functional interests engage in political exchange with state agencies over public policy outputs which involves those organizations in a role which combines interest representation and policy implementation through delegated self-enforcement.'[22] Critical for Cawson's definition is the fusion of representation and policy implementation in the hands of groups. We argue, instead, that the fusion about which Cawson speaks can occur in three distinctive forms: clientele pluralism, concertation, and corporatism. In each case, the balance of power among societal groups and between groups and the state varies, yielding quite different policy consequences.

In the case of parentela pluralism, a close relationship exists between owners or managers of individual firms and the dominant political party. Such a relationship has distinct implications for ties between the sector and the bureaucracy. Joseph Lapalombara identifies several defining characteristics of this network.[23] The party in power dominates the state and members of the government are willing, indeed eager, to intervene, employing a partisan calculus in the administrative process. Ordinarily, interest groups will have attained a prominent place inside the party organization, but in the Canadian context, where there is high sub-system autonomy between the party and interest-group systems, it is individual firms that are crucial to the party organization. When it comes to the bureaucracy, decision-making authority is dispersed, technical expertise is weak, and a professional, bureaucratic ethos is scarcely, if at all, developed. Accordingly, individual politicians have more freedom to exert pressure at regional or local levels where decisions on specific allocations are made.

The remaining three networks – corporatism, concertation, state direction – vary significantly from the pluralist models. In the case of corporatism, arguably the most familiar of the three, an autonomous but divided state seeks to place the onus for decision making in the hands of conflicting socio-economic producer groups. On the macro plane, the conflict at issue has normally been between capital and labour. However, when one drops to the sectoral level, other patterns of conflict emerge: the struggle may involve business and farmers,[24] or even two or more fractions of business.[25] Whatever the level or the groups involved, corporatism arises when the parties are in a position of 'mutual deterrence.'[26] Each can prevent the other from realizing its interests directly. A corporatist network provides a means for incorporating two or more classes or class fractions into forums where policy is formulated and implemented.[27] This process of incorporation makes demands on the producer groups in question. They must develop structures that permit comprehensive representation of their domain and facilitate the internal expression and integration of competing interests. All these properties have been identified by Schmitter in his influential portrayal of corporatist systems.[28]

Meso-corporatism differs from its macro-political analogue in the relationship that prevails between producer groups and political parties. In the macro version, corporatism requires a degree of co-ordination and leadership exchange between a social-democratic party and the representatives of organized labour. At the sectoral level, however, co-ordination with the party system is more likely to involve informal arrangements between the socio-economic partners and groups of legislators drawn from a range of parties who represent the *territory* relevant to the sector. In a parliamentary system, legislators from the government party often become the key intermediaries in group/state relations.[29]

Corporatism at the meso level, as on the macro plane, arises when the state, acting with some restraint, delegates sufficient authority to conflicting groups to permit them to resolve their differences without further state interference. The arrival of corporatism is, as Marin suggests, a two-step process that begins with a stalemate between two or more producer groups.[30] In the first stage, the state devolves decision-making authority onto these conflicting groups. At this point, informal coalitions of regionally organized legislators may provide additional co-ordinative capacity by acting as mediators between the conflicting parties and relevant state agencies. When a tentative agreement is reached, the sanction of the state is sought to legitimize the rules needed for implementing the agreement. In this manner, the state attains a degree of autonomy it would normally not possess. Schmitter writes: 'State agents acquire the capacity to make an independent and significant contribution towards the negotiation of a more stable and institutionalized interest compromise and, at the same time, are empowered to extract some "public-regarding" concessions from the bargaining associations.'[31]

Corporatism must be distinguished from a closely related network that we have labelled concertation. Some of the organizational requirements of concertation resemble those of corporatism: the need for inclusive, hierarchical, and non-voluntary associations will not have diminished. But in a concertation

TABLE 4.1
Conditioning factors for policy networks

	State structure			
Mobilization of business interests	High autonomy High concentration	Low autonomy High concentration	High autonomy Low concentration	Low autonomy Low concentration
Low	State-directed	Pressure pluralism	Pressure pluralism	Parentela pluralism
High	Concertation	Clientele pluralism	Corporatism	Industry-dominant pressure pluralism

network, it is business, and usually just a single element or fraction of business, that shares policy-making responsibility with the state. Labour is involved only in a marginal way, if at all, in negotiations about the investment decisions of individual firms. Even in the area of labour mobility, the formal participation of labour groups is extremely limited. In Canada, where labour organization is weakly developed, the prospects for a concertation network are particularly good. Direct negotiation between a strong business association and strong state agencies at the sectoral level is a more likely development than corporatism.[32]

The second feature of the concertation network that requires emphasis is the strength of the state. Unlike a corporatist network where state action is circumscribed, concertation involves an autonomous state agency. To build a common frame of reference, including a common set of objectives and an agreement on the appropriate means of achieving them, the state must, paradoxically, have its own agenda. State officials must articulate objectives that are more encompassing than those of their private-sector partners and insist on standards that they alone set. In short, there are areas of policy making and implementation that are non-negotiable. At the sectoral level, state officials seek an accommodation with business that not only meets the latter's need for freedom of action and economic support, but also is in step with a set of broader political objectives. Some of these objectives will be established by the government of the day, but most will be the legacy of a series of policy decisions.

The final policy network depicted in table 4.1, state direction, is characterized by a weak system of business representation, as found in the pressure pluralist case, combined with a high degree of state autonomy. In this network, the privileged position of business in advanced capitalist systems is put to a severe test. With little warning, and sometimes with little explanation, the state embarks upon economic projects that have serious repercussions for the investment decisions of business. Business is typically divided and, in any event, considered untrustworthy by officials. Politicians and bureaucrats are often self-righteous and manipulative. Officials are not in the mood for concertation, and they are by no means neutral with respect to outcomes and instrumentalities. The political-administrative style is one of managerial directive followed by a polite briefing. Business/state relations are barely cordial.

There are those who imagine that the state is perpetually ready to assert its independence.[33] In Canada they point to episodes such as the National Energy Program (NEP) to illustrate the poignancy of this perspective. But the NEP notwithstanding, circumstances are rare indeed in which the state has both the room to act independently and the will to do so. Not only must conditions of autonomy and concentration be met, but a significant measure of political direction will be required. Although these elements might be forthcoming on a regular basis in some countries, we pointed out in chapters two and three that Canada is not one of them. Achieving the necessary level of centralization at the sectoral level may be marginally easier, but autonomous state action in Canada requires a commitment that can come only from the political centre.

Policy Networks and Industrial Policy

If there is a single legacy of the macro-institutional framework presented in the previous two chapters, it is the widespread importance of pluralism in Canadian politics. No analyst of Canadian politics would be surprised to find pressure pluralist networks in any policy arena. Nevertheless, networks conforming to one of the other types defined above also obtain in Canadian politics and specifically in the industrial policy arena. Under conditions that we shall define, networks other than pressure pluralism may develop in any given sector. In this section, we identify several factors that favour the emergence of a particular policy network in different types of sectors. We show that the mix of policy networks is likely to vary across sectors and within sectors depending on a host of factors.

The nature of industrial policy employed in a sector is closely linked to the character of the policy network. In Canada, the most common arrangement involves a reactive approach to industrial policy and a pressure pluralist network. Even at the sectoral level, where business organization is often more mobilized and state structure more variable, the state is predisposed to leave business alone. Policies are responses to political pressure from business. They tend to be ad hoc, uncoordinated with previous decisions, and oriented almost entirely to the short term. Other than discussions about specific, short-term problems, the state administration requires little from business and business makes few demands of the state.

Although reactive industrial policy often will constitute an effective response, a number of developments – including major shifts in trade patterns, fiscal crises, and changes in government – may disturb the equilibrium on which this approach depends. Particularly important at the sectoral level are changes in the industry cycle. The sector may have reached a point where new expansion is imminent, a different technology has destabilized the production cycle, or perhaps the sector is faced with precipitous decline. The disturbances in policy arrangements resulting from changes in the industry cycle may not be accommodated well by the combination of reactive policies and pressure-group politics. If adjustments are made to the policy objectives of a sector or to the policy instruments employed, a new network, based on different assumptions about business/state relations, may be required.

The question of appropriate policy networks becomes particularly acute when policy change involves a move from a reactive to an anticipatory strategy. What distinguishes an anticipatory approach from a reactive one, it will be recalled from chapter one, is the predisposition on the part of the state to intervene in the industrial organization of the sector. At the sectoral level, anticipatory policies seek to shape industrial organization, including the size and number of firms and their sources of equity. Thus anticipatory policies have a greater range than reactive ones and a greater depth: they aim beyond existing products and organization.[34] Finally, anticipatory policies at the sectoral level are well integrated: they are co-ordinated and mutually reinforcing.

State officials and political leaders may consider a shift from reactive to anticipatory policies in order to ensure significant expansion of a sector following a successful start-up. Their rationale is twofold: they wish to enhance the ability of firms to appropriate privately the benefits of innovation (i.e., improve their profitability) and they hope to generate social benefits in excess of those that would have emerged from the operation of competitive markets.[35] An anticipatory approach to these objectives would favour the promotion of mergers and the gradual restriction of inefficient domestic competition to prepare firms better for intense international markets. Product innovation and greater efficiency would be the target of extensive support for research and development. These initiatives might be augmented with financial assistance and market intelligence to help secure a foothold in export markets. Governments might even move, at this point, to develop a set of chosen firms or 'national champions' in the given sector.[36]

The Japanese semiconductor industry provides an example of anticipatory policy at this expansionist phase. In the early stages of industry development, between 1960 and 1974, the Japanese government protected the domestic market using production quotas and strict limits on foreign investment.[37] During the same period, the Ministry of International Trade and Industry (MITI) pushed firms into a series of mergers with a view to realizing the economies of scale required for international competition. In 1975, having cultivated a group of highly competitive, large firms, MITI, in close consultation with the industry, assisted these firms to establish co-operative research laboratories where they could combine their expertise in a further drive for product innovation. Rationalized and well equipped for future developments, the industry was able to maintain and expand positions already secured in export markets in the United States and Western Europe.

For industries in a stable phase, where the main problem is one of maintaining markets for standardized products, an anticipatory approach may seem less attractive. Even here, however, the state may discover, or invent, strategic reasons for planning comprehensive policies for industry. When planning occurs, emphasis will likely be laid on regulatory instruments. These will be used to stabilize the price of inputs and other operating costs, maintain product quality, restrict the entry of new firms, and ensure domestic political stability. Research and development support emphasizing product improvement and production efficiency will continue to complement these regulatory systems. Because the firms involved are mature, more of this R&D can now be carried out by the firms in-house rather than by government laboratories or universities. Finally, competition policy may be relaxed to afford industry the opportunity to construct mergers for export purposes or resist the intrusion of foreign firms. Firms and the state share responsibility for the future of the sector.

A good Canadian example is the pulp-and-paper industry. Input costs have been stabilized somewhat through price regulation schemes that take into account both market conditions and longer-term regeneration of the resource. Timber-access policies favour larger companies and, as such, provide a barrier to entry.[38] The federal and some provincial governments have supported an extensive modernization of plants in the industry through the federal billion-dollar Pulp and Paper Modernization Program. The federal government has also provided the facilities, as well as some operating support, to the industry's research institute, Paprican. These measures may have helped forestall a threatened decline in an important traditional sector of the Canadian economy.[39]

In declining sectors, the state will find anticipatory policy attractive if only because the alternatives implied in a reactive policy – chiefly increased levels of trade protection – are either unpalatable or unavailable. The ideal typical anticipatory policy approach in a declining sector is planned positive adjustment. The state seeks to reduce production capacity to a level that matches demand and to encourage modernization in order to ensure firms can meet this demand efficiently. The most inefficient plants will be closed, and the remaining firms will be merged and their assets consolidated. Most important, labour-adjustment programs will be established to retrain and relocate workers. Programs may even be launched that will attract new firms to areas abandoned by declining industries.

Jon Pierre provides a useful example of such an approach in his analysis of the termination of three shipyards in Sweden.[40] Although there were special features in each of the three cases, the overall approach used took the following form. The closing of the shipyard was anticipated years in advance. Committees composed of local labour unions, industrialists, bankers, and research institutes were formed and given funding to search out new industries to replace the soon-to-be-abandoned shipyards. These committees searched for industries with growth potential that could be operated on a market-conforming basis. Governments aided in the transition by providing subsidies for worker retraining, the winding down of the old industrial plants, and the building of new industries. In each case, new jobs helped compensate for the loss of the shipyards, and the communities that had existed on the basis of the industry remained viable.

None of these anticipatory strategies could have been sustained with a pressure pluralist policy network. Competition among producer interests and among state agencies is antithetical to planned positive adjustment. Anticipatory policies, by their very nature, require close co-operation between business and the state. Either business must be highly mobilized – capable of looking to the longer term and sufficiently strong to keep state intervention under control – or the state must be autonomous from business – capable of articulating its own vision of the industry's future, and sufficiently co-ordinated to implement a range of policies. The requirements of an anticipatory policy are best met when centralization and autonomous state agencies meet business interests that are mobilized into hierarchical and inclusive groups. The result is a concertation network and collaborative policy making. Thus, table 4.2 indicates that concertation is the preferred policy network for the delivery of anticipatory policy.

Such concertation arrangements emerged in both the Japanese semiconductor and the Canadian pulp-and-paper examples. Both partners shared the same definition of the industry's problems and its requirements. The state had its own objectives, more general than those of business, but they did not pose an obstacle to collaboration. At all stages of industry development, and regardless of the specific character of industry problems, divisions between state officials and business leaders were increasingly regarded as artificial. Public policy making and private interests were progressively integrated.

TABLE 4.2
Policy approach, sector type, and policy networks

Sector type	Policy approach	
	Anticipatory	Reactive
Expansionist	**Concertation** / state-directed	**Pressure pluralism** / parentela pluralism
Stabilizing	**Concertation** / clientele pluralism	**Pressure pluralism** / clientele pluralism
Declining	**Concertation** / corporatism	**Pressure pluralism** / parentela pluralism

Needless to say, these organizational demands are exceedingly difficult to meet. Business and the state will often be out of step, even at the sectoral level where macro-level factors, like the operation of the country's party system, are only remote obstacles. There will be instances, for example, in which the state possesses all the required organizational attributes of centralization and autonomy, but business is not highly mobilized. Under these circumstances, a state-directed network often becomes the vehicle for anticipatory policy. This outcome is particularly likely where state support is required to achieve the product and process innovations necessary for the establishment of competitive positions in international markets. The subsidization of high-risk R&D, the negotiation of state-to-state purchase of volatile technologies, and the transfer of technical innovations from government laboratories to those of industry are measures that autonomous state agencies can initiate in support of innovative firms. These are activities that even Schumpeterian firms, regardless of their market-place potential, are often reluctant to perform for themselves or to accomplish through collective political action.

There are, of course, some instances in which it is business and not the state that possesses the necessary organizational properties. When business interests are highly mobilized, but state agencies are unable to co-ordinate or take the lead in decision making, producers will demand a political structure to accommodate their interests. Under these circumstances, anticipatory policy is entrusted to a corporatist network and sectoral corporatism becomes the alternative to concertation (see table 4.2).

A corporatist network will often arise when a sector is faced with the problem of stemming serious decline. Such a sector will typically have had a long history presided over by a host of state agencies each dealing with a different aspect of the industry, including international trade, home markets, employee training, and quality control.[41] At the same time, the long experience of the industry with a series of problems is likely to have fostered a highly effective industry associational system.[42] This associational system will often house sophisticated policy expertise and possess experience in dealing with other social groups, particularly labour. The state, lacking the organizational capacity to resolve the social conflicts and the hardships involved in decline, delegates to organized interests the problem of formulating a long-term policy solution to these problems.

The Swedish shipyard case followed this pattern, with labour organizations, industry associations, and financial firms co-operating to formulate an alternative industrial strategy for the community. Once formulated, these associations took responsibility for implementing the strategy, using funds provided by the state. Hence, the state continued to take advantage of the high mobilization of sectoral interests but achieved some distance from the delicate political questions of winners and losers in the adjustment process.

There are two reasons why anticipatory policies and their associated networks seldom arise in Canada. First, macro-level variables, including a weak state tradition, the centrality of the legislature, and the presence of a firm-centred industry culture, make it difficult to meet the organizational requirements for concertation, state-directed, and corporatist networks. Second, the most convenient, and often the most appropriate, response to many of the problems inherent in the life cycle of an industry is reactive policy devised and implemented through pressure pluralist networks.[43] In the case of expanding sectors, small programs designed to assist in product and market development may be sufficient. Once stabilized, a sector can be supported by a minimal regulatory scheme designed to keep product quality high and competition 'fair.' If an industry is in decline, governments are free to react ad hoc with higher tariffs, import quotas, and bail-outs. None of these policy scenarios places demands on either the state or business that cannot be accommodated within a pressure pluralist network. For officials anxious only to distance themselves from the structural sources of unemployment and to associate with high profile, firm-specific successes, selective aid to industry is more than sufficient.

Reactive policies can, of course, be sustained by other types of pluralist networks. Table 4.2 indicates the phases of the industry cycle when other pluralist networks might substitute for pressure pluralism. Parentela pluralism, for example, may dominate during either expansion or decline. In the early stages of sectoral development, collective action by firms is often at an elemental stage, while the state has not yet adjusted its structures to take account of the new industry. Similarly, when the industry has been pitched headlong into decline, competition for the remaining markets may become so fierce that collective action in a sectoral association becomes impossible. Within the state structure, officials may be demoralized and governments unwilling to devise a policy response to the problem. These sunrise and sunset scenarios leave a path open for parentela pluralism and the employment of partisan criteria for intervention.

Pressure pluralism may develop into clientele pluralism when the state seeks to capitalize on industry expertise without signaling a change in policy. For example, during the stabilized phase of the industry cycle when state agencies develop limited regulatory systems for quality control and 'fair competition,' they normally establish regular contact with firms in the sector. The technical expertise necessary for running such systems lies initially with the firms. If state agencies are able to learn from these firms and transfer some of this expertise in-house, a pressure pluralist network will persist. Alternatively, these sectoral agencies may be content to leave expertise with the industry, particularly if it is accessible through an interest association. This association is then incorporated into the policy-making process, penetrating the state in a way consistent with the clientele pluralist network.[44]

In summary, when it comes to countries with a weak state tradition, such as Canada, our analysis of the conditions underlying policy networks suggests two conclusions. First, anticipatory policies are likely to be attempted only on those exceptional occasions when circumstances combine to render reactive policy inappropriate. This response will normally occur where state agencies are strong – that is, officials and politicians have succeeded in concentrating resources and decision-making power – or where business mobilization is high. It is unlikely to happen often. The second conclusion follows directly from the first. Where the political conditions for anticipatory policy are not met – that is, when policy networks are not based on concertation, corporatism, or state direction – and anticipatory policies are attempted anyway, frustration will follow. Not only will these policies fail, but the exceptional resources committed will fall into the hands of the strongest vested interests in a pressure pluralism network.

We have argued that although pluralist principles underlie the industrial policy process at the macro level, a wide variety of political arrangements become possible in different sectors of industry. Similarly, although industrial policy at the macro level is largely reactive in character, anticipatory experiments should be expected in those industrial sectors that have established congruent policy networks. Hence, our focus in this chapter has been on policy networks and state/society organization at the meso or sectoral level.

The chapter presented a framework for the analysis of policy networks at the sectoral level. These networks may take on a variety of forms and we have every reason to expect that any given liberal democratic polity will possess most of these policy networks in varying numbers at any given time. As Philippe Schmitter and Luca Lanzalaco indicate, the meso level may provide a propitious environment for experimentation.[45] It is less subject to international or meta-regimes than the macro level, and unlike the micro level of the firm, it is less bound by forms of traditionalism and personalism. The sectoral level may also often be much less visible politically than either the macro or micro levels, a point also made by Arthur Wassenberg.[46] In the face of these weaker constraints, margins of manoeuvre widen and alliance possibilities increase.

None the less, it is also reasonable to expect that the relative frequency of different types of policy networks will vary systematically across democratic polities depending on the macro-political institutions. For example, sectoral associations are likely to assume a highly mobilized form when the interest-intermediation system that exists at the macro level is hierarchical, vertically integrated, and highly representative. By contrast, an undifferentiated, weakly integrated, and poorly representative interest-intermediation system on the macro level will offer few incentives for high mobilization on the meso plane. Under these circumstances, meso-corporatism or sectoral concertation becomes much less likely.

Similar macro/meso relationships obtain when it comes to state structures. While suggesting the need for more sectoral analysis, Stephen Wilks and Maurice Wright stress the possible importance of 'administrative continuity' resulting from a more general bureaucratic culture. They also note the relevance of industry culture, particularly as it bears upon the legitimate limits of state intervention as perceived by business and the state. Hence the 'rules of the game' at the sectoral level draw significantly from these more macro conditions.[47]

In the sectoral chapters that follow, we draw on the discussion of policy networks begun here. We seek to determine whether the policy approach adopted in each of these sectors is appropriate given the sector's structural characteristics and the policy networks in place. We contend that the success or failure of Canadian industrial policy will depend heavily on the shape of these institutional arrangements.

PART TWO

The Political Economy of
Industrial Policy

5 The Political Economy of International Expansion: Telecommunications Manufacturing

Since the very beginnings of settlement in British North America, political leaders have viewed transportation and communications as instruments of both economic and political integration. The Canadian Pacific Railway was built with a view to nation building and Trans Canada Airways (later Air Canada) was created to serve the goal of political integration by setting up an east-west trunk line through which smaller firms could link remote settlements in the north, west, and east to the metropoles in central Canada. Improving technology for long-distance communications has occupied a similar if less glamorous role in the process of nation building. Harsh winters and widely dispersed settlements have encouraged use of the most modern communication technology available, whether it be the wireless, the telegraph, the telephone, microwave transmission, or direct broadcasting satellites. The need to adapt and improve communications technology to serve dispersed communities has brought Canadian scientists and technicians to the forefront of research and development in this field. Canada's geography has required sufficient expertise and inventiveness to give it a comparative advantage in an industry that is one of the fastest growing in the world.

The telecommunications equipment industry includes a range of goods designed to accomplish three functions: the origination and reception of signals, the transmission of signals, and the switching and routing of signals from one transmission link to another.[1] Corresponding to these functions are three basic types of equipment: terminal equipment such as the telephone; transmission equipment such as coaxial cable, microwave radio, and satellites; and switching equipment.[2] The manufacture of these traditionally electromechanical products has been protected through linkages between private and public monopolies in the telecommunications carriers sectors. The advent of semiconductors and modern electronics, combined with the deregulation of carriers, has diminished traditional barriers among a range of industrial sectors. Firms devoted to computers and office equipment have begun to take aim at the rich telecommunications industry, while manufacturing firms in the latter sector have begun to eye the other two as potential areas for expansion. The development of satellite technology, long unrelated to telecommunications equipment, has brought still another industry, aerospace, into the picture.

The telecommunications equipment-manufacturing industry in Canada contains two sub-sectors: on the one hand, the manufacture of communications satellites, and, on the other, the production of other transmission, terminal, and switching equipment. For the purpose of this discussion, we refer to the first as the space sub-sector and to the second as the telecommunications equipment sub-sector.

The state-directed policy network in the space industry departs from the norm in Canadian industrial policy making. It has emerged in the face of the strong obstacles to anticipatory policy-making discussed in part one. Several factors account for significant state direction in the space industry: a highly sophisticated research and development program operating within the Department of Communications, an infant industry structure, the need for state-to-state bargaining, and the ability of the Canadian state to design and implement megaprojects. Over time this state-directed network has fostered a space industry that has become a significant exporter on world markets and an international leader in selected market niches.

The telecommunications equipment sub-sector, with a weak pressure pluralist network, presents a direct contrast to the space industry. This industry has flourished under the leadership of Northern Telecom, one of the world's leading telecommunications equipment-manufacturing firms. Where related product lines in the electronics field have suffered heavy losses to foreign competitors in the post-war period, this sub-sector has achieved unparalleled success. Moreover, it has done so with little help from the state. State agencies have worked on the margin of this sub-sector. Consequently, as Northern Telecom and other firms have moved more and more production abroad, the state has been left singularly unprepared, if not confused, by these developments. It lacks a strategy for the treatment of these multinational corporations and hence any capacity to capitalize on the success of these firms.

These circumstances are traced in this chapter, beginning with a description of the industry structure of the two sub-sectors. There follows a discussion of the policy networks dominant in each industry, state directed in the space case and pressure pluralism in the telecommunications equipment sub-sector. The final section of the chapter examines the configuration of policies that these networks have yielded and evaluates their successes and failures.

Industry Structure

The Telecommunications Equipment Sub-sector

The most prominent feature of the telecommunications equipment industry in North America has been its organization into large, vertically integrated groups. The two major telecommunications carriers in the United States, AT&T and GTE, integrated backward to form their own equipment-manufacturing facilities. The two largest Canadian companies, Bell Canada and B.C. Telephone, were founded originally as subsidiaries of these American carriers. They, too, had companion equipment-manufacturing firms. Northern Electric was a Bell subsidiary, while Lenkurt Electric (Canada) Ltd and Automatic Electric (Canada) Ltd, both owned by GTE, supplied B.C. Tel. When Bell Canada became Canadian-controlled in the 1950s, it retained its share in Northern Electric (since renamed Northern Telecom). The remaining shares continued to be held by Western Electric, the equipment manufacturing arm of AT&T.

Today, Bell Canada Enterprises Inc. owns 53.2 per cent of the shares of Northern Telecom Ltd, the sole Canadian firm offering a complete range of switching and transmission systems, wire and cable, and terminal equipment.[3] Northern, in turn, is the major shareholder in Bell-Northern Research (with Bell Canada a minor holder), the largest private research and development firm in Canada. B.C. Tel has recently rationalized the GTE holdings in Canada by instigating the merger in 1979 of Lenkurt Electric and Automatic Electric creating the new firm, Microtel Ltd. B.C. Tel then purchased Microtel (its principal supplier) with a view to rationalizing its operations and increasing its international competitiveness. Microtel, in turn, has created its own research and development subsidiary, Microtel Pacific Research Ltd.

These ties between the equipment firms and the carriers are of great economic importance because of the monopoly enjoyed by the telephone companies. Regional monopolies provide telephone services in Canada with the largest, Bell Canada, serving about 60 per cent of the telephones and B.C. Tel an additional 11 per cent.[4] The nine major telephone companies have formed a corporation called Telecom Canada, which co-ordinates their traffic within a North American context. Teleglobe Canada, until recently a federal crown corporation, takes charge of overseas communications. The telephone companies participate in a duopoly with CNCP Telecommunications in providing other services such as data communications, private-line services, and video transmissions.

The shift from electromechanical to electronic technology has brought important changes to the internal dynamics of these vertical groups in both Canada and the United States. Semiconductors, specifically integrated circuits, have altered product lines, the way firms organize themselves, and the nature of their markets. The manufacturing process has increasingly become a matter of assembling ready-made components produced in a variety of sites around the world. This process has simplified manufacturing in any given location, but the testing of the finished products has meant vastly increased costs for individual firms operating in highly specialized markets.[5] In addition, new types of research and development now allow firms to take full advantage of digital technologies, which have been used to facilitate decentralization and the local control of communications. With decentralization and a wide range of localized needs, the development of software has grown in importance: it now consumes about 60 per cent of R&D expenditures.[6] Overall, R&D costs have soared in the 1980s, forcing companies to search out wider international markets to cover the increase. As usual, given the public goods character of R&D, governments have been subject to increased demands for support.

The arrival of semiconductors has had another impact as well: it has removed a serious technological obstacle to deregulation in the industry. Electromechanical switching had posed a major barrier to entry because the technology was sui generis to the sector. Advances in telephone technology had little relevance for adding machines and typewriters. Government regulations allowed carriers to favour their equipment subsidiaries when it came to procurement. The carriers and the state agreed that the complexity of electromechanical technology required intense collaboration between equipment manufacturers and carriers. Breaking the hold of these vertically organized industrial groups was close to impossible for outside firms.

Other technological developments have contributed to the erosion of traditional industry barriers. The arrival of digital electronics has made it easier to adapt technology from the office and data-processing industries for use in telecommunications.[7] Even semiconductor firms have become potential entrants to the industry because access to efficient semiconductor design and manufacturing facilities has become an important determinant of competitive performance in the manufacture of switching devices.[8] Some of the larger communications equipment firms have acquired their own semiconductor manufacturing facilities primarily through the purchase of established firms. The confluence of telecommunications equipment, computing, and office equipment has been hastened further by changes in transmission material, specifically the arrival of fibre optics technology.[9]

Finally, governments have accelerated market cross-over by removing many of the regulations that required consumers to purchase equipment from the subsidiaries of the telecommunications carriers. The customers of Bell, for example, have been required to rent their telephones from Western Electric. Key court decisions in the United States removed these requirements by deregulating terminal equipment markets and long-distance services.[10] The US experience has had something of a 'demonstration effect' on Canadian regulators.[11] Since 1980, the federal government and, in particular, the CRTC have made changes in regulations allowing for increased competition in some markets, although not to the degree that has occurred in the United States. Recent CRTC decisions have opened up markets for terminal attachment, allowed new firms to offer enhanced services, and permitted the resale and sharing of terminal equipment. But they have not allowed CNCP Telecommunications to break into the long-distance market held by Telecom Canada and the major telephone companies.[12]

These technological changes, in combination with the growing importance of information processing and transmission, falling costs, and the increasing freedom of consumers to pick and choose equipment to suit their purposes, have encouraged high economic growth in the industry over the past decade. The telecommunications carriers have moved to replace their analogue switches with digital devices, and large institutions such as corporations, government departments, and universities have purchased their own digital personal branch exchanges (PBXs). The terminal equipment market has grown even more quickly as falling prices and new entrants have brought a wave of consumer interest.

The Canadian telecommunications equipment industry has capitalized on the opportunities that this volatility has created. Between 1973 and 1982, shipments in the communications equipment industry grew at an annual rate of almost 30 percent.[13] By the mid 1980s, growth had slowed to 8 per cent, but the industry remained one of the fastest growing in the electronics sector.[14] Equally important, telecommunications equipment, unlike other electronics products, showed a positive balance of trade in the mid 1980s. Exports of telephone apparatus equipment and parts rose by over three and one-half times to $820 million between 1979 and 1984, while exports of other commercial telecommunications equipment increased by two and one-half times to $400 million in the same five-year period.[15] Most of this expansion took place in the US market.

Practically speaking, the industry is heavily dominated by Northern Telecom. In 1982, Northern accounted for more than 45.5 per cent of all Canadian shipments.[16] Since 1960, when Bell Canada bought out Western Electric's share, Northern has moved to develop its own line of products. In 1970, only 10 per cent of the firm's manufacturing sales were of its own proprietary design; by 1980, 82 per cent of its sales were products of its own designs.[17] Northern has been a world leader along with the Swedish firm L.M. Ericsson in the development and sale of digital switches and digital multiplex equipment. The company has moved gradually into the office communications field with the introduction of the LAN (local area network) capability and the Meridian line of fully integrated digital data and voice systems. Northern has entered into a deepening alliance with Apple Computers that will, it expects, further facilitate its progress in the office-products industry.[18] In 1984, Northern operated twenty-five manufacturing plants in Canada, fifteen in the United States, one each in the Republic of Ireland, Brazil, and the United Kingdom, and two in Malaysia. Research and development takes place in twenty-six centres located at these facilities. In addition, Bell-Northern Research operates eight dedicated R&D facilities in Canada and, together with affiliated companies, five in the United States and one in the United Kingdom.[19]

The expansion of Northern into the United States has been remarkable. As late as 1977, the US market absorbed only 15.8 per cent of the firm's sales valued at $193.5 million.[20] By 1985, fully 67 per cent of the firm's revenues totalling $3.9 billion came from sales in the United States, largely on the strength of central-office switching devices.[21] Of particular significance here is the line of digital DMS switches and the SL-I, the world's best-selling digital private branch exchange (PBX). Progress in the US market has been facilitated by an advantageous tariff situation: the tariff on telecommunications products in Canada is 17.8 per cent compared to 4.3–8.5 per cent in the United States.[22] Northern has also increased its sales in Europe and Japan but at a far slower pace than in the United States. It was the sixth leading manufacturer of telecommunications equipment in the world in 1980[23] and represents a prime example of a successful Canadian multinational.[24]

A number of firms trail far behind Northern including Microtel, Mitel, Electrohome, Canadian Marconi, Spar Aerospace, and Gandalf Technologies. The most noteworthy of these is Mitel. Established in 1971, Mitel grew spectacularly from $0.3 million in sales in 1975 to $255.1 million in 1983.[25] With the introduction, in 1979, of a complete range of PBXs, Mitel broke into export markets with unprecedented success. However, the growth of the firm slowed in the mid 1980s as it experienced delays in the introduction of the SX-2000, its first digital switch. British Telecom purchased a significant block of the company's shares, helping to diminish Mitel's decline in the 1980s. Recovery has been slow, but the firm does seem likely to remain a significant exporter of equipment into the next decade.

In a sense, the policy problems posed for governments by the structure of the telecommunications equipment sub-sector are more tractable and pleasant than those in such sectors as textiles and clothing and dairy products. The industry is growing quickly, and competition is increasing with new entrants from the data-processing and office-equipment industries. Unfortunately, foreign governments have put increased pressure on multinationals like Northern Telecom to locate production facilities in the markets they wish to serve. For the Canadian state, the policy problem has become one of ensuring the continued growth of these firms while retaining as much production and R&D in Canada as possible.

The Space Sub-sector

Canada's launching of the *Alouette 1* in 1962 was the first attempt by a power other than the United States and the Soviet Union to explore the uses of space technology. Since that early first attempt, Canada has fashioned a competitive place for itself in what has become a burgeoning industry. The manufacture of space equipment is a technologically innovative sector, requiring a high level of R&D, a number of experimental projects, and highly trained personnel. The *Alouette* project and the later *ISIS* and *Hermes* projects were designed to draw on the resources of other countries and establish a pattern of co-operation that continues to characterize the industry. The fact that the early Canadian projects were overseen by the Defence Research Telecommunications Establishment, later renamed the Communications Research Centre, points to a third characteristic of the industry.[26] In all countries where the industry is active, governments have taken the lead in laying the foundations of it.

By linking two or more points, including moving points such as ships and aircraft, satellites offer a flexible, competitive response to the problems of communicating over long distances.[27] They provide high-quality transmission for areas with low population density, and they handle large information flows quickly. The technology involved has proved reliable and costs are decreasing annually. Satellites, accordingly, are now used not only for standard telephony, but also for televison broadcasting, weather forecasting, remote sensing, search and rescue, and TTC (telemetry, tracking, and control).

Production in this sub-sector involves three distinct activities. First, there is the development and manufacture of satellites, which differ according to their function – telecommunications, remote sensing, weather forecasting, and so on. Satellite production further subdivides between the manufacture of the 'platform' (metal skeleton and panels, solar panels) by aerospace firms and the 'payload' (onboard electronics) by electronics firms.[28] Second is the manufacture and launching of vehicles that place the satellites in orbit. The third activity, and the largest in terms of expenditure, involves the manufacture of earth stations that relay and interpret signals received from satellites. Normally manufactured by telecommunications or electronics companies, these, too, vary, depending on the purpose to which they are being put. Canadian firms have participated in only two of these activities, satellite production and earth-station manufacture.

The industry clearly conforms to what we called in chapter four an expansionist sector. The market for satellite telecommunications is growing steadily; since 1980, growth has doubled every four years.[29] The OECD has predicted that between 1983 and 1990 investments 'will amount to about four billion dollars for launches, 4.5 billion dollars for satellites, and eight billion dollars for earth stations.'[30] Compared to the market for satellites, markets for earth stations are much more competitive with more firms and a more diversified customer base.

The Canadian industry has grown up under the umbrella of a series of contracts let by the Defence Research Telecommunications Establishment (DRTE) in the early to mid 1960s and, during the 1970s, by the Department of Communications and Telesat Canada, the latter an industry/government corporation created in 1969. In the 1960s, DRTE sponsored the *ISIS* program for scientific exploration of the ionosphere. The prime contractor for this project was RCA Victor; de Havilland Aircraft was the major subcontractor. In 1968, the Special Projects and Research Division of de Havilland provided the core for a separate firm, Spar Aerospace. Spar continued in a subcontractor role in the *Anik A, B,* and *C* series of communications satellites commissioned by DOC and Telesat, finally becoming the prime contractor for the *Anik D* series in the late 1970s. In 1977, it purchased the government and commercial systems of RCA Canada in Ste-Anne-de-Bellevue and additional facilities from Northern Telecom. These moves strengthened Spar in its transition to the status of a prime contractor. In the 1980s, Spar was successful in its bid to become the prime contractor for a Brazilian communications satellite and for the *Anik E1* and *E2* satellites to be launched for Telesat Canada in 1990. The firm is at present a major subcontractor to Hughes Aircraft for the *Intelsat VI* series of satellites that provides intercontinental telephone traffic. It is also a significant participant in the European Space Agency's *Olympus* satellite program. Besides providing components for this satellite, Spar has the contract for testing it in the David Florida Laboratories of the Department of Communications. Finally, Spar has been designated the prime contractor for the mobile servicing system for the proposed US space station. This servicing system will be Canada's major contribution to the space station program.

Other smaller firms have also enjoyed success, particularly in international markets. These firms (and products) include Comdev (satellite multiplexers), SED Systems (telemetry, tracking, and control earth stations and satellite receivers), Canadian Astronautics Ltd (search and rescue satellite [SARSAT] terminals), Microtel (space telephony terminals), and Raytheon Canada Ltd (earth terminals).[31] Overall, space has emerged as one of Canada's most rapidly expanding high-technology industries. It has recorded strong gains in manufacturing output and employment and spectacular increases in labour productivity. Most important, much of this success has been accomplished in export markets. John Kirton notes that 'alone among the world's space industries, Canada's exports exceed domestic consumption, with a full two thirds of its output going to the fiercely competitive international market.'[32]

The space sector poses a problem for policy makers similar to that of the telecommunications equipment sub-sector: How is growth to be sustained and even increased over the next two decades? In some respects, the space industry is even more exposed than telecommunications to rapid downturns. The space industry is more cyclical and much more reliant on major projects to foster rapid innovations. Although the Canadian industry resembles that found in other countries, especially in its degree of dependency on the state, its development has differed by being restricted overwhelmingly to commercial rather than military applications.[33] As the industry has moved from the infant stage to a more expansionist, internationally competitive stage, the state will have to continually re-evaluate its role.

Policy Networks and Policy Outcomes

The Space Industry

By the mid 1970s, a well-articulated, anticipatory policy was developing in the space sector. The Canadian state took the lead in formulating this policy, capitalizing on a state-directed policy network that had grown up over the previous decade. The organization of the state agencies impinging on the sector concentrated decision-making responsibility. These agencies possessed both considerable in-house expertise and research and development facilities, which gave them a measure of autonomy from the industry. Business interests in the sector were not highly mobilized; the interest organizations that existed were nascent in form. Business/state interaction in the sector was conducted primarily through direct negotiations between firms and relevant state agencies. Policy making was characterized by the formulation, within the confines of the state, of long-term objectives and the pursuit of these objectives through medium-term planning exercises. Both these characteristics constituted departures from the pluralist bias of Canadian industrial policy making.

It is true that until 1987 there were numerous bureaucratic participants in this policy network. Five government departments or agencies had a direct interest in the space industry:

1 the Department of Communications, which managed most of the communications experimental programs including *Hermes* and *Anik B*, and indirectly oversaw the operating satellites *Anik C* and *Anik D*;
2 the National Research Council, which operated a Space Science Program and had been the lead agency in the development of the Shuttle Remote Manipulator System (the Canadarm) by Spar;
3 the Department of National Defence, which assumed policy responsibility for the search and rescue experimental project (SARSAT);
4 the Department of Energy, Mines and Resources, which directed remote-sensing satellite programs and operated the Canada Centre for Remote Sensing;
5 the Department of the Environment, which had a strong interest in meteorological satellites.

In addition to these agencies, the field has included three more specialized entities:

6 Teleglobe Canada, a recently privatized crown corporation responsible for providing Canadians with efficient overseas radio, television, telephone, and other communications services;
7 Telesat Canada, a corporation jointly owned by the federal government and the telecommunications carriers, which has assumed responsibility for the launch and operation of commercial communications satellites;
8 Canadian Radio, Television and Telecommunications Commission (CRTC), which regulates the communications and broadcasting industries.

Despite the number of bureaucratic actors, decision-making responsibility was not seriously diffused among these many agencies. The five government departments noted above were joined by the Departments of Fisheries and Oceans, External Affairs, Regional Industrial Expansion, and Science and Technology in a rather unique body – the Interdepartmental Committee on Space (ICS). This committee was formed in 1969 and operated for its first five years like most other such committees: the member departments met to discuss their respective projects but went to Cabinet individually for the required funds. In 1974, when a longer-term space policy was formally adopted, the ICS was given a small permanent secretariat housed in the Ministry of State for Science and Technology. By the late 1970s, ICS had developed to the point where it could assume responsibility for integrating and presenting to Cabinet all new program proposals relating to space. This was a key step, as the British example has shown. Without this responsibility, decision making tends to be confused and ineffective.[34] The ICS became, accordingly, a mechanism for co-ordinating the various agency interests, integrating these interests in developing an overall plan, and consulting with industry in assessing the viability of the plans. In this respect, it provided the core for the eventual creation of a new space agency.

The natural tendencies toward diffusion in the space sub-sector were checked further by the lead role assumed by the Department of Communications. Traditionally, the three other entities noted earlier – Teleglobe, Telesat, and the CRTC – have reported to Cabinet through the minister of Communications. In addition, the department houses the Communications Research Centre which includes the David Florida Laboratory. This centre has served as the focal point for research and development on satellite technology in Canada, transferring the fruits of its labours to industry. In addition, DOC has gradually expanded the David Florida facility: it can now provide on a cost-recovery basis all the necessary equipment and assembly areas needed to perform integration and environmental testing of space aircraft. The commercial satellites *Anik C*, *Anik DI*, and *Anik D2* were tested there, as will be the *Olympus* satellite for the European Space Agency. These bureaucratic linkages and this internal expertise enabled DOC to rise above its own departmental mandate to attempt enthusiastically to co-ordinate industrial and communications policy.

The combination, then, of a strong lead department plus the ICS planning framework has served to concentrate decision-making responsibility for the space industry. Yet it should be appreciated that this accumulation of authority, particularly the lead role of DOC, has been strongly contested within government. The former Department of Regional Industrial Expansion, particularly in its still earlier incarnation as the Department of Industry, Trade and Commerce, consistently opposed DOC recommendations. Central to the struggle between these departments were principled differences over the role of the state in industrial development. An assistant deputy minister in DOC summarized the disagreement in the following way:

There is a fundamental difference – the government can be either a court, if you like, who says, 'Well, we're sitting here as the judge. We have some money. You, the private sector, send us in some proposals, and you show us why they will work, and we will try to defeat you in that.' That has been, unfortunately, the attitude of ITC and other departments in the past. Opposed to that is the one where we say that government and industry are partners. We share common objectives ... certainly in the area of industrial development. And what we should do is sit down, get ideas, we should encourage people to put in ideas. Then, instead of trying to shoot them down, we sit down and work with industry and develop programs so we can effectively and efficiently apply the limited resources that we have.

Almost in direct reply, a senior official in DRIE distinguished his department's approach from that of DOC: 'I can tell you we sure wouldn't do that. What we're in the business of doing is leveraging private investment. Private investment – leveraging private investment – that's what this Department is all about. And that does not mean, in my judgment "fully funded." And it does not mean government sponsorship and commitment.' These differences over how the state should approach industrial development were deeply felt, particularly on the ITC/DRIE side. Bureaucrats in this department were bitter and often caustic in their descriptions of the activities of DOC.

The Department of Communications has not been seriously deterred by these challenges to its approach. The expertise at its fingertips gave it a decided advantage over its opponents. An official in the space directorate of DOC put it bluntly: 'Industry, Trade and Commerce try to run their programs with very few people understanding what's going on. In contrast, because of a lot of things, we try to run our programs here having a little better understanding of what the technology is, and what people are trying to do in the industry. There are so many choices, and yet so little cash, that our basic philosophy, albeit not written, is to bring better technical judgment on which area to attack than is available generally from ITC.' Officials in DRIE acknowledged their department's lack of technical expertise. Speaking of the knowledge base of the industry in his own department, a DRIE official said: 'Quite frankly, at the risk of washing dirty linen in public, that knowledge base is very fragmented. It's highly idiosyncratic. It's uneven. It's not very accurate in many cases. It's very difficult to tap right now ... which says more about our internal operations than it says about the companies.' The industry department, whatever its incarnation, acts very much on the margin in the space sub-sector. It has vociferously criticized DOC initiatives, but it has had little to offer by way of an alternative.

Business interests in the space industry are at an emergent stage of organization. Most of the relevant firms belong to the Aerospace Industries Association of Canada (AIAC) and speak through the Space Committee of that association. DOC officials have used this committee as a sounding board when they wish the opinion of the 'industry' on a particular matter. Yet the committee remains far from an organization in its own right. The AIAC has provided a forum for business/state interaction and the support necessary for the committee to play a policy role, but until recently it has not been active itself in the policy network. Most of the contact between business and industry continues to involve individual firms rather than the Space Committee.

The state-directed network in this sector has its origins in the decision by the government's Defence Research Telecommunications Establishment to create a space industry, beginning with the first Canadian satellite, *Alouette 1*. In 1963, the government announced its intention to transfer this technology to industry over the course of the *isis* ionospheric testing program, with RCA in Montreal and de Havilland (both later to become part of Spar) being the primary recipients.[35] In the latter part of the 1960s, the government shifted its research and development efforts from studies of the ionosphere to the more applied problems of domestic communications. The results of these efforts were also transferred to industry, a practice continued by Telesat Canada (created in 1969). This corporation, jointly owned by the telecommunications carriers and the federal government, was put in charge of, among other things, the promotion and development of a domestic space and communications industry.[36]

Channelling the state's resources toward the Canadian space industry would not have occurred, it appears, without the unflagging energy and determination of one man, Dr John Chapman. Chapman did his doctoral research on the radio field characteristics of the ionosphere at McGill University and continued this research first at the Defence Research Board and subsequently at DRTE. His experiments led directly to the *Alouette* series and later to the family of *Aniks*. Beginning in the early 1960s, in the words of Larry Clark, 'Dr. Chapman, as the federal government's representative, stood in the wings as a sort of godfather ensuring that Canadian industry was ready, willing, and able to rise to the challenges as they evolved. Above all, Dr. Chapman was determined that the Canadian industry must establish itself on a competitive basis so as to be able to expand from its domestic sales base into the world market.'[37] Chapman's success indicates that in a state-centred policy network, there are opportunities for political entrepreneurship for both bureaucrats or politicians.

Chapman's efforts met with some success when, in 1974, the government tied these various initiatives together in a new document, 'A Canadian Policy for Space.' Central to this policy was the following statement: '*The government endorses the principle that a Canadian industrial capability for the design and construction of space systems must be maintained and improved through a deliberate policy of moving government space research and development out into industry.*'[38] It was the Canadian state that took the decision to create a Canadian space industry. In so doing, the state indicated that by continuing to transfer the results of its own research and development to the industry, it intended to take the lead in the industry's development. But Canada would remain reliant on other nations for launch vehicles and services. The Canadian industry would be confined to the manufacture of satellites and of earth stations.

Several instruments have been used in support of this policy objective, the most important being government procurement. To date, virtually all purchases of satellites in Canada have come through Telesat Canada and various government departments. The 'Policy for Space' directed these agencies to develop purchasing policies with a view to establishing a 'viable research, development and manufacturing capability in Canada.'[39] It was at this time as well that the Interdepartmental Committee on Space was given its permanent secretariat, in part to ensure that departments submitted plans that conformed to the principle: 'Canada's satellite systems are designed, developed and constructed in Canada, by Canadians using Canadian components.'[40] This policy was elaborated further when, in 1975, the government opted to move toward a Canadian-based prime-contractor capability for satellite manufacture. In turn, it expanded the David Florida Laboratory to provide the required testing facilities and finally selected Spar as the prime contractor for the *Anik D* series of satellites. Spar parlayed this contract – and the exposure it received from another product, the Canadarm – into its selection as the prime contractor for the Brazilian communications satellite.[41]

In seeking to direct the development of the Canadian industry, the government not only needed to create the technical capabilities required for the manufacture of specialized products, but also had to ensure that the highly skilled and technologically sophisticated work-force required was kept busy. The state was uniquely situated to phase in its own requirements and avoid a peak loading of an industry with scarce human resources. But to do so required a commitment to co-ordination and longer-term planning, highly unusual in the realm of industrial policy. An official associated closely with ICS described the committee's thinking:

We've tried to propose, we were the first I think ... a multi-year plan to the government. We proposed a five-year plan, they approved a three-year plan. And this helped a lot because we could tell the industry, 'Well don't worry, this project is funded and it's all written here in a cabinet decision for three years ... And this made them feel much better. On the other hand, since space projects usually are seven to ten years in length, it might be more realistic to approve them for the full period. We did this once with the LSAT program with the European Space Agency. That's a six-year program and there was no way that we could commit ourselves to it without getting approval for the total amount, because the Europeans wouldn't have allowed us into it otherwise.

This form of stewardship requires a priority-setting capability and eventually intensive industry/government collaboration.

DOC's nurturing of a prime-contractor capability was stoutly resisted by the Department of Industry, Trade and Commerce. ITC carried its fight to the Cabinet table with each successive expenditure proposal. An approach involving state direction in close consultation with a chosen firm raised the hackles of the more laissez-faire ITC officials. A senior policy adviser in the Electrical and Electronics Branch of the department made the point this way: 'The Space program isn't a space program, it's a Spar program.' He added: 'Here is a company whose crowning glory is that it can touch a button in Ottawa and the money comes out. It's like a perpetual slot machine and they're able to rig the numbers. They just get money out of government like nobody's business.' Yet the same official upon reflection admitted that ITC's rather automatic opposition to DOC initiatives may not have been well advised. 'We may be wrong there. Their success in Brazil suggests that we might be wrong.'

The Department of Communications continued to use its own special resources in this field in the pursuit of the objectives announced in 1974. It provided funding to Spar to support development of the next generation of (*Anik E*) communications satellites and let contracts to industry for further development of sub-systems, components, and processes for satellite communications.[42] The department took over from the National Research Council the administration of the Pilot Industry / Laboratory Program (PILP), which provided funding for the transfer of technology from government laboratories to firms.[43] Finally, the department offered marketing support to firms in the industry. It supported Canadian firms bidding to provide earth stations in New Guinea and the Peoples Republic of China. More important, it participated in critical government-to-government negotiations and provided guarantees that assisted Spar to secure the Brazilian contract. DOC continues to manage the $8 million Spar-Embratel training program, which was funded by CIDA (Canadian International Development Agency) to train engineers and technicians to operate Brazil's communications satellite.

This brief overview illustrates that policy formulation in the space sub-sector has been distinguished by its long-term planning horizons and a hands-on approach to the development of the Canadian space industry. Such an approach continues to be followed in the late 1980s. The government announced in the spring of 1986 a comprehensive, planned program designed to orient the industry's development well into the next decade.[44] In addition, it unveiled plans to create a new space agency that represents the culmination of the development of the ICS. The planning approach of the earlier years continues to be favoured. For example, in 1989, in co-operation with the United States, a special satellite (*MSAT*) will be launched to improve mobile communications, particularly from remote areas. In order to use such a satellite, new ground-station technology currently not available in Canada will be required. DOC's reaction to this situation is instructive. In 1985, it published a discussion paper whose purpose was to identify an industrial strategy for the *MSAT* ground segment.[45] It suggested that planning was needed to ensure that demand for ground terminals could be met from Canadian sources and set the objective that at least 80 per cent of the domestic market be captured by Canadian firms. It also targeted 10 per cent of the US market for Canadian industry. The plans set out in the document were very detailed both as to products and components, and to timing. The paper was then used as the starting point for discussions between likely participant firms in industry and the department's own scientists.

We shall reserve our evaluation of the policy network in the space sub-sector for the conclusions of this chapter. Suffice it to say that, in the space sub-sector, Canada has a rather distinctive policy formation process, one that is state directed. This state-directed network has developed, in part, because of the character of the industry itself. The space industry in Canada is driven by large-scale projects, is R&D intensive, and has been characterized by a firm-centred industry organization. The result is an industry heavily dependent on the state. The state, for its part, has concentrated decision-making responsibilities, accepted the ideas of political entrepreneurs, and embraced the need for anticipatory policy making.

The Telecommunications Equipment Sub-sector

The policy network dominant in the telecommunications equipment industry and the policy instruments used differ widely from the space example. Decision-making responsibility for the sector is diffused among several competing agencies and virtually no attempt has been made to co-ordinate their activities. These agencies are much less autonomous from industry than their counterparts in the space sub-sector. They lack technical expertise and an independent knowledge base. The organization of business interests mirrors government organization. Instead of a single industry representative, there are two competing ones, each with a somewhat different approach to the policy process. The resulting policy network assumes a pressure pluralist form with many of the most important business/state interactions taking place between firms, particularly Northern Telecom, and relevant agencies. Policy making is highly reactive and poorly co-ordinated, with state bureaus inclined to carve up the industry and claim narrow responsibilities.

The state bureaus responsible for this sub-sector differ most significantly from those overseeing the space industry in their weaker knowledge base. Research and development in the telecommunications equipment industry takes place outside government, particularly in the laboratories of Bell-Northern Research and Northern Telecom. In the realm of telecommunications, and informatics in general, no state agency has the type of expertise that DOC has drawn upon for space technology. Decision-making responsibility for the industry is divided between DOC and DRIE, the latter having a longer history of relations with the industry through the offices of an electrical and electronics-sector branch staffed with industry personnel. For years, observers complained that these sector branch officers had lost touch with technological developments in the industry soon after they were recruited to the public sector, and that they had become captives of the industry. By the early 1980s, disenchantment with these officers led to reductions in personnel, accomplished in the midst of significant (and seemingly endless) reorganizations.

DOC's interests in the development of this industry grew out of its responsibilities for regulating the use of the radio-frequency spectrum and for setting standards for radio and telecommunications equipment. These responsibilities, when combined with its laboratories' interest in communications problems, created a natural interest among its officials in such new technologies as fibre optics, teletext (Telidon), mobile radio, and office communications. In each of these cases, DOC followed the approach used in the space sector, seeking monies from Cabinet to fully fund projects in these areas, and suffering, in the process, routine resistance of DRIE. With each successful award of funds, the department gained a stronger policy role in the telecommunications equipment industry until its voice on these matters has become at least as strong as that of DRIE. Yet its knowledge base in this industry pales compared to its expertise in space. Neither DOC nor DRIE have a mandate or a knowledge base sufficient even to contemplate anticipatory policy making.

Like the configuration of state agencies, the representation of business interests is fragmented, in this case into three parts. Smaller Canadian-owned firms interested in exports belong to the Canadian Advanced Technology Association (CATA), while larger foreign multinationals with a primary interest in the Canadian domestic market are members of the Electrical and Electronics Manufacturers Association of Canada (EEMAC). With its own vice-president for public affairs and a politically astute chairman (Walter Light), Northern Telecom is a power unto itself. Although a member of EEMAC, Northern is very much a single player when it comes to industry/state relations.

The industry's traditional home had been the Electronic Industries Association of Canada, which merged with the Canadian Electrical Manufacturers Association in 1976 to form the Electrical and Electronic Manufacturers Association of Canada. EEMAC compares favourably in size to other major sectoral associations discussed in subsequent chapters. It employs twenty persons and has annual expenditures of about $1 million. Headquartered in Toronto, the association has sporadically maintained an Ottawa office for on-site lobbying. The Electronic Systems Division of EEMAC oversees telecommunications equipment manufacturing and enjoys the active support of Northern Telecom.

Not unlike their close associates in DRIE, EEMAC's position as the industry's main representative was challenged in the late 1970s. In 1978, several of the emerging Canadian-owned firms in the industry, including Mitel and Gandalf, created their own association, the Canadian Advanced Technology Association. It is CATA's conviction that Canadian-owned firms have different interests from most of the multinational corporations active in electronics manufacturing in Canada. These differences are particularly evident in the realm of exports. Accordingly, CATA has restricted its domain to firms that are at least 51 per cent Canadian owned. The association received some initial assistance from government; its first executive director, Bob Long, was seconded from the federal public service. CATA's aggressive style and deliberate attempts to cultivate public opinion contrasted directly with the tactics of EEMAC. Early in its history, CATA singled out the traditional sector-branch organization of ITC as an example of outmoded government organizations responsible for high-technology industries. The old sector boundaries among electronics components, telecommunications, and office and data-processing equipment were collapsing quickly, and ITC, among others, had yet to respond. The association was to find a more suitable partner in the Department of Communications.

With interests fragmented in industry and responsibilities divided within the state, policy making in the telecommunications sub-sector has tended to be reactive and short term. It has been defensive in rationale, environmental in scope, and fragmented among a variety of instruments and agencies. These instruments have included tax expenditures, subsidies, and commercial measures. The tax system has been the most important vehicle, with firms being permitted to deduct all their R&D expenditures from taxable income and (until 1988) a further 50 per cent of increases over a three-year average. Commercial measures employed by the federal government include a tariff on telecommunications products of 17.8 per cent (considerably higher than the US tariff) and a government procurement program that favours Canadian manufacturing in both the telecommunications equipment and computers markets.[46]

During the last several years, an elaborate system of subsidies has been created to promote innovation in the electronics industry in general. Assistance has been made available under a number of umbrella subsidy programs, including the Industrial Research Assistance Program (IRAP), the Defence Industry Productivity Program (DIPP), and the Industrial Regional Development Program (IRDP). In 1982 the Liberal government unveiled yet another program – Strategy for Technology Enhanced Productivity (STEP) – intended specifically for electronics firms. Unlike the others, this program was a relatively targeted instrument, driven by a perceived technology gap created, in part, by the subsidization practices of other countries.

The state has accepted industry's call for 'framework' policies and has avoided the articulation of public goals. It has rarely embarked on schemes of equity participation in the electronics-manufacturing industry, and employs no policy instruments specifically designed to pool the risks associated with the development of volatile technologies.[47] Those instruments that have been employed have operated at the macro level and have never been co-ordinated to the point that it is possible to discern an element of strategy in the policy response. Implicit in the approach that has developed is a decision to let the market-place determine the industry's trajectory. The programs of industrial support currently in place are intended solely as adjuncts to competitive markets. The narrow window of effective public policy intervention in this sector closed long ago and now the problem is to retain sufficient industry intelligence to avoid being entirely surprised by developments.[48] Unfortunately, programs such as the ones described above have operated at such a distance from industry that they have provided few opportunities to address the problem of an inadequate information base. An official in DRIE summarized the situation well:

What's fascinating is that the policy process is so disconnected from fact. (Laughter.) Very often policies, ideas, programs, and so on are dreamt up in somebody's head, and they're based on a very impressionistic, personalized, fragmented view of industry which is gained just through a process of osmosis. There is a great dash of conventional wisdom, combined with a certain amount of myopia, and a bit of hyperbole. You know, it sounds like Stephen Leacock's recipe for humour. Some of it is very humorous. But you know the notion of somebody sitting down, and analyzing the industry, identifying the principal issues and problems, ranking them, analyzing the priority ones in depth, and so on, just is not the case. It doesn't happen. The time frames do not allow it. The information is so uniformly bad, it just doesn't happen.

Overlapping jurisdictions, imprecise mandates, and competing bureaus reinforce reactive policy making. Many officials in DRIE have complained about this lack of direction and predicted that policy paralysis will result. 'You know what happens in a situation like that is that people begin to retrench. It just becomes too difficult to do anything. So they fall back into the area of responsibility that they can very clearly say is theirs. And they limit their initiative and their scope and their perception of issues and everything to that narrow little dimension. And you know, nothing happens, nothing happens ... And that's what happened to this case. This bureaucracy has reached the point where it doesn't work.'

The organization of business interests in the sector constitutes another obstacle to co-ordinated policy making. As one official noted, firms have only a primitive knowledge of the policy process. 'On the part of companies, I would say they don't understand the policy process at all. They don't understand how

Ottawa decides. They don't understand how ideas can be formed. They fundamentally don't understand the enormous importance of making an analytical case for any measures that you want to carry forth. That, of course, is not part of the business culture. There you make your decision on the basis of whatever information you have on hand at that day, and you go with it.' What is more, the industry associations do not seem capable of compensating for the ignorance of the firms. EEMAC and CATA cannot be described as 'policy organizations,' that is, organizations capable of formulating their own policy proposals and discussing their analytical merits with officials. EEMAC has occasionally tried the patience of politicians and bureaucrats with what officials described as 'unbelievably foolish proposals.' For its part, CATA is a very flat organization with an ineffective committee structure and hence little capacity for in-depth policy analysis.

In short, co-ordinated policy making becomes extremely unlikely in such a policy network. We find, instead, that the two leading departments have pursued their own programs, each with its own rationale and its own policy instruments. Two examples, among the many available, illustrate these differences and the lack of co-ordination they produce. The STEP program, sponsored by DRIE, is the first of these. It grew out of an earlier program targeted at the electronics industry, the Special Electronics Fund (SEF). STEP had two objectives: to increase awareness of possible uses of electronics by firms in all industry sectors and to support innovative research and product development by electronics firms. It followed the standard DRIE approach to such programs: firms applied to the department describing their project and specifying how much capital they could contribute. The department assisted these firms to develop a business plan, and offered a measure of financial support often intended to lever contributions from commercial lending institutions. DRIE has rejected the fully funded approach followed by DOC, arguing that shared-cost programs with specific objectives are more attuned to market forces. Over the course of its existence, the SEF/STEP program made large contributions to leading firms in the telecommunications equipment industry, including Mitel, Nabu, and Northern Telecom. The department did not monitor closely how the grants were used, arguing that because the firms themselves were contributing there was no need to do so. As one official put it, 'We don't have to monitor it because no company will squander its own money.'

During this period, DOC was also active in the electronics field, offering to industry the Office Communications System (OCS) program. This program was targeted at the same electronics sectors as the DRIE program and the same firms took advantage of the opportunities provided. Recognizing the growing integration of data processing, telecommunications, and office equipment, noting the immense market that was unfolding in this field, and feeling intense pressure from CATA to assist Canadian firms, DOC commissioned a series of studies to determine the need for automated office equipment and how demand might be met by domestic manufacturers. Based on the results of these studies, DOC made $12 million available to support field trials of new office equipment in federal government departments. In the end, five field trials took place:[49]

1 Bell Canada, Northern Telecom, and Bell-Northern Research in the Customs and Excise division of Revenue Canada;
2 a consortium consisting of Mitel, Nabu, Gandalf, CNCP Telecommunications, and three cable companies in the Department of the Environment;
3 Systemhouse using equipment furnished by AES, Canstar, and several other Canadian companies in the Department of National Defence;
4 Officesmiths, an Ottawa-based software company, in Energy, Mines and Resources;
5 Comterm in the Department of Communications.

In projects of this sort, DOC normally establishes advisory committees composed of government officials and industry personnel to help it monitor the results. In the case of the OCS, the department created an OCS Users Group of government departments and an Industry Consultative Committee chaired by Carl Beigie. Members of the consultative committee represented CATA, EEMAC, the Information Technology Association of Canada (formerly the Canadian Business Equipment Manufacturers Association), the Canadian Association of Data Processing Organizations, and various telecommunications carriers.[50] This committee in turn created three subcommittees: Standards, Federal-Provincial, and Field Trials Evaluations. The use of such committees reflects DOC's belief that successful technological applications require programs in which industry is involved in design, implementation, and evaluation. Committees are also used to ensure that business develops a stake and a commitment to a program, rather than treating it as an initiative simply imposed by government.

The organization of state and industry in the telecommunications equipment industry has produced a pressure pluralist policy network in which agencies and associations are in open competition and the policy style of the state conforms to disjointed incrementalism. The programs just described reflect these characteristics. Most noticeably, policy making in the telecommunications industry has been poorly co-ordinated. Reactive in character, the policies are not underpinned by a planning process and have incorporated no vision of the future of the industry. Yet the telecommunications equipment industry is in many respects a Canadian success story, as noted at the outset of this chapter.

Is a pressure pluralist policy network the most appropriate in this sector of the economy? This question is central to our evaluation of outcomes in the space and telecommunications equipment sub-sectors.

Evaluation and Conclusions

The assessment of the appropriateness of particular policy networks and the policies they have yielded must be based on two factors: the degree of current success and the future direction of these sectors. Comparing the space industry in its early years against the policy objectives articulated in 1974, it is evident that anticipatory policy has achieved some success and that most of the objectives are being met. State intervention has shaped the institutional characteristics of the sector (development of a prime-contractor capability), has contributed to product development based on a partnership between government research laboratories and firms, and has succeeded in planning for future developments. These effects were made possible by a state-directed policy network well suited to the industry's early stage of development.

The general objectives defined in 1974 continue to provide the overall framework for Canadian space policy. They have led to an increasingly mature industry and one that is likely to continue to expand in the future. An official with considerable expertise in the sector reflected this view: 'I think that what will happen is that through greater use of satellites, not only the way Telesat is using them for point-to-point type of communication, but when you start adding satellites for mobile communications, satellites for direct broadcasting, satellites for remote sensing – the sum total of all these satellites and the need to replace them with new replicas or improved versions will probably create a sufficient domestic market to keep one satellite builder in operation and busy all of the time.'

Each of the uses identified by this official will continue to require state involvement in the industry. The cost of providing communications to remote areas through mobile satellite technology (whether this be telephone or broadcasting) and the use of remote sensing for mineral exploration will inevitably demand state participation. The Canadian state is already involved in telephony through Telesat Canada, has a direct interest in broadcasting through the CBC, and is the sponsor of the Canadian Centre for Remote Sensing, which leads the way in this application.

Nevertheless, there are two reasons why growth will not necessarily continue if the status quo, a state-directed network, is maintained. Once an industry has advanced beyond the infant stage to a more mature level of development, state direction becomes less and less appropriate. The imbalance that once existed between the industry's expertise and that of the state becomes less pronounced. With industry more mature (especially in the area of communications satellites) and possessed of its own research and development agenda, firms and associations will insist that they become more directly involved in policy planning. All these factors suggest that a transition to a concertation network is under way. This transition may not be an easy one. The requisite structures are not in place, especially on the side of business. Alex Curran, head of SED Systems and a former assistant deputy minister for space in DOC, has written:

Currently, there is no management process by which priorities and schedules can be jointly assigned to the projects undertaken within Canada's national space programme. Yet, because Canada's domestic requirements cannot support all the capabilities it must develop, and because the space industry must aggressively pursue exports, it is essential that Canada manage effectively the resources assigned to applications development. Recently, the Aerospace Industries Association sent the prime minister a proposal for a much stronger managerial structure. If that proposal – or something similar – is not acted upon, Canada will not meet its achievable goals.[51]

As Curran has indicated, the AIAC has recently taken a more active policy role in this subsector; the new space agency will need to use the association and the expertise of its members in its planning framework.

Second, despite its success, the Canadian space industry is still too small to do everything on its own. It will continue to rely on research and development done in government laboratories. An official in the Space Directorate at DOC described this problem well. 'In the space industry, we are below threshold. That is to say that the company revenues, the revenues of the principal companies, are not high enough to generate a threshold of activity that allows the companies to be self-sufficient.' The same official bluntly added that without government and development support, 'we'd pretty well strangle the industry out of existence.'

It is not obvious, however, whether the state's expertise will be up to the task. Kirton notes that the first generation of space scientists that led Canada to the forefront of the industry is now retiring.[52] It is unclear that the current generation will possess all the resources it needs to compete internationally because of cut-backs in provincial funding to universities and federal cut-backs at the National Research Council (NRC). Yet, as the Swedish case suggests, an independent scientific base is crucial to Canada's maintaining its position and further diversifying its markets.[53] Without such a continuing state presence, concertation will devolve into pressure or clientele pluralism. Anticipatory planning will give way to short-term reactive policy making, and Canadian prominence in this sub-sector will likely suffer as a consequence.

A rather different question arises in the telecommunications equipment subsector: Can Canada afford to continue to rely entirely on reactive policy making in this industry? Two aspects of industry development suggest that this question must be answered in the negative. Technology in telecommunications has come to depend heavily on semi-conductors, specifically integrated circuits of microprocessors. The Canadian semi-conductor industry is virtually non-existent. Canada's deficit in electronic components was close to $2 billion in 1984 and is growing rapidly.[54] Aside from Northern Telecom, which manufactures its own integrated circuits for internal use, there is no major manufacturer of semiconductors in Canada, only a limited number of small ones.[55] The response of many officials and politicians to this situation has normally taken the following form: Canada has no comparative advantage in semiconductor manufacture, better that it import what it needs. Smaller Canadian firms can take the basic semiconductors, customize them, and then find a particular niche for their more specialized product.

The problem with this view is that it is increasingly difficult to divorce the technology of semiconductors from their end use. An OECD study has noted: 'From a policy perspective, the increasing interrelationship between integrated microelectronic circuit technology and technological developments of end-use sectors implies that a technologically backward semi-conductor sector could have severe consequences on developments and growth in the end-use sectors.'[56] The telecommunications equipment industry is just such an end-use sector and the decision to take a laissez-faire attitude may have unfortunate consequences, especially for the smaller manufacturers. As well, technological change is overtaking the ability of small firms to customize their chips and to market them in specialized niches. Developments in product and process technology, particularly the use of computer-assisted design systems, have made it feasible for large companies 'to change gate arrays quickly and cheaply to meet custom requirements.'[57] Hence, even in the context of large mass-production facilities, firms are able to customize and adapt semiconductors for rather specialized end uses.

Other countries have responded strategically to these events. They have increased support for research and development. They have entered into specific R&D projects with firms and, in the case of Japan, have even brought firms together to develop a co-operative research capacity.[58] So far, Canadian public policy has been market-driven; it has eschewed any large-scale collaborative projects with industry. Although Northern Telecom, with its own semiconductor research and manufacturing capacity, will almost certainly be spared the consequences of reactive policy making, it is less clear that the rest of the firms in the sector will be so fortunate.

Ironically, perhaps, Northern Telecom presents the second major problem for Canadian policy makers. Despite its commanding position within the Canadian market, Northern Telecom now generates less than one-third of its revenues in Canada. Sales and production in the United States, however, have mushroomed to the point that the United States is now by far the firm's major market. The presence of a pressure pluralist network in the telecommunications equipment sub-sector means that the state in Canada will not figure largely in these developments. Unlike the case of Sweden where L.M. Ericsson has developed, following a path planned in consultation with government, Northern has been left quite alone.[59] How does a country capture maximum rent, technological spin-offs, and economic growth from multinationals like Northern? Can Northern Telecom's success be used to spur further development of the telecommunications equipment industry in Canada or will Northern transfer even more of its research capacity and eventually its head offices to the United States? All these questions would appear to be vital to the future of the Canadian telecommunications equipment industry. Yet our research shows that a policy network that might address them does not currently exist in Canada.

6   The Political Economy of
Domestic Expansion:
Pharmaceuticals

The pharmaceuticals industry is truly a twentieth-century creation. The home preparation cure-alls of the nineteenth century have given way to an industry of astounding size and profitability. Exponential growth in the industry began with the discovery and patenting of the antibiotics penicillin, streptomycin, and tetracycline in the 1930s and 1940s, followed by the coricosteroids, antihistamines, antidepressants, and diuretics of the 1950s and 1960s.[1] These preparations have had a dramatic impact on diseases such as tuberculosis and pneumonia and have ushered in an era of drug therapy in the treatment of mental illness. While improved diet, hygiene, and public health have aided in reducing mortality and morbidity rates in advanced industrialized countries, the pharmaceutical industry can claim some of the credit as well.

Like all high-technology industries the success of pharmaceuticals depends on investment in innovative capacity. Massive research and development costs have compelled drug companies to exploit therapeutic breakthroughs on a world-wide scale, often exporting drugs to countries whether or not they are consonant with local demand. Faced with such exigencies, the more successful drug companies have become multinational in form, establishing plants and distribution outlets in a host of countries. And in virtually all countries public authorities have adopted measures to regulate pharmaceuticals for safety, efficacy, and price. The scope and intensity of regulations vary from country to country, but in every case the competitive strategies of drug companies must include an appreciation of government regulation.

The metaphor of battle is appropriate for describing the history of the pharmaceuticals industry in Canada during the past quarter-century. By the late 1950s, the multinational drug companies were at war with the consumers and politicians over the question of price. When the Canadian government introduced compulsory licensing in 1969, it brought an end to a decade of open hostilities. The decision to allow greater competition from domestic generic manufacturers also marked the start of a new cold war during which the isolated multinationals reorganized for a second round of open conflict. The policy settlement imposed on the industry in 1969 created a complex pressure pluralist network that dominated state/industry relations through the 1980s. The firms in the sector, largely through the offices of their industry association, mounted an intensive lobbying effort against compulsory licensing. This effort was met by competing associations representing the generic drug companies and consumers. Divisions on the part of industry were matched by parallel alignments within the state apparatus at both federal and provincial levels.

The industry also found itself fighting on a second front in the early 1960s after the thalidomide scandal raised searching questions about its testing and evaluation procedures. In contrast to the pricing issue, this problem was resolved more quietly when the state and the industry agreed on a series of procedures to be implemented in the context of a clientele pluralist network. The emergence of such a network was important for two reasons. First, the issues of safety and efficacy were, to a large extent, kept off the public agenda, thereby allowing the industry to concentrate its energies on the questions of price and compulsory licensing. Second, the close collaboration that developed within this clientele pluralist network generated some sympathy among federal health officials for the industry's position on compulsory licensing. This sympathetic posture was sufficient to neutralize the health consumers' bureaucratic advocate, a potential supporter of compulsory licensing, and further marginalize the industry's opponents within the state.

In the early 1980s, the federal government reconsidered the position of the pharmaceutical industry. Dismayed at the lack of investment by a high-technology industry, the Canadian state gradually made domestic industrial expansion a principal policy objective.[2] With a pressure pluralist network already well entrenched, the only serious option was that of major public concessions to the industry. Lacking the requisite bureaucratic resources and forced to deal with a mature, well-organized industry, a state-directed network, like the one that had emerged in the space sub-sector, was out of the question. Rather than negotiation and planning, pressure pluralism promotes bargaining, posturing, and the art of the quid pro quo. The industry succeeded in exchanging a promise of increased investment for an effective end to compulsory licensing. This new settlement was not reached quietly in negotiations between bureaucrats and the industry but in a public forum involving political leadership at the highest levels. While these changes hold out some potential for a remarkable shift in the tone of industry/state relations, it is unlikely that they will bring an abrupt end to the reactive policy making that has long characterized the sector.

In this chapter we explore the relationships among three sets of variables: the structure of the industry, the instruments of state intervention, and the networks that have developed to sustain public policy objectives in this sector. We conclude with an evaluation of the prospects for industrial policy based on a consideration of the dynamics of policy networks outlined in chapter four.

Industry Structure

Very large firms, originating primarily in the United States, Switzerland, the United Kingdom, Germany, and France, dominate the world's production of pharmaceuticals. The twenty-five largest of these firms account for the majority of international sales.[3] Given that no single firm accounts for more than 5 per cent of the world market, and none has acquired more than 20 per cent of any major national market, the level of concentration in this industry appears, at first blush, to be rather low. In fact, however, the industry is divided into a number of self-contained sectors within which a considerable degree of concentration ordinarily exists. Oligopolistic competition is the norm, and in most product lines firms compete on the basis of innovation and product differentiation rather than price. Competition is genuine in the sense that fortunes wax and wane within these sub-sectors, but the major players tend to remain the same. One author has characterized the phenomenon as a game of musical chairs played by the same set of large drug firms: 'When the music stops, the participants in each game have changed, but merely in order to effect a mutual exchange of one oligopoly situation for another.'[4]

These large pharmaceutical firms engage in a pattern of production premised on a very extensive international division of labour. Research is the critical activity and is normally highly centralized in the company's country of origin. None of the largest firms has more than eight research units altogether, and most have fewer, with one or two of these units ordinarily accounting for 80 per cent of total effort.[5] The second activity, the production of fine chemicals (raw materials and intermediates), is more decentralized. Even here, however, scale economies dictate a relatively few establishments whose precise location is determined by the internal economies of the multinational corporation (MNC). For example, firms take advantage of tax havens such as Ireland and Puerto Rico to engage in transfer pricing that will maximize profits at the points of lowest tax burden. Of course, the production of fine chemicals does require a minimum standard of skill and training because preserving purity is imperative at this stage. For this reason alone, production cannot take place just anywhere. None the less, the absence of serious tariff barriers and the ease of transportation make this part of the industry relatively 'footloose.'

In the third and final stage, the formulation and packaging of products, plants are frequently established in the national markets they are intended to serve. These plants import fine chemicals and combine these with fillers, often to meet special local requirements. The value added at this stage is minimal. The finished drugs are then marketed and promoted by a substantial sales force that is attuned to local traditions and medical practices. Domestic companies are emerging to duplicate these activities – that is, to import and assemble products that are bioequivalent to those of the MNCs – but efforts to induce these companies to engage in the innovative activities that lead to chemical advances typically have met with little success.[6]

In 1980 the value of world trade in pharmaceuticals was $14 billion (US), $8 billion of which was in the form of finished drugs and $6 billion in raw materials and intermediates.[7] With the exception of Japan, which is relatively self-contained, there is a very strong relationship between a country's capacity for innovation and its overall trade balance in pharmaceuticals. Countries that are the home nations for the world's leading pharmaceutical companies have a history of success in innovation and an overall positive balance of trade. In contrast, those countries in which the industry has a low capacity for innovation are dominated by foreign MNCs and are net importers of either fine chemicals, finished products, or both. Unless, like Ireland, they have taken measures specifically designed to attract the production of fine chemicals, their prospects for developing an export trade are, other things being equal, very poor.

Canada clearly belongs among these low-capacity countries. Not only does it lack a single large firm to rival those of the major exporting nations, but Canadian firms also have a very low commitment to R&D by international standards. Their R&D expenditures have varied between 3.5 and 4.8 per cent in the period 1967 to 1982,[8] considerably below the 12–14 per cent levels that are the norm in high-capacity countries. More important perhaps, basic research accounts for only 15 per cent of the R&D expenditures of pharmaceutical companies in Canada. Most of this work is done by a handful of firms, one of which, CDC Life Sciences (formerly Connaught Laboratories), is Canadian owned, and two of which are foreign subsidiaries that were once Canadian firms with well-established R&D facilities in Canada.[9] Another 15 per cent of the industry's R&D effort goes toward process research aimed at reducing costs or improving quality. The remainder, the vast bulk of expenditures, is devoted to research concerned with safety and clinical effectiveness.[10] Without denying the importance of this latter type of research, the point is that Canada makes a negligible contribution to the store of knowledge from which new drugs are ultimately derived.

None of this means that the drug industry in Canada is unprofitable. Whatever the method used for calculating profitability, the conclusion is the same: relative to the profit levels of other Canadian industries, those of the pharmaceutial industry have been consistently high since at least 1968. In fact, the Eastman commission was moved to remark that 'the profitability of pharmaceuticals clearly exceeds that for all manufacturing industries, and also for that of chemicals and chemical products.'[11] International comparisons are notoriously difficult, but the information assembled by the commission suggests that firms operating in Canada enjoy profits as high as, if not higher than, those in the United Kingdom, a country usually defined as a high-capacity performer.

High profits have not attracted many new firms to the industry. The fact that these profits have been captured by the established firms suggests that there may exist some serious barriers to entry into the pharmaceuticals industry. Considerable evidence shows how R&D acts as just such an entry barrier. A monopolist, faced with a set of potential entrants, invests heavily in R&D, thus making entry costly for would-be competitors.[12] In the absence of a firm or set of firms that can break the monopoly by an offensive strategy of R&D investment, public policy becomes the only other means to bring market forces to bear on the industry. Such was the Canadian approach beginning in 1969, when an amendment to the Patent Act required that firms holding a patent on a chemical product be required to license other firms to produce it. In the wake of this legislation, several generic drug companies appeared to produce low-cost equivalents of the products supplied by multinational firms.

Generic firms are distinctive in several ways. First, they engage in a modicum of R&D, typically only enough to satisfy safety and efficacy requirements. Second, they are not part of a world-wide production process. Canadian-owned firms, for example, are prominent generic manufacturers. They have little or no vertical integration and are organized primarily to serve the domestic market, especially hospitals and pharmacies. Third, they produce a restricted range of products, specifically those for which there is a high demand. Economies of scale prevent generic firms from producing a wide range of products for the small Canadian market. Finally, and most important for the consumers of pharmaceuticals, generic firms price their products below those of the multinational firms whose R&D efforts originally led to the development of the drug. Because generic firms are not constrained to recoup gigantic R&D investments, or spend large sums promoting their products, their pricing policy is very attractive to consumers. The average price of generic producers' multiple-source drugs has been about one-half that of the patentee's.[13] Indeed, price competition has supplied the rationale for legislation limiting the effective life of drug patents in Canada.[14]

What emerges clearly from this discussion is a picture of a well-established, internationally rationalized drug industry. The Canadian component industry is not a dynamic one, being organized only for the rudimentary manufacture, promotion, and sale of products developed elsewhere. In the 1980s, the Canadian government began to ask whether the trade-off between price competition and investment was an appropriate one. The multinationals argued in the negative, suggesting that without some modification to the existing patent law, investment would continue to decline. Both Liberal and Conservative governments in this period were forced to take these arguments seriously, because an alternative strategy premised on the mobilization of domestically owned firms was unavailable. Division within the industry between multinational and generic firms, and within the state between those interested in increased investment and those committed to affordable drugs, virtually ensured persistence of a pressure pluralist network. Major policy changes have occurred, but the Canadian state cannot achieve the goal of increased investment directly, as it could in a concertation or state-directed policy network. In a pressure pluralist network with a foreign-controlled multinational industry, the state must rely on inducements to achieve the policy goal of domestic expansion.

Policy Instruments and Policy Goals

In recent years, Canada, like most Western countries, has pursued with considerable intensity two policy objectives in the pharmaceuticals industry: the reduction and stabilization of price, and the provision of safe and efficacious drugs. Two other objectives have been pursued less strenuously: the encouragement of R&D investment in the industry and the insurance of a rapid and steady supply of drugs to the Canadian market. These latter goals are not unimportant, but officials have found it exceedingly difficult to develop a policy formula in which all four objectives can be pursued with equal vigour. In practice, both the state and the industry have tended to separate the safety and efficacy and the supply objectives from those of price and investment. The connection between the price and the investment issues has been a direct one. The manner in which Canada has sought to reduce the price of pharmaceuticals has seriously alienated MNCs whose parent firms have been denied monopoly profits. In this respect, Canada's experience resembles that of Britain, where the government's concern to reduce health-care costs and hence drug prices resulted in a major battle with the industry.[15] Firms in Canada have reacted by attempting to restrict investment in Canadian-produced R&D despite the fact that Canada, with a large number of highly trained personnel, would ordinarily be a very attractive site on which to establish some types of R&D undertakings.

Arriving at a balance between pricing and investment policy has involved highly politicized interchanges in a pressure pluralist policy network. In contrast, the safety, efficacy, and supply objectives are dealt with in a bureaucratic-administrative fashion in a clientele pluralist network. Generally speaking, the issues of safety and efficacy have been isolated from those of price and investment, allowing the industry to concentrate most of its political energies on the removal of compulsory licensing.

Safety, Efficacy, and Supply

Canada has a reputation for insisting upon high standards in the testing of pharmaceutical preparations. These high standards take the form of numerous stages of clinical and pre-clinical testing in which prodigious amounts of research material are assembled to buttress claims for both safety and efficacy. Multinational drug companies have expressed their disapproval of the high costs of this regulatory system. The costs are located in the administration of the system and in the delays that are frequently encountered when the submissions of pharmaceutical companies cannot be processed quickly enough to avoid accumulating a serious backlog. These delays, in turn, affect the availability of new drugs to Canadians.

The system itself is operated almost entirely by the Health Protection Branch (HPB) of Health and Welfare Canada.[16] It begins with the pre-clinical testing (usually on animals) of a new chemical entity in which information is obtained on the toxicity of the drug and its pharmacological effects. A firm that wishes to proceed to clinical testing must prepare a Preclinical New Drug Submission based on the evidence accumulated to date and on information relating to the drug's manufacture. This submission is reviewed by HPB, where an estimate is made of the advantages of this new drug and of the risks involved in human testing. Once clinical tests are completed, the firm prepares a New Drug Submission, often comprising hundreds of volumes, that documents all the results of testing and requests permission to market the drug. This permission is granted upon issuance, by HPB, of a Notice of Compliance accompanied by a Product Monograph detailing the uses to which this drug is to be put and the precautions that must be followed.

Delays are experienced at each stage in this regulatory regime. Some of these originate with the firms themselves because it takes time to prepare submissions, especially when protocols are changed. But most of the delay is the responsibility of the regulatory authorities, who diligently pore over the assembled materials at each point in the process. Canadian approvals take substantially longer than those obtained in the United States, France, Britain, and West Germany. The average time for a Notice of Compliance to be given in Canada is almost twenty-five months, compared to six months in Britain and France and twelve to twenty months in the United States, where drugs that promise major therapeutic advances receive even faster consideration.[17] Regulatory authorities in these countries are frequently required to respond to submissions within about a month, and then only to acknowledge, not review, the clinical trials contemplated. In the United States, for example, the Federal Drug Administration has only thirty days in which to examine the safety aspects of clinical research and although it may veto a drug company's plans (an option rarely exercised), the research proceeds automatically if no refusal is forthcoming.

It is a testament to the esteem in which Canadian authorities are held that compliance with Canadian regulations is deemed sufficient for many other countries. In Canada itself, however, the delays created by the regulatory system appear to have had adverse effects on other policy goals. Quite apart from the impact that delays may have on the appearance of new drugs on the Canadian market, the slow and deliberate quality of the approval process seems to have discouraged MNCs from conducting clinical research in Canada. They would prefer to conduct a full battery of tests in the United States. Between 1981 and 1984 the average duration of MNC clinical research on a new drug in Canada was only thirty-three months, whereas in the United States the corresponding figure was sixty-nine months.[18] It may be that changes to the regulations that would reduce the amount of required documentation and see the withdrawal of HPB from some aspects of regulatory control, including the review of all changes to Product Monographs, would encourage firms to place more clinical research in Canada. That said, it must be noted that such an increase in research effort could not have been seriously anticipated before changes were forthcoming in compulsory licensing provisions.

The presence of this elaborate regulatory system does not mean that the state has the upper hand in this policy area. To the contrary, in the area of safety and efficacy, the state does not possess the wherewithal to undertake the elaborate clinical and pre-clinical trials required. In order to achieve the goal of safe and efficacious drugs, the state in Canada must relinquish some of its authority to private-sector actors – especially with respect to information on new drugs that is supplied by the industry and forms the basis on which regulatory decisions are made. HPB reviews this information and assesses the procedures carried out in company laboratories. Because this system seems to work (albeit with the delays discussed earlier), and because of staff shortages, there is increasing pressure to transfer more of these review activities into the private sector. A clientele pluralist system has evolved in which political authorities rely on the goodwill and the technical capabilities of industry, while scientists on both sides of the public/private sector co-operate in a mutually beneficial project, namely the careful assessment of new pharmaceutical compounds.[19] What the clientele pluralist network requires is consultative machinery that will mediate the objectives of state and industry and remove the risk of confrontation.

Crucial to the success of a clientele pluralism network is an association on the industry side capable of participating fully in the formulation and implementation of policy. The Pharmaceutical Manufacturers Association of Canada (PMAC) represents sixty-four pharmaceutical firms, almost all of which are foreign-owned, patent-holding companies. These members account for approximately 90 per cent of the sales of prescription drugs in Canada. As associations go, the PMAC is highly institutionalized. It maintains an elaborate committee structure organized on the basis of five divisions: financial, marketing, medical R&D, personnel, and plant operations. These committees are composed of representatives from member companies and are charged with achieving consensus on issues and fostering relationships with other associations.[20] The PMAC has maintained a full-time staff since 1958. At present it includes the president and treasurer as well as the directors of three divisions: Professional Relations, Government Liaison, and Publications. These officers of the association are responsible to a board of directors drawn from the senior management of fifteen of the largest member companies. Ad hoc committees, some devoted to liaison, others to specific problem areas, round out the organizational complex.

There are two general consultative mechanisms that link the state and industry to one another, and in both cases the industry association plays a large role. In the first of these, officials from HPB and PMAC meet regularly in joint committees to work out regulatory changes and their accompanying guidelines. In addition, senior officials in HPB, including the assistant deputy minister, meet twice yearly with the board of directors of the association to discuss any major changes in the regulatory regime. A second consultative mechanism, the information letter, gives firms in the industry advance notice of contemplated changes and solicits their reaction. This reaction is usually provided by PMAC itself, following consultation with its membership. In fact, HPB makes a practice of discussing these matters with the association even before an information letter is drafted.

There are no serious regulatory obstacles to the practice of consultation. The regulations defined under the Food and Drugs Act tend to be brief and general, with considerable scope for negotiation and discussion. An official in HPB described the situation in the following manner: 'They [the regulations] are not that great now. There are about six or seven pages and that covers all there is in Canada about new drugs. In the usual way, following the old British tradition, we keep things very vague. For example, what is your regulation for testing the safety of a new drug? Well, what's asked for in our regulations is submission to us of details of the test carried out to establish safety. That's the extent of the regulation ... So we need to have, and we do have, a fair amount of guide-lines explaining what we interpret that regulation to mean.' In classic clientele pluralist fashion, the regulatory system is weak on specifics and the state and the industry must collaborate on the development of appropriate practices.[21]

The success of consultative mechanisms, combined with the open-ended character of Food and Drugs Act regulations, has encouraged the state to experiment with the delegation of authority to industry. For example, although the inspection of manufacturing establishments is conducted by HPB officials, they employ guide-lines drafted by a joint committee composed of state and industry representatives. These guide-lines have no legal force, but PMAC acts as a self-regulating agency requiring companies, as a condition of membership in the association, to formally agree to respect these guide-lines. Member firms must also agree to abide by the association's 'Code of Marketing Practice,' which states that claims made on behalf of a product must 'reflect accurately and clearly the intent and spirit of the Product Monograph as accepted by the Health Protection Branch.' Responsibility for enforcing this code has been delegated to a private body, the Pharmaceutical Advertising Advisory Board. This board is composed of representatives from the PMAC, the medical and pharmaceutical associations, and the Consumers Association of Canada, with a representative from HPB sitting as an ex-officio member. It is charged with reviewing advertisements and comparing their claims against the indications contained in the Product Monograph. Thus, the state has relinquished to a private-interest government the responsibility for enforcing those parts of the Food and Drugs Act that prohibit misleading advertising.[22] In both cases, the state and industry are co-responsible for the formulation of policy, but it is the association that is responsible for implementation.[23]

Delegation in Canada has not reached the point that it has in France and the United Kingdom, where the decision to market a new drug rests with a com-mittee of 'experts' composed of pharmacologists, chemists, and physicians. Such a move was suggested, however, by the Eastman commission. The com-mission expressed the opinion that public servants are highly sensitive to adverse reactions and for that reason may be inclined to discount the advantages that could attend the early introduction of a new drug. The commission argued that 'however talented the staff of a government agency, an expert committee drawn from universities, hospitals, research institutions, and industry has a better chance to make a properly balanced judgement on a particular drug.' The Eastman commission did not want to eliminate HPB – it would continue to blish appropriate guide-lines and procedures' – but it suggested that the clientele pluralist network, which already exists in nascent form in this sector, be strengthened in an important way.[24] The result would, of course, be a further blurring of the boundary between state and industry, a concomitant of clientele pluralism.

In Canada, the issues of safety, efficacy, and supply have been dealt with by bureaucrats rather than politicians, with the industry playing a strong role in policy formulation and implementation. Such a system is popular in other countries as well, even though breakdowns have occurred, as the introduction of Opren/Oraflex in the United States indicates.[25] Whatever its impact on health, the clientele pluralist network in place to mediate these issue areas has broader implications for policy making in this sector. First, among officials of HPB, this network provides PMAC with a measure of legitimacy as a responsible participant in the policy process. PMAC's status in this network helped shape the rather ambiguous role played by the Department of Health and Welfare in the debate over pricing and investment policy. Second, it allowed PMAC to concentrate its political attentions on compulsory licensing. Unlike the early 1960s, when the industry found itself fighting and losing on the two policy fronts, clientele pluralism kept the politics of safety and efficacy off the public agenda during the 1980s.

Compulsory Licensing and the Politics of Investment

The present pricing system and the level of investment by the industry are largely the products of a political arrangement with which neither party, business or the state, has been entirely happy. In its attempt to regulate the price structure of pharmaceuticals in Canada, the state has sought to manipulate the patent system as it applies to ethical drugs. In 1969, following almost a decade of hearings, the then-Liberal government introduced an amendment to Section 41(4) of the Patent Act requiring that a licence be granted to anyone seeking to import pharmaceutical products that had been produced by patented processes. Previously, compulsory licences had been granted only for manufacture, use, and sale of the patented processes themselves. The extension of the act to cover imports of pharmaceuticals led to a dramatic increase in the number of licences applied for and granted. Of course, they were not granted for free. The Commissioner of Patents determined that a royalty rate of 4 per cent of the net selling price of the drug in its final dosage form was a sufficent tribute to the research and development efforts of most patent holders. Thus, a small amendment to the Patent Act opened the way to companies, many of them

Canadian, wishing to manufacture generic substitutes for a host of pharmaceutical products that had previously been the sole preserve of patent holders.

The Liberal government justified compulsory licensing by noting the need for increased price competition. It argued that as long as the pharmaceutical companies enjoyed a monopoly over the production of fine chemicals, they would engage in monopoly pricing. The patent system created that monopoly and, it was alleged, excess profits because rents accruing to successful innovations have been greater than expenses arising from unsuccessful ones.[26] The numerous hearings and task forces that assessed drug prices in the 1960s determined that prices in Canada were unjustifiably high as a direct consequence of this monopoly. By giving other firms the opportunity to produce a generic equivalent, the government believed that a measure of price competition could be introduced with little immediate sacrifice, other than the political support of the multinational drug companies.

The benefits of drug licensing turned out to be, as expected, quite sensational. Drug prices in several categories were reduced by 50 per cent and more. Moreover, because provincial governments, through 'pharmacare' plans, reimburse consumers the costs of approximately 43 per cent of pharmacy drug sales,[27] the potential benefits of compulsory licensing extended to taxpayers as well as consumers. These latter benefits were often unrealized, however, because provincial governments did not insist on the substitution of generic equivalents for patented drugs. None the less, the opportunity to substitute existed because of compulsory licensing. And the incentive existed as well. Pharmacare programs constituted a large and growing drain on provincial public treasuries sufficient, in all likelihood, to encourage at least some provincial officials to lobby for a continuation of the compulsory licensing system that kept these savings within reach.

This compulsory licensing policy represented a frontal attack on the policy preferences of MNCs. They argued that the existence of monopoly pricing in the first place is a direct outcome of market failure in research and development. Pharmaceutical products are high-technology items. They embody a considerable amount of information and skill, and these have a public goods character. The costs associated with developing new products outstrip, by a considerable margin, the costs of manufacturing them. Somehow the originators of these products must be afforded an opportunity to recoup their costs. If no such opportunity is provided, the incentive to engage in innovation is diminished and public access to new pharmaceutical preparations is diminished with it. In short, the private returns to R&D are less than the social benefits.[28]

From the industry's perspective, then, patents exist to close the gap between public and private returns to innovation by providing innovators with the opportunity to supply their products temporarily free from competition. The precise period for which this privilege should be extended is always a matter of debate, but in principle it should be long enough to ensure that innovators do not provide sub-optimal levels of R&D, but not so long that the marginal benefits of R&D spending are insufficient to justify continued protection. Thus patent policy, in this reading, is first and foremost a matter of balance. If patent coverage is too short, there will be too little innovation; if it is too long, resources that should be invested elsewhere will be used by the patent holder to extend the period of monopoly profit-taking.

PMAC's position was that the effects of compulsory licensing were not limited to price competition but had an impact on the general environment in which innovation took place. Specifically, compulsory licensing discouraged the performance of R&D in Canada by multinational firms. In a number of submissions to the Eastman commission, firms cited compulsory licensing, and the generally hostile attitude of the Canadian government toward foreign investment, as the reasons that patent-holding firms were unwilling to carry out R&D activities in Canada. The chairman of Warner-Lambert explained his company's position this way: 'There was no way we could in good conscience ask our board of directors for funds for pharmaceutical research facilities in the only major country in the world that deprives the innovator exclusive market rights to compounds that would be developed in those facilities.'[29]

Critics of the industry position replied that it was not patent policy that determined the location of R&D activities but scale economies and the preference of MNCs for establishing facilities in countries of origin.[30] They suggested that there was little evidence that the introduction of compulsory licensing had had a serious adverse affect on the amount of R&D performed in Canada.[31] Before and after 1969, the ratio of intramural R&D expenditures to factory shipments remained low by international standards, inviting the conclusion that foreign ownership, and not patent policy, was the reason for low levels of R&D spending in Canada.[32] The Eastman commission came to the 'inescapable' conclusion that either cost conditions were not as favourable for R&D as they appeared, or competitive pressures were not severe enough to force MNCs to swallow their political convictions and use Canada as an R&D site.[33] In either event, the repeal of compulsory licensing would do little to improve matters. This logic did not discourage MNCs from promising increased R&D facilities in exchange for a change in the Patent Act provisions, and, as we will see, it did not discourage politicians from responding to these inducements.

The regulation of price competition has been the central focus of a pressure pluralist policy network involving state agencies and industry representatives.

Two groups have been especially prominent as industry representatives: PMAC and the Canadian Drug Manufacturers Association (CDMA). Other groups, including the Canadian Medical Association, the Canadian Association of Pharmacists, and the Canadian Association of Non-Prescription Drug Manufacturers, have all played ancillary roles. The two primary combatants have little in common except, of course, the problems intrinsic to collective action. PMAC is a large, well-institutionalized association; the CDMA is much smaller, with twenty-one members. The largest, Novopharm, had sales of $49.9 million in 1986.[34] Membership in CDMA is confined to Canadian-owned companies, all of which are generic drug manufacturers. Membership has not been stable; for example, one of the association's two largest financial contributors, Apotex, is only a recent participant. Such instability arises from the intensely competitive character of relationships among a handful of generic firms. This instability, the absence of a permanent staff, and an ad hoc organizational structure have prompted some to describe CDMA as a 'fledgling' interest association.[35]

The PMAC, in contrast, is a formidable pressure group. Since moving its headquarters to Ottawa in 1962, the association has been on a war footing. In describing institutional changes coincident with the move to Ottawa, the then executive director, Guy Beauchemin, observed that the association was being 'designed to pressure.'[36] It was being organized to keep in close touch with other interested groups and to spearhead the attack on plans to remove patent protection. Its present organizational format, discussed earlier, suggests that it has not wavered from that commitment.

The divisions between PMAC and CDMA have analogues within the federal bureaucracy. As befits a pressure pluralist network, bureaucratic politics, complete with what Allison calls 'pulling and hauling' among players, has characterized interchanges in this network.[37] Each bureau has its interests and its allies in the associational system. Bureaucratic players articulate these interests and use their alliances to press their advantage along regularized circuits in the policy process (Allison calls them 'action channels').

Officials in Consumer and Corporate Affairs (CCA) are the industry's perennial critics. They evince a thoroughgoing scepticism about the needs and promises of the multinational drug companies. Pointing to the transnational organization of the industry, they have insisted that a fully integrated research operation in Canada is an unrealistic expectation. As one CCA official argued: 'What benefits can we expect from stimulating this industry? No reasons are normally given except that it is a sexy, clean industry, one that employs a lot of immigrant ladies stuffing capsules ... It is obviously an international industry. If we were to develop any drugs here, they would end up benefiting other countries and not Canada.' Little wonder, then that PMAC has foresworn contact with its bureaucratic enemies in Consumer and Corporate Affairs. PMAC has been convinced (probably correctly) that no amount of discussion would persuade these officials to set aside the goal of increased competition in order to protect the profits of multinational drug companies. For much the same reason, and because in terms of resources they are pygmies compared with PMAC, CDMA has largely confined itself to encouraging these same officials, their only bureaucratic allies.

On the other side of the fence, bureaucratically speaking, has been the Chemicals Branch of DRIE, especially the Health Care Products Division. In its 1980 sector analysis of the pharmaceuticals industry, DRIE attacked compulsory licensing as an obstacle to the growth of a research intensive pharmaceuticals industry.[38] Officials in CCA ridiculed this position:

Since 1969 DRIE has been trying to come up with a strategy for fostering the development of the Canadian industry and has failed. They think that the only way to have an industry is to dance with the MNCS. But this will not give us anything worth having. They are convinced that Smith, Klein, and French would build a plant if the policy were changed, but the members of PMAC would do nothing if the policy were changed ... If it wasn't Section 41 it would be something else. Why does Leslie Dan [the former president of CDMA] infuriate those guys? Because they have to compete, that's why ... This is the only country in the world where the generics are loose and it drives them crazy.

In the middle of this debate has stood the Health Protection Branch of Health and Welfare Canada, by far the largest of the health-care bureaucracies. As the representative of the health consumer, the department might have been expected to support compulsory licensing. Instead, officials in the department expressed some sympathy for the complaints of PMAC and ended up taking a rather more passive role than might have been expected. As we have seen, HPB has sought, above all, to maintain cordial relations with the industry, often begging its indulgence, particularly when it comes to delays in the approval of new drugs – delays that violate regulations. Thus, officials have expressed rhetorical support for a modification of compulsory licensing, but have stressed that their mandate is to provide safe and efficacious drugs. A senior HPB official put the matter this way: 'I think we have tended to drive out the research-based industry, maybe as much on perception as on reality, but I think we have driven them out. But that doesn't bother us directly. Our legal mandate is to make sure that the drugs that are available are safe and effective. I think that the country is poorer when we don't have a research-based drug industry here, and maybe we don't get drugs introduced as quickly as they might be otherwise.

But it's easy to ignore that because my legal mandate is just to look at what comes on the market.'

HPB's neutrality on the compulsory licensing issue robbed CCA of one potentially significant ally. However, the debate between CCA and DRIE on this matter was not particularly crucial to policy outcomes. Neither of these bureaus had much influence by the mid 1980s. The fact that DRIE's view prevailed speaks more to the effectiveness of the strategy used by PMAC than it does to the actions of the department.

In a pressure pluralist network, politics is not regularized. Issues reach the political agenda in haphazard ways, sometimes because of an unexpected crisis (thalidomide, for example), sometimes because of a change in government, and occasionally in response to international pressures. These exogeneous factors offer opportunities that are quickly seized on by existing groups. In the interim, these groups must rest content with maintaining a constant barrage of criticism and comment. Because they do not control the political agenda, they must build alliances within the bureaucracy that can be mobilized at the opportune time. When that day arrives, the groups seek to politicize issues immediately, draw as many participants as possible into the battle, and forego longer-term concerns. At the outset at least, no middle ground exists. Politicians and bureaucrats are pressured to choose sides and are discouraged from forming a side of their own. And because, in a pressure pluralist network, the state lacks the singularity of purpose to generate its own position, interest groups assume the task of defining the alternatives. It is possible, of course, to buy some time and perhaps generate some political leverage by creating an independent inquiry, such as the Eastman commission. Ultimately, however, politicians must choose, and they do so largely without the support of independent bureaucratic advice, because it is a commodity that no longer exists.

The break in the decade-long trench warfare over compulsory licensing came with the election of a Conservative government in 1984. Events in the 1980s, however, had prepared the way for a new political initiative. Groups of MPs from Quebec had been expressing concern about the closures, and threatened closures, of pharmaceutical plants in that province. The 1982 decision by Hoffman-LaRoche to close its Montreal plant was a case in point, as was the decision by Ayerst to close its research facility in Montreal and open a new one in New Jersey. In 1983, the minister of Consumer and Corporate Affairs, André Ouellet, had responded to these concerns by tabling his review of Section 41 of the Patent Act.[39] His successor, Judy Erola (who became president of PMAC in 1986), claimed that by the time she arrived in office she was unable to reverse the momentum toward a reconsideration of the act's compulsory-licensing provisions, although at the time she apparently had little enthusiasm ercise.[40] With the arrival of the Mulroney government, the impetus toward change was suddenly coming from the Prime Minister's Office. Evidently a significant amount of pressure for the abandonment of compulsory licensing had been applied by the then US Trade Representative, William Brock. The Americans argued that Canada was not shouldering its responsibility toward the regulation and protection of intellectual property. The suggestion that this attitude might constitute an obstacle to the achievement of a free-trade agreement added whatever further incentive was needed to proceed with a review of the act.

PMAC was well prepared to take full advantage of the break in the policy stalemate. It responded by concentrating attention at the political level, lobbying the ministers of Health and Welfare, Regional Industrial Expansion, and Consumer and Corporate Affairs. And because it promised increased investment that would be distributed on a regional basis, the PMAC included MPs in their lobbying strategy. This approach worked particularly well with members of the Quebec caucus of the Conservative party, who had expressed considerable concern over the closing of a Gulf refinery in the east end of Montreal. Tory MPs were particulary sensitive to the argument that patents constitute inalienable rights rather than privileges granted by the state; Liberals were attracted by the possibility of increased investment in R&D and urged a wait-and-see attitude. Only the NDP, which held no seats in Quebec at the outset of the 1984 Parliament, favoured the status quo.[41] Thus, PMAC succeeded in orchestrating a bipartisan regional alliance of MPs who were either pledged to open support for an end to compulsory licensing or prepared to acquiesce quietly in the project.

No policy instrument has provoked more controversy in the pharmaceuticals industry than compulsory licensing. Although many observers heartily approve of the policy goal of reduced drug prices, they are dismayed that pursuit of this goal has jeopardized other objectives. Other approaches to regulating drug prices are available and have been tried. In the United Kingdom, for example, drug prices are regulated directly. Patents are left intact, but there is a limit imposed on the prices companies can charge for drugs for which they are the sole source. In Canada, some industry analysts have sought to modify compulsory licensing itself. For example, the Eastman commission recommended retaining compulsory licensing, while creating a Pharmaceutical Royalty Fund to which generic firms would contribute based on their sales, the industry's world-wide R&D expenditures, plus 4 per cent to reflect promotion costs. The proceeds from the fund would be distributed to patent-holding firms based on their sales and R&D intensity in Canada. This modification to the existing compulsory-licensing system would still have resulted in higher drug prices, but it would also have rewarded firms prepared to make R&D investments.[42]

Neither of these options found favour with politicians. In 1987 the Conservative government of Brian Mulroney introduced and passed legislation extending significantly the protection afforded to patented drugs, thus gutting the compulsory-licensing provisions of the Patent Act. The legislation was passed over the strenuous objections of consumer and public advocacy groups and the Canadian Senate, which evidently had its own political agenda. For its part, the industry, acting through PMAC, promised $1.4 billion in new investment (that is, beyond the present trend in the industry) over the next ten years. The industry refused to bind itself formally to these plans and the government refrained from pressing the issue further. The passage of the legislation and the informality of the industry's commitment were a testament to the power of the drug lobby and a classic illustration of policy making in a pressure pluralist policy network.

Evaluation and Conclusions

The policy that emerges in this environment conforms well to the reactive model in two respects. First, it is operational in character and oriented to the short term. In the face of intransigent interest groups and ineffective bureaucracies, it is more realistic to concentrate on concrete, short-term problems than to address longer-term, abstract issues. When it comes to the trade-off between price regulation and domestic expansion, the policy settlement of 1987 contains no strategy for the long-term development of the industry. Similarly, both sides have been reluctant to tackle directly the question of just prices in the context of monopoly pricing. In a pressure pluralist policy network, with a minimum capacity for strategic thinking, it is impossible to determine how much firms in Canada should be contributing to the world supply of new pharmaceuticals. The solution to these dilemmas is again classically pluralist: both are redefined as procedural issues and a Patented Medicine Prices Review Board has been created to answer them on a case-by-case basis. In a pressure pluralist network no one, and this includes the state, is in a position to articulate more general principles or to define the public interest entirely free from challenge.

Second, the policy is reactive in the sense that it is a one-time exchange between the state and the industry. There is no provision for continuous monitoring of progress toward policy objectives. Instead, the major actors, public and private, have settled for a political arrangement based on immediate concrete benefits. In exchange for a period of exclusivity in the production of patented preparations, multinational drug firms, orchestrated by PMAC, have made their $1.4 billion investment promise. Through this process of partisan mutual adjustment, a new pluralist equilibrium has been reached, but nothing more. Policy making will stop until the next crisis arises. Unlike the space and petrochemical industries, the drug industry has no organizational framework for planning domestic expansion over even the medium term.

Can the objective of domestic expansion be attained through spasmodic bargaining in a pressure pluralist network? There will be some difficulties. Expansion will not continue to come easily to this sector. The international pharmaceutical industry has gone through a number of stages, but the period of dramatic breakthroughs followed by rapid advance is no longer the norm. It is true that patent activity continues apace, but many of these 'new' drugs are of the 'me-too' variety: minor changes in chemical composition that succeed in breaking patents but not in providing significant improvements in treatment. The industry has apparently entered a period in which the early advances and insights, having been exploited, can no longer nourish new discoveries. A hiatus in drug development has occurred, and the industry can only hope for yet another wave of spectacular change that will ultimately feed a second 'revolution.'[43]

In short, the Canadian state has made domestic expansion a priority at a time when growth will, at best, be steady. In a period in which there will be no strong market inducements to expand R&D facilities, the present government expects increased private-sector investment in general and more R&D in particular. But a pressure pluralist policy network provides it with no mechanism to extract this investment or even monitor the achievement of public policy objectives. It offers no opportunities for the systematic co-ordination of industrial policy instruments with firms' investment decisions. The government's own company, CDC Life Sciences, is highly profitable but technologically unadventurous. It cannot be used to lever new investment. If anything, the 1987 settlement weakened even further the state's capacity to influence industry behaviour. The delegation of some key decision-making powers to a drug prices review board can be expected to tip the balance toward a clientele pluralist network. If so, greater responsibility for the implementation of policy will be transferred to industry. The task of persuading firms to live up to the implicit bargains that have been struck – in particular the agreement to invest in exchange for patent protection – will likely be passed on to industry associations. In a sense, the state is indicating even more strongly its unwillingness to take direct responsibility for implementing its own policy objectives.

There is little doubt, therefore, that industrial policy in the pharmaceuticals sector will remain reactive in character. There are two reasons why such an assumption seems reasonable. First, the transnational organization of the most important firms ensures that the state can influence investment decisions only at a distance. These decisions remain primarily subject to the logic of internal markets. As a result, the inducements of state agencies are merely one of a number of factors (and by no means the most important) that firms must weigh. Second, in the case of pharmaceuticals, prospects are poor for creating a concertation policy network on which anticipatory policy could be erected. Although dominated by PMAC, the associational system is fragmented by the presence of other associations representing generic and non-prescription drug firms. Each of these associations has developed some capacity for high-intensity lobbying but not for longer-term policy planning. In this sector, the state itself is ill prepared to engage in the type of long-term planning that is critical to anticipatory policy. There currently exists no single, autonomous state agency capable of integrating the wide variety of policy objectives. Without a significant augmentation and concentration of resources, the state is in no position to collaborate with industry in planning for domestic expansion. It is clientele pluralism, pressure pluralism, and reactive policy – not concertation and anticipatory policy – that are most likely to prevail in the pharmaceuticals sector.

7 The Political Economy
of Transition:
Petrochemicals and
Meat Processing

This chapter examines the formation of industrial policy in two mature sectors of the economy, petrochemicals and red-meat processing. Both these industries felt the effects of a slow-down in the 1970s after a long growth phase. As such, they pose similar problems for policy makers: how to maintain market share in the face of slower growth and increasing international competition; how to reconcile resource, industrial, and regional development policies.

These industries share several other properties as well. First, both derive a comparative advantage in international markets from the Canadian resource base: petrochemicals from oil and natural-gas feedstocks; meat processing from feed grains. Partly as a result of these backward linkages, these industries depart from the Canadian norm in manufacturing by playing a large role in the prairie economy, specifically in Alberta, as well as operating important facilities in central Canada. Second, both have developed under the auspices of major national policies that have given primacy to the growth of manufacturing in central Canada or the United States rather than western Canada. In the case of petrochemicals, the National Oil Policy, formalized after the Borden commission report of 1960, effectively divided the Canadian petroleum market. Western oil was diverted to the American midwest, and markets east of the Ottawa River were served by imports of Venezuelan crude.[1] Federal policy on freight rates for the transport of grain, especially the so-called Crow rates, discouraged the processing of meat in western Canada and encouraged the shift of pork processing from the west to Quebec, particularly by the late 1960s and 1970s.

The red-meat industry is defined here to include the processing of beef, veal, and pork. In the mid 1970s, this sector employed about 35,000 workers, but this number fell by over 6000 in the ensuing decade as thirty-five plants, most of them old and inefficient, closed their doors.[2] The slow-down in growth affected the beef and pork sub-sectors differently. Pork production continued to grow in the late 1970s and early 1980s, albeit at a slow rate, while beef and veal began a slight decline. In the period 1976–83, per capita consumption of beef declined by 22.1 per cent while pork and poultry use increased.[3] Similar trends in the United States also contributed to the growth of over-capacity in the industry. As the major red-meat-producing countries in the world stepped up their competition for shrinking markets, all governments, including those in Canada, were increasingly urged to fashion policies to help stabilize the industry.

Increasing competition also affected the petrochemical industry. The production of petrochemicals is normally divided into three main stages.[4]

1 *Primary petrochemicals* These are obtained directly from feedstocks and have few direct end uses. They include ethylene (the most widely produced), propylene, butylene, butadiene, acetylene, benzene, methanol, and ammonia.

2 *Intermediate petrochemicals* Obtained from the primary group, these too have few direct end uses. Examples include ethylene oxide, ethylene glycol, styrene monomer.

3 *Petrochemical products* These include such end-use sectors as plastics, synthetic fibres, solvents, synthetic rubber, fertilizers, and agricultural chemicals.

Each element of the petrochemical industry showed a remarkable rate of growth from the end of the Second World War until the late 1960s when production began to level off. Several factors account for the end of the rapid growth phase. The basic petrochemical technologies had matured and the field of potential applications had narrowed.[5] The penetration of markets by petrochemical-based synthetics had slowed as market saturation became increasingly common.[6] These trends were accentuated further when economic growth in western countries slowed in the 1970s. The oil-price shocks in the same decade – events that made the price of feedstocks by far the most important cost in the production economies of petrochemicals – virtually ensured the continuation of a flat growth curve. By the end of the decade, the international industry found itself in the midst of a capacity crisis. Hardest hit were Western Europe and Japan, but even the United States was forced to shut down about 20 per cent its ethylene and 25 per cent of its ammonia capacity.[7]

Primary petrochemicals are manufactured from three main types of hydrocarbons: natural gas, natural-gas liquids (extracted in the processing of raw gas), and oil products (especially naphtha and LPG [liquefied petroleum gases]). Oil feedstocks are the more flexible in the sense that a wider range of petrochemicals can be produced from them. But the second oil shock in 1979 raised the price of these feedstocks, strengthening, in the process, the competitive position of the natural-gas-based component of the industry.[8] Translated into the Canadian context, these developments turned the Alberta industry, which uses natural-gas feedstocks, into a significant player in the world market, but placed extreme pressure on the two eastern-based complexes in Sarnia and Montreal, both of which used oil fractions as feedstocks. These circumstances created a complex set of policy problems,[9] many of which, as in the red-meat case, had serious regional implications. The internationally competitive western industry required assistance to expand on world markets, while the eastern portion of the industry was in dire need of contraction and rationalization. Selected regions, particularly Ontario, demanded a more rational management of energy resources, and some assurance that the national community as a whole would receive some of the benefits of whatever economic success was achieved.

We argue in this chapter that, during this critical period, both the red-meat and petrochemical industries, with their backward linkages to Canada's resource sectors, were candidates for anticipatory sectoral policies. No such policy emerged in either industry, although an attempt was made in the case of petrochemicals. For a brief period, the Canadian state sought to capitalize on a vertically integrated industry structure, a highly mobilized business community that has been at peace with labour, and a policy system in which decision-making power is relatively concentrated. None of these features is present in the red-meat industry. A vertically segmented industry structure inhibits policy planning; business interests are poorly mobilized and locked in a life and death struggle with labour; and decision-making power is diffused. Our treatment of these two sectors begins with an analysis of industry structure, followed by a description of the policy networks in place in the early 1980s. We conclude with an evaluation of the policy prospects in each sector.

Industry Structures

Production in the petrochemical industry is international in scope; all major producing countries export a significant portion of their output. As a result, no domestic industry can be entirely protected from changes in international prices. Traditionally, intensive research and development has been necessary to survive in the industry, especially as production processes have become more technologically sophisticated and complex.[10] The construction of processing facilities, accordingly, has required huge infusions of capital, making the sector highly capital intensive.[11] Such high capital requirements have encouraged the domination of the industry by a relatively small number of multinational companies. Within this select group, there are two families: oil and gas enterprises that have integrated forward into the production of primary and intermediate petrochemicals (e.g., Exxon) and basic chemical companies (e.g., Du Pont, Union Carbide, and Imperial Chemical Industries).[12]

Those petrochemical companies whose production is based on natural gas (ethane, butane, propane) are obliged to locate close to the source of their feedstock. The remainder, whose production is based on oil, are relatively 'footloose' and tend to locate near petroleum refineries. With ethane's lack of co-products and significantly lower plant capital costs, the 'cracking' of ethane has been potentially the cheapest means of producing ethylene, the most widely used primary petrochemical. However, as long as oil costs remained low, international capital-cost differentials were such that an ethane cracker constructed near natural-gas reserves, such as in the Middle East or Alberta, had no chance of being internationally competitive.[13] But the two oil shocks of the 1970s gave these natural-gas-producing areas a sudden advantage in the world petrochemicals market-place.

The Canadian industry follows the world pattern inasmuch as it is dominated by a relatively small number of large, vertically integrated, companies. Only three companies participate in the manufacture of the ethylene chain of products, the so-called backbone of the petrochemical industry.[14] Of these, the largest, with control of about 80 per cent of Canadian ethylene output, is NOVA/Polysar. This chemical company, which is ranked ninth largest in North America, took its present form in 1988 when NOVA, an Alberta-based company, took over Polysar, the leading ethylene producer in eastern Canada.[15] The western and eastern wings of the corporation have thus had distinct histories.

Polysar began its life as Polymer Corporation, a crown company created during the Second World War for the manufacture of synthetic rubber. Polysar became a participant in the manufacture of ethylene during the 1970s when it joined Union Carbide Canada and Du Pont Canada to form a new company, Petrosar. Polysar, currently the world's largest producer of synthetic rubber and latex, initiated this project in a bid to obtain competitively priced raw materials. But scarcely two years into its operation, Petrosar, which relied on oil feedstocks for its production of ethylene, was hit hard by the oil shock of 1979. It floundered throughout the early 1980s until oil prices finally began to decline. In 1985, Polysar acquired full control of Petrosar and integrated it into its other feedstock operations. A major plant conversion program at Petrosar allowed the company to crack natural-gas liquids shipped from western Canada in addition to naphtha.[16] With this increased flexibility, Petrosar had returned to profitability by the end of 1986, becoming in the process an attractive acquisition target for NOVA.

NOVA entered the ethylene market at about the same time as Polysar. The first world-scale ethylene plant in western Canada, owned by Alberta Gas

Ethylene (AGE), began operating in Joffre, Alberta, in 1979. A second, even larger, AGE plant came on stream in 1984.[17] AGE is 100 per cent owned by Novacor Chemicals Ltd, itself a wholly owned subsidiary of NOVA, and uses ethane drawn from natural gas as its feedstock. Ethane is piped to AGE by four 'straddle plants' owned by PetroCanada, NOVA, Pan Canadian Petroleum, and Dome.[18] AGE then relays its ethylene to the Dow Chemical of Canada plant in Fort Saskatchewan. The OECD describes the Alberta-based industry as one of two new export centres (the other being the Middle East and North Africa) that could fundamentally alter the market structure of petrochemicals in the Western bloc.[19]

The remaining two ethylene producers in Canada are smaller operations. Esso Chemical Canada owns a petrochemical complex in Sarnia, Ontario, which uses either oil-based gases or natural-gas liquids as feedstocks. Ethylene is also produced by Pétromont, a company formed in 1980 by the Quebec government's Société générale de financement in conjunction with Gulf Canada and Union Carbide Canada. Initially, Pétromont used naphtha and oil-off gases drawn from Montreal-area refineries for its feedstocks. Its processing facilities are not world scale and were crippled through much of the 1980s by the rise in oil prices.

In industries such as petrochemicals, where there are high levels of concentration and firms are routinely exposed to the vicissitudes of international demand, the prospects for state-driven, plan-rational industrial policy are ordinarily very good. This is especially the case during crisis periods. In Canada, the crisis period was the early 1980s. The industry itself was organized for the task of anticipatory policy making. Vertical integration permitted co-ordination of all industry activities from the acquisition of raw materials to the end uses of petrochemicals. More important, there were few obstacles to the political mobilization of business interests. Because individual companies tend to dominate particular products,[20] the divisive effects of competition are reduced. The major players in the industry are few in number and have often co-operated with one another in joint ventures. In short, the industry structure has been conducive to the growth of a cohesive, policy-capable industry association. The state sought to take advantage of this highly mobilized industry organization in the early 1980s, but the weakness of its own organization ultimately inhibited the development of a concertation network and anticipatory policy.

A more segmented industry structure in the red-meat sector presents a greater obstacle to the mobilization of business interests and hence to anticipatory policy. The Canadian market functions as an integral part of the much larger North American market with the result that the organization of meat production in Canada tends to be similar to that in the United States.[21] In contrast to the vertical integration found in the petrochemical industry, the meat industry is vertically segmented. Typically, the production chain breaks into the following segments: new-born calves are raised for a few months only on a cow/calf operation and then are sold to a feedlot farm. The feedlot farmer keeps the calves until they reach maturity, at which time they are sold to a meat-packing firm, either directly, through a terminal market, or at a country auction. The slaughtered animal is either sold as a whole carcass to a retailer or another processor or is processed by the packer into smaller cuts and boxed for sale to retail outlets ('boxed beef'). At each stage in this process there is a separate market with its own characteristics and perturbations. In addition, farms or plants at every stage are usually independently owned. Both this diverse market structure and pattern of dispersed ownership contribute to the segmentation of production in the sector.

Overlaying this industry structure in Canada is a critically important regional difference. The western region is a surplus agricultural area while the eastern region operates at a deficit.[22] How is this surplus to be transferred from west to east? In principle, several possibilities exist. Western grain might be sold to livestock producers in eastern Canada; calves might be grown in the west and shipped to eastern feedlots; mature cattle might be grown and slaughtered in the west with whole carcasses being shipped east for processing; or cattle might be slaughtered and processed in the west and shipped east for final consumption. In practice, each of these alternatives is used. The first two are preferred by eastern interests because they increase the value added in eastern Canada. For identical reasons, the latter two processes are preferred by western industry. In this tug of war, eastern agricultural interests have won some important battles. The federal government's feed-freight assistance programs have given a subsidy for the movement of grain from Thunder Bay to points east. Similarly, the old Crow rates and the present-day western grain-transportation policy encourage eastern meat production and processing at the expense of the same activities in the west.[23]

The province of Quebec, in particular, has taken advantage of these policies to increase substantially its production of pork. Since 1971, the percentage of pork processing accounted for by the western provinces has declined from 46 per cent to below 30 per cent, while production in Quebec has increased from 20 per cent to 34 per cent.[24] Quebec's expansion has been spearheaded by agricultural co-operatives, which, contrary to the Ontario and western pattern, have encouraged the vertical integration of the industry under the aegis of the Coopérative fédérée du Québec.

Since the late 1970s, the Canadian industry has faced a serious problem of over-capacity, forcing it to search intensively for export markets. Unfortunately, all surveys of potential export markets show that only two, the United States and Japan, hold any promise, and gaining access to them will not be easy. The US market is mature and very competitive. In recent years, processors in the United States have driven wages down, virtually forcing Canadian companies to do the same, just to hold their market share. The result has been several long and bitter strikes in the industry in the mid 1980s. Americans have also become very skilled at using grading regulations as a non-tariff barrier, a practice that has forced Canadians to ship live cattle rather than higher value-added products. The Japanese market has been even less accessible, particularly because of the use of non-tariff barriers.

The structure of the red-meat sector is more conducive to a reactive rather than an anticipatory approach to these problems. Vertical segmentation undermines producer co-operation; regional cleavages exacerbate the problem. As a result, the industry is ill equipped to organize an assault on export markets. For example, the Japanese market requires an entirely different product than does the Canadian market.[25] Japanese tastes demand a product with relatively more fat than that preferred by Canadians, but the Canadian grading system is geared to entirely different tastes. Nor is it easy to reorganize processing in order to cater to the Japanese market. When the feedlot operator sells his cattle at an auction or terminal market, he has little idea of the market in which his product will eventually be sold. Accordingly, he will grow cattle to suit Canadian tastes in order to maximize opportunities for sales. At each stage in the production chain, sellers and markets respond in the same way. Hence, the packer that wishes to arrange an export deal faces virtually impossible obstacles in undertaking the necessary planning.

In addition to the vertically segmented industry structure, the conflict between the western and eastern industries constitutes a persistent obstacle to anticipatory policy. As we have suggested, eastern and western participants disagree over how to capitalize on the western agricultural surplus. These disagreements frustrate the mobilization of firms into strong, policy-capable associations. If the state was sufficiently autonomous to manage its side in a concertation arrangement, it is unlikely it would find a strong industry partner to share in planning the future of the red-meat industry.

Policy Networks and Policy Outcomes

The Petrochemical Industry

During the period from 1973 to 1985, public policies in the petrochemical industry were overwhelmingly reactive in character. They were neither broadly conceived nor well integrated. This reactive approach to policy was not the one to which the state and industry had aspired. During the crisis years of the early 1980s, both state officials and industry representatives had expressed interest in an anticipatory approach to policy. Unfortunately, state structures were not suited to the task. State bureaucracies lacked sufficient autonomy from the industry and the necessary concentration of decision-making responsibility. At the same time, business interests in the sector, although not as highly mobilized as their counterparts in Britain and Germany, had achieved a significant degree of success in developing an effective policy-capable association. The combination of weak state structures and a high level of industry mobilization opened the way for a clientele pluralist policy network between 1980 and 1984. The policies that emerged from this network continued the basic reactive approach that had been pursued throughout the 1970s. In turn, reactive policy making encouraged a return to the pressure pluralist norm after the crisis had passed.

Both primary and intermediate petrochemical (including plastics resins) manufacturers are represented by the Canadian Chemical Producers Association (CCPA). Manufacturers of plastics resins may also belong to the Society of the Plastics Industry of Canada (SPI). This association represents manufacturers of plastic end products, and resins manufacturers join in order to develop linkages with these firms.[26] But it is CCPA that best represents their interests as intermediate petrochemicals manufacturers. In fact, CCPA has succeeded in mobilizing business interests in this sector to the point that *all* of Canada's petrochemical producers belong to the association and the chief executive officers of the largest firms always sit on the association's board of directors. The association's staff of twenty people is a highly professional body, quite capable of generating information on the industry of sufficient quality to be used extensively by public officials as well as by association members. CCPA has significant competence in the area of environmental issues and is involved with the departments of the Environment and Transport in formulating policies for waste disposal and the transport of dangerous goods.[27] Yet it is important to note that the CCPA does not act as a 'private-interest government.'[28] It is not given legal responsibility for the implementation of public policies or for enforcing the compliance of its members. Its authority is moral rather than legal. When the association reaches a consensus, members adhere to it on the basis of mutuality and commitment rather than legal coercion.

Decision-making authority in the policy arena for petrochemicals is diffused between levels of government. With its ownership over natural resources and its ability to influence the price of feedstocks, the government of Alberta has successfully encouraged the growth of a petrochemical complex in the province.

The encouragement of this complex has never really been a source of conflict between the two levels of government, although the industry suggested to both levels that it preferred to pipe the ethylene manufactured in Alberta to Sarnia. The province countered that a greater proportion of manufacturing value-added should take place within Alberta. The federal government supported this point of view. Much more conflict has been generated by the matter of oil prices. Because the Alberta industry is based on natural gas, the Alberta government has had little interest in policies that would price oil feedstocks low enough to give the Sarnia and Pétromont complexes a competitive edge. But the federal state, with the support of Ontario and Quebec, did seek a special lower price for feedstocks that became a source of many disputes on petroleum pricing in the late 1970s and early 1980s. Frictions eased only after the signing of an oil-pricing agreement with Alberta in 1981. Policy making became more consensual after this date, with policy discussions taking place primarily at the federal level.

Decision-making responsibilities were also horizontally diffused within the federal level between the Department of Energy, Mines and Resources (EMR) and the Chemicals Directorate (formerly Chemicals Branch) of the Department of Regional Industrial Expansion (DRIE). DRIE is responsible for the industry in the sense that it interprets and articulates industry demands, while EMR has a signficant influence over the industry's future because of its commanding position on matters of energy pricing. An official at DRIE described the potential for differences between the two bureaus. 'The competitive position of the Canadian petrochemical industry is determined, internationally at least, to a very major extent by the cost of energy in feedstocks that are used by industry ... To the extent that Energy, Mines and Resources views a higher price as a necessary factor to developing industrially the mineral resources, that puts us in conflict by definition.' Officials at DRIE added, however, that the conflicts that did occur were quite restrained and even described them as 'a necessary ingredient for healthy policy development.'

In fact, the two bureaus were able to pool their expertise and co-operate when a crisis hit the industry in 1980. Already faced with the longer-term problems of slow growth in the markets for petrochemical products and international over-capacity, the industry was confronted by a sharp rise in feedstock prices and, by 1982, an economic recession. EMR and DRIE set up a joint interdepartmental task force to study the problems brought on by this chain of events. The question of policy response was then turned over to an industry task force. Both departments collaborated in preparing a reply to the task-force report. By the early 1980s, then, the earlier pattern of diffused decision making had been replaced by a more concentrated authority structure with DRIE taking the lead role.

By forming the industry task force, DRIE was offering the industry an opportunity to initiate the development of an anticipatory policy strategy. Ironically, however, DRIE itself lacked the expertise and resources needed for extensive collaboration with the industry. The Chemicals Directorate had traditionally exhibited little autonomy from the industry and nothing had changed during the 1980s to alter this state of affairs. Several properties of the bureau illustrate the state's dependence on industry. Central to this relationship is the perception on the part of officials in the bureau that their primary responsibility is that of promoting and serving the industry. In the words of a senior DRIE official: 'Our fundamental job is industrial development and how we go about that, I suppose, has a number of bases. The most obvious thing we do is deliver the department's and branch's assistance programs, such as the Enterprise Development Program ... That is the sort of obvious thing we do. We provide service to the industry in terms of putting them in touch with the right people. It's always difficult for firms that don't deal with government on a regular basis to know where they should be going for this or that or some other information.' At the core of the agency's ideology is its service to the industry: its task is to speak for industry in the halls of government.

Recruitment of officials from the industry is one of the reasons why this ideology prevails. Even the appointment of the Chemicals Directorate's senior official would normally be a matter for discussion with industry representatives. In addition, the department does not have a strong regulatory mandate with respect to petrochemicals and, as a result, there is no corpus of law that sets the bureau apart from the industry. Finally, the bureau depends on CCPA for reliable statistical information on the industry. Because petrochemicals is not a statistical entity for Statistics Canada,[29] CCPA carries out an annual statistical survey of the sector and a member of the Chemicals bureau in DRIE sits on the association's statistics committee, which compiles the report on the survey. Each of these aspects of the bureau's relationships with industry – its service role, its personnel, and its weak information base – lay the groundwork for a clientele pluralist network.

In the petrochemicals industry, a sectoral bureaucracy possessed of relatively centralized decision-making capacity but a low level of autonomy from business confronted a well-mobilized industry association. The result, in the early 1980s, was a clientele pluralist policy network. Clientele pluralism is not the normal state of affairs, however. Prior to 1980, and subsequent to 1984, pressure pluralism characterized state/industry relations. The clientele pluralist relations of the early 1980s developed when, in the face of an industry crisis, the state sought to collaborate with the industry in the formulation of a longer-term policy. Unprepared itself for such an exercise, the state then gave considerable responsibility to the industry for policy design, with the result that CCPA played an important co-ordinating role in this process. State officials found it easier, indeed natural, to let the industry define the outlines of policy: 'Sometimes it's easier to let the association mediate and come up with an industry/association position, in which they convene their committees, get all the companies' inputs, reach an agreed position on particular issues, and present that position to us. That saves a lot of work, but you don't always get, I guess, what would be, what we would consider a good answer.' This explicit inclusion of industry and its association in the policy formulation process signals the shift to clientele pluralism. The industry is given a public role in the development of policy and is no longer merely a policy advocate as it would be under pressure pluralism.

The shift to clientele pluralism took place against a background of reactive policy making. Prior to 1980, policy for the industry had been organized to accomplish the following five objectives:[30]

1 balanced growth: the continued growth of the Ontario and Quebec complexes plus development of a strong complex in Alberta;
2 secure supplies of feedstocks at competitive prices;
3 maximum upgrading of primary petrochemicals in Canada;
4 improved access to world markets;
5 orderly growth: new plants should be large enough to be internationally competitive, but at the same time, companies should not add new facilities, given the dangers of over-capacity.

The realization of these policy objectives had required minimal federal intervention. The most important exception was the effort of federal authorities to keep the prices of feedstocks competitive through various energy policies, including the gradual elimination of some taxes.

Consistent with reactive policy making, the government of Alberta had intervened in the industry independently of the federal government. Throughout the 1970s, Premier Lougheed had argued that the Province of Alberta required a larger say in the disposition of its resources. Lougheed argued strenuously against the building of the Petrosar complex and threatened to deny it feedstocks.[31] His government played an important role in putting together the consortium of investors for the Alberta petrochemical complex.[32] But the Alberta government did not plan or direct the investment. It reacted to industry proposals. In this respect, its approach to policy was consistent with that of the federal government.

The oil shocks of 1979 coupled with a pricing policy for oil that lacked responsiveness to international market conditions led to an attempt to reconsider policy for the petrochemical industry. As this attempt proceeded, the industry itself became progressively more involved in the policy process. Policy consultations began with the CCPA early in 1980 and culminated in a report by an Interdepartmental Task Force late in 1982. This report reviewed in detail the various policy options for the government, utilizing extensive information gathered from the industry. Following this report, DRIE and EMR convened the industry task force (mentioned above) and asked it to make specific policy recommendations. The task force was co-chaired by the national director of the Energy and Chemical Workers Union and the president of Shell Canada Chemical. The other members were all business persons, chief executive officers from the following companies: Esso Chemical, Pétromont, Celanese Canada, Polysar, Ocelot Industries, C-I-L, Dow Chemical, Union Carbide Canada, Hercules Canada, Novacor Chemicals, and Du Pont Canada. No state officials or politicians were formally included, but officials from several federal departments attended and provided advice. The secretary for the task force was Jean Bélanger, the long-standing president of CCPA. With Bélanger in this position and all the other members drawn from the board of the CCPA except, of course, labour's representative Neil Reimer, the CCPA now occupied a central place in the policy process. The task force reported in February 1984; in June of that year the government responded by endorsing many of its proposals.

The recommendations of the task force reaffirmed the reactive policy-making tradition of the sector. Governments were asked to make natural-gas pricing more 'market responsive' and to lower the price of gas feedstocks. The industry suggested a further reduction in barriers to trade with the United States and Japan. It also recommended that transportation become more 'market responsive' and that regulatory reciprocity on cross-border transport of dangerous goods be negotiated with the United States. The only structural question addressed was the weakness of the oil-based segment of the industry. Here, the task force recommended continued protection of these complexes while a transition program to increase feedstock flexibility was implemented. Rather than asking whether each of these complexes should be retained, the task force suggested the program be made available to all, with the specific terms to be negotiated with each individual firm.

The Liberal government had already announced assistance to Pétromont in 1983 to cover operating losses in 1983 and 1984. Petrosar was offered loan insurance at the same time, but did not accept it. After the report of the task force, the Liberals refused the request from Pétromont and the government of Quebec for additional assistance. But after the 1984 election, the new Conservative government reversed this decision and agreed to co-operate with the

Quebec government in another set of bail-outs for the long-suffering Pétromont complex in Montreal. The task force had suggested providing support for retooling at Petrosar to allow the Sarnia complex to receive natural-gas liquids as feedstocks as well as oil. Although the federal government agreed with this recommendation, no further offer was, in fact, made.[33]

With a new policy direction established, the clientele pluralist network dissolved. Industry continues to be an influential player but the institutional arrangements that drew state and industry together in the early 1980s are no longer deemed necessary. Reactive policy does not require elaborate consultation. However, the dependency relationship described earlier continues. Industry lobbies a weak state agency and the latter refuses to contemplate significant change in policy without industry support. The return to pressure pluralism and the rejection of anticipatory policy are not without their costs. In particular, there has been no resolution of the inconsistency between policies calling for regional balance and for international competitiveness. With the oil shocks of the 1970s and the growing importance of natural-gas feedstocks, it has become increasingly difficult to maintain all three complexes and still obtain orderly growth and internationally competitive products. We return to this point in our conclusions.

The Red-Meat Industry

Public policy making in the red-meat industry, in addition to being reactive, appears to be more rudimentary than in the petrochemical industry. Whereas in petrochemicals a process existed for the systematic review of policy, and several such reviews had taken place in the 1980s, there is no process of policy review in the meat industry. Neither government nor industry has engaged in even a medium-term assessment of where the industry is going. Accordingly, the public policies in this sector tend to be more ad hoc, more short-term oriented, and less integrated than those in the petrochemicals industry.

Industry/government relationships conform best to the pressure pluralist model. As expected in such a network, the red-meat industry is presided over by a set of sectoral bureaucracies, each having some measure of decision-making responsibility for the sector and operating quite autonomously from the industry. Business interests in the sector are poorly mobilized by contending associations, which tend to mirror and reinforce divisions within the state.

Unlike officials in the petrochemicals industry (where federal/provincial conflict at times inhibited policy co-ordination), officials in the red-meat industry described their relations with provincial counterparts as essentially co-operative. The weakness of state organization in this sector lies primarily with the diffusion of decision-making responsibilities within the federal bureaucracy. This diffusion occurs in both of the sector's two main policy arenas. In the first of these – industrial development – responsibility is divided among three bureaus: the Policy (formerly the Marketing and Economics) Branch of the Department of Agriculture, the Food Branch of DRIE, and the trade development side of the Department of External Affairs. In addition to the number of bureaucratic units involved, co-ordination is confounded further by their different approaches to industrial development. Agriculture aggressively seeks to locate markets for *commodities* and then tries to find firms capable of serving those markets. Such an approach is consistent with the interests of farmers, the primary clientele of the department. DRIE and External Affairs, in contrast, take the view that *firms* should search out markets and then, only where absolutely necessary, apply for limited state support to assist in serving them.

Three bureaus also participate in the second policy area, product quality control: the Food Production and Inspection Branch of Agriculture, the Health Protection Branch (HPB) of the Department of Health and Welfare, and the Department of Consumer and Corporate Affairs (CCA).[34] Each approaches the question of food quality from a different perspective. Agriculture's grading service is devoted to maintaining quality control to ensure that competition among producers in the market place is 'fair'. Agriculture's Meat Hygiene service emphasizes protecting the safety of meat consumers. HPB stresses standard setting for food additives used in processed meats. CCA also acts on behalf of consumers, this time to ensure that there is no fraud involved in the packaging and merchandising of food products.

As is perhaps obvious, these respective mandates are far from mutually exclusive. Indeed, they have invited a certain degree of bureaucratic conflict. In the early 1980s, this conflict took the form of an attempt by Agriculture to consolidate all aspects of food regulation under its own umbrella. This attempt met strong resistance from the other bureaus. A senior official in HPB expressed his displeasure in these terms:

They would like to take over the whole food sector. It would be totally wrong if that occurred. It would be wrong because there is an intrinsic producer-oriented bias in Agriculture, and that's a reasonable bias. I mean, somebody has to look after the producer. But there are other legitimate factors in society besides that of the producers. One of those factors is health. Our experience with commodity-related departments is that if producer concerns and health concerns are run up against one another, health concerns will lose and producer concerns – because they have a political impact primarily – will almost always prevail.

Throughout the food bureaucracies, officials argue that a plurality of agencies is the best means of achieving their objectives. Only in Agriculture is there concerted support for a single food agency.

For the moment at least, the pluralists prevail. At the federal level alone, the six bureaus discussed above all have policy responsibilities affecting the development of the meat industry. None of these is pre-eminent. Nor have there been mechanisms in place for the co-ordination of their activities.[35] An assistant deputy minister in one of these departments expressed his frustration with this lack of co-ordination in clear terms: 'There isn't the kind of overall policy determination which should exist ... There's no overall integration of policies and so we end up with a situation where we may have the aims of one department, the policies strategic for that department, really not very much in sync [sic] with health considerations. And there's no overall integration. This doesn't occur; the notion that Cabinet does it is just nonsense. It doesn't do it at all.' In short, decision-making power is widely diffused in this sector, a property inherent in a pluralist policy network.

Operating with distinctive mandates and differing policy instruments, these various bureaus have charted their own course in establishing relations with the industry. The three bureaus concerned with industry and market development are quite independent of the industry in the sense that officials do not depend on associations for information in doing their jobs. Firms are the primary contact point for these bureaucrats, and many spend their time processing applications and delivering programs. These bureaus are highly responsive to the industry, but this process has not required close collaboration.

At the same time, the three quality-control bureaus work more closely with industry. Successful regulation in capitalist systems demands a large measure of state and industry co-operation. Much of the day-to-day work of running the regulatory system involves informal contacts between the bureau, association staff, and chairpersons of the 'technical' (read quality control) committees of the associations.[36] In addition, all three bureaus hold formal meetings, at least annually, with the boards of directors of the relevant associations. These formal meetings serve to review larger issues and potential changes to the regulations. An official in HPB described these meetings in the following terms: 'These will involve major impending regulatory change, major impending policy determination, almost exclusively. For example, if we were interested in nutritional labelling, we'd talk to GPMC [Grocery Products Manufacturers of Canada] about nutritional labelling, long before it gets to the information letter stage, long before we've asked for formal comments. We get their ideas on whether it makes some sense. It's essential for us to deal with the industry in that way, because they know what's technically feasible far better than we do.'

While the close ties between food associations and these regulatory agencies suggest clientele rather than pressure pluralism, the former network does not, in fact, prevail in this sector. The divisions among the various bureaus when coupled to similar divisions among the industry associations prevent the establishment of the stable one-on-one relationships between groups and bureaus that characterize clientele pluralism.

Business interests in this sector are represented by a wide variety of groups. The association with the best claim to represent the red-meat-processing industry is the Canadian Meat Council (CMC). This claim, however, has been strongly challenged by the Grocery Products Manufacturers of Canada (GPMC), an association that represents brand-name grocery-products firms. In practice, its membership is drawn heavily from multinational, primarily US, food-manufacturing firms. In the early 1980s, the CMC could claim to represent only about two-thirds of the production in the industry while GPMC represented about one-third.[37] The GPMC members not in the CMC tended to be large *western*-based meat-packing firms that were dissatisfied with the CMC's activities. An official in DRIE summarized the situation well: 'The attitude in western Canada is that the Meat Council's done nothing for them, that it's too heavily influenced by Canada Packers. It should not be sitting in Toronto, but should be in Ottawa. That if they want to be truly effective they have got to move their office. They've got to be seen as more of an interest group ... Burns is an example. Their CEO makes no bones about the fact that he thinks that the Meat Council is a moribund organization. Their people are not doing anything and he puts all his emphasis on GPMC.'

This split in the representation of the industry tends to reinforce divisions among bureaus in Ottawa. The CMC works more closely with Agriculture, while GPMC has established cordial relations with HPB and DRIE. In practice, therefore, both industry and the state are divided from within and each tends to accentuate the fissures in the other. Pressure pluralism becomes in such circumstances the dominant pattern for industry/state relations.

Reactive, and especially short-term, policy making has predominated in this pressure pluralism network. Moreover, it has been reactive policy making without an overall framework. Policy for the industry is dominated by a series of programs that can loosely be grouped into three types:

1. Protectionist policies: the most important example is the Meat Import Act, which is administered by the Department of Agriculture and allows the department to set quotas on imports in circumstances when the industry can demonstrate it is being seriously harmed.

2. Horizontal policies not specific to the industry: a prominent example is the policy on rates for the transportation of grain, which, as we have argued,

have a wide-ranging impact on the meat-processing industry.

3. Market-development policies: these include assistance provided for the types of activities such as trade fairs, trade missions (including visits to Canada of potential buyers of Canadian products); market and feasibility studies; and promotion of the technical qualities of a product or industry. Programs offered under this heading include the Program for Export Market Development (DRIE), the Promotional Projects Program (Agriculture), and the Canadian Agricultural Market Development Fund (Agriculture).

These various programs are not explicitly co-ordinated with one another. They are offered by different bureaus and have tended to duplicate each other, or even to compete with one another for clients. They lack the depth and resources associated with anticipatory policies. Officials in DRIE and Agriculture admitted as much in their own internal evaluation of these programs. 'Canadian export programs generally do not provide assistance for the comprehensive activity ... necessary for export market development. Canadian programs tend to be restricted to specific types of activities, of fairly short duration. At the same time, agricultural export promotion, with the exception of grain, tends to be ad hoc, noncontinuous and superficial. It does not seem possible for a potential exporter to receive assistance for an overall marketing plan which involves longer term activities of one to five years, for example.'[38]

The simple fact that existing programs operate without even a one-year planning horizon illustrates how the diffusion of authority in the state bureaucracies and the low mobilization of business interests in this sector have created a pressure pluralist network that is incapable of supporting anything but reactive policy making.

Evaluation and Conclusions

We have described both the red-meat and petrochemical industries as mature, implying that they have achieved a measure of stability in terms of technology. An assessment of the appropriateness of reactive policy making and pressure pluralism in such circumstances must begin with a consideration of the future of these industries. Prospects for the red-meat industry appear less attractive than those of the petrochemicals sector. Simply put, there are few new export markets for Canadian meat. With a free-trade agreement, openings may arise in the United States, particularly California, but making gains in this market and in Japan will be difficult given the presence of non-tariff barriers and fierce competition. In the case of petrochemicals, Canada is one of the leading suppliers of natural gas in the world. As oil prices climb, the natural-gas-based petrochemical industry in Alberta is poised to make significant gains in world markets.[39] The critical question becomes whether the present configuration of policies and the structure of policy networks are appropriate for the challenges that these sectors must face.

The minimal degree of state intervention currently found in the red-meat sector enjoys clear support from the industry, its associations, and state officials. No strong argument is being made for an anticipatory approach to policy making in this sector. The red-meat industry is the largest sector in the Canadian food-processing complex, with a significant export trade. Fierce competition in international markets coupled with changes in the consumption patterns of North Americans, who increasingly favour poultry and fish over beef and pork, has slowed the growth of the Canadian industry. In spite of its large size and its growing predicament, both state officials and firms are inclined to leave resolution of these problems primarily in the hands of the firms themselves. The policies in place are designed to help individual firms improve their access to specific markets in the very short term.

A major reversal in this pattern of policy is highly unlikely. With no significant pressure for change coming from either the industry or the state, responsibility for the industry within the state will remain widely diffused and the industry will continue to be divided within itself. In such circumstances, the only significant question is which types of reactive policies are more appropriate to the mature state of the sector. Rather than financing trade fairs, the state might consider support for research designed to modernize processing techniques and to foster more product innovation. Transportation policies might be modified to assist the western-based industry, which enjoys a comparative advantage in feed grains, to enter new markets in California and Japan. Unfortunately, the reactive policy approach found in the sector has not encouraged a broader assessment of policy instruments or industry economics that might eventually reorient priorities.

Although reactive policy making may remain the most appropriate approach to policy in the red-meat sector, the argument in favour of anticipatory policy is more compelling in petrochemicals. During the crisis in the early 1980s, state and industry went some distance toward an anticipatory approach but lacked the will and the policy network needed to sustain it. On the surface, at least, some movement toward a concertation network, in which both parties jointly plan the future of the industry, could be detected. This network failed to materialize, however, and the eventual policy outcome conformed to the reactive tradition in the industry. The task force that finally reported in 1984 was an 'industry' task force – the state requested that industry supply the direction. Either the bureaus concerned could not establish the appropriate policy response or they interpreted their role as one in which they accommodated the industry's suggestions. In either event, a clientele pluralist, not a concertation, network emerged in this sector.

This reaffirmation of long-standing reactive policies can be questioned in light of several structural characteristics of the petrochemicals industry. The Japanese, for example, have argued in favour of anticipatory policies in this sector because of several obstacles to the proper operation of market mechanisms:[40]

1. Factors of production, particularly capital, are insufficiently mobile.

2. Variations in relative prices are not predictable. Without some predictability, industry response is delayed and some firms are unable to cope on their own.

3. Changes in the economic environment are not gradual. Industry is thus unable to pass on the steep rise in costs in the short term, weakening its profitability and thereby making it more difficult to adjust over the medium term.

4. Change-overs to new production technologies that might help counteract cost increases cannot be introduced quickly simply because of the time required to adapt technologies to new conditions.

These arguments apply to the Canadian case as well. But there would be a further, additional advantage to anticipatory policy in Canada, because these structural problems are accentuated by the continued maintenance of three geographically dispersed petrochemical complexes. There is little doubt that the presence of these three complexes has been a very costly proposition. The problem is summarized by an official in DRIE:

In the United States, for example, the petrochemical industry is concentrated in one area. So you've got pipeline interconnections between the plants, you've got services available at the drop of a hat to the whole industry. You've got a concentration of fabricating and tradesmen and construction workers that are available at a level which is adequate to accommodate the requirements of the industry. And that is the standard of competition in the world, around the world. We have petrochemical industries now in Quebec, in Ontario, and in Alberta ... But as an industry, none of these locations is really what we would call world scale simply because you are missing those large concentrations of construction tradesmen and skilled tradesmen ... I suppose, if you put everything else aside, ideally you would have one petrochemical centre in Canada.

Growth in the Canadian petrochemical industry has been based on a series of ad hoc decisions. It is questionable whether the industry structure that has resulted remains appropriate for the 1990s and whether it makes sense to continue following a reactive strategy based on company-led growth. The success of the newly created NOVA/Polysar will be the key. With its near-monopoly position in Canada, private intra-firm planning becomes a possible substitute for concertation with the state.

To date, neither party – the industry or the state – has ventured to put these questions on the policy agenda. Consequently, decisions in the industry remain very much reactions to current conditions and, in some instances, to short-term electoral considerations. Continuing to follow such an approach runs the risk that growth opportunities in a mature, but very important, sector of the Canadian economy will be squandered. The weak link in the network is the state: it appears to have neither the capacity nor the will to intervene.

8   The Political Economy
of Retrenchment:
Textiles, Clothing, and
Dairy Products

Dairy products and textiles and clothing provide examples of industrial sectors engaged in a process of retrenchment: special and stringent trade-protection measures have been required to prevent a precipitous decline. Both are sectors where, with one or two specific exceptions, Canada enjoyed no comparative advantage in the 1980s.

The primary-textiles industry developed late in the last century and gradually prospered as a consequence of the growing population, favourable tariffs, access to hydroelectric power, and the availability of relatively cheap labour. Selected parts of the textile and clothing industries continue to prosper, but many others, especially in the clothing sector, have seen their competitiveness eroded by newly industrializing countries (NICs) whose strategies of export-led growth are built around the exploitation of a reservoir of labour power.

The dairy-products industry also enjoyed a period of prosperity when, at the turn of the century, it developed export markets in Great Britain. However, as other countries began to produce dairy products, Canada's climate took its toll on the industry's competitiveness. The feed and heating costs incurred over the winter months put Canadian products at a disadvantage compared to those entering from countries with more temperate climates, such as New Zealand and Australia. Moreover, domestic per capita consumption of dairy products has long since peaked and the industry has had to fight strenuously to maintain present consumption levels.

These sectors are similar in other respects as well. Both industries are concentrated in Ontario and Quebec. In 1983, Quebec accounted for 41 per cent of the value added in dairy products, while Ontario contributed a further 30 per cent.[1] In the same year, Quebec was responsible for 54.5 per cent of value added in textiles and clothing and Ontario for an additional 33.6 per cent.[2] In both cases, significant numbers of workers are involved. Textiles and clothing employed about 185,000 workers in Canada in 1985.[3] The dairy-processing industry employed far fewer workers – 25,306 in 1983 – but to these must be added 46,859 dairy farmers.[4] The important place of these industries in Quebec's economy made them focal points in the debate over political sovereignty that took place in the 1970s.

The exceptional status of both sectors in the international trading system established under the General Agreement on Tariffs and Trade (GATT) constitutes a final important similarity. The textile sector has been an exceptional case since the signing in 1961 by GATT members of the Short Term Arrangement (STA), which was, in effect, a 'voluntary export restraint arrangement.' This agreement evolved into the Multi-fibre Arrangement (MFA) signed in 1974 and subsequently renewed in 1977, 1981, and 1986.[5] At each juncture, it became more comprehensive in terms of the fibres covered and more restrictive in terms of the trading practices permitted. In the clothing sector, it has been Article XIX of GATT that has played the prominent role. A clause in this article allows a nation to raise tariffs or impose quotas on imports in order to protect a domestic industry. Although it was meant to be an emergency provision to which a country might resort in order to relieve short-term hardships caused by imports, it has been used extensively.

For dairy products, Article XI of the original GATT agreement eliminates quantitative restrictions on trade but allows exceptions for agricultural products in two circumstances. Restrictions may be imposed when governments seek to eliminate temporary surpluses or wish to limit quantities of a product being produced for the domestic market.[6] In 1981, an International Arrangement on Dairy Products was signed committing GATT members to the expansion and liberalization of trade in dairy products while seeking greater stability by setting minimum prices for certain basic commodities.

Despite these political and economic similarities, public policies in the two sectors have developed in quite different directions. Policy making in the dairy sector has featured long-term planning horizons and significant industry restructuring – in short, anticipatory policy. In the textiles and clothing sector, policy is uncoordinated, contradictory, and short term in character. It conforms to the reactive model of industrial policy. The comparison of these two sectors, then, is instructive because it affords an opportunity to compare alternative approaches to positive adjustment and to assess their political requirements. We begin by examining the institutional structures of the respective sectors, highlighting the problems they pose for policy makers. The policy networks in each sector – corporatism in the case of the dairy industry and pressure pluralism in the case of textiles and clothing – are described and the resulting differences in policy outcomes analysed.

Industry Structure

Textiles and Clothing

The manufacture of textiles products has traditionally involved three main steps.[7] First, raw fibres, predominantly cotton and wool, are treated and transformed into yarn. The yarn is then woven or knitted into fabric, with knitting having become increasingly popular in the 1950s and 1960s.[8] The final stage is the manufacture of finished products including clothing, industrial goods (such as seat-covers for automobiles), and household goods (carpets, sheets, and towels). The introduction of such synthetic fibres as polyester, nylon, and polypropylene, combined with advances in technology, has contributed to the blurring of the first two steps in the production process and made the industry more capital intensive. This chapter focuses on primary textiles – the making of yarns and fabrics – and on the clothing industry, which absorbs approximately 40 per cent of the primary textiles manufactured in Canada.[9]

The standard technologies for all three steps of the cycle from fibres to garments are diffused world-wide and do not demand highly skilled labour. Differences in labour productivity for a given type of equipment do not vary significantly from one location to another, making sites with a low-wage labour force especially attractive. The OECD notes that 'for the bulk of the textile industry, a strong comparative advantage is enjoyed by countries (and regions) which offer a favourable socio-cultural environment and general infrastructure for such industries, but where the cost of unskilled labour is still low relative to its potential productivity.'[10] A number of countries in the developing world meet these requirements and have become important sites for the manufacture and export of textiles and clothing.[11]

Nevertheless, the OECD adds that the developed countries are not powerless in the face of these circumstances. NICs rely on textiles exports for foreign-exchange earnings and the developed countries continue to be the world's principal importers. In 1960, the United States alone absorbed 15.1 per cent of the world trade in textiles and clothing and was able to use access to this market to influence trade negotiations with Japan and the low-cost countries. Gradually the United States lost its pre-eminent position and by 1980 it was the European Community (EC), with almost 20 per cent of world trade, that had taken the lead role among developed countries in the textiles negotiations.[12] In addition, to preserve domestic industry, developed countries have taken advantage of lower costs for factors of production other than labour. Capital costs are often higher in low-wage settings where highly trained technicians, required in some facets of the production process, may be scarce. Wage costs as a proportion of total costs have also declined with the introduction of new technologies. Because these technologies are usually developed in the advanced industrialized countries, the dynamics of the product cycle ensure these countries at least a marginal head start.

The impact of these developments has been very different, however, in the clothing and primary-textiles sector. In textiles, innovations such as shuttleless looms, robots, and computer controls have allowed extensive rationalization of production.[13] In the cotton industry, new technologies have allowed firms to integrate the process of spinning yarns with that of fabric weaving, thereby increasing significantly the minimum efficient size of the average plant. In the wake of these technological changes, smaller firms, unable to raise sufficient capital, have either closed down or been absorbed by larger ones. In Canada, for example, the number of producers has fallen to the point where there were no more than two major producers in any one sub-sector and, in most cases, one or two firms accounted for 100 per cent of the sub-sector's production.[14] Overall, the Canadian industry has come to be dominated largely by three firms: Dominion Textiles, Celanese Canada, and Du Pont Canada.

In becoming highly capital intensive, the primary-textiles sector has diverged increasingly from the clothing industry. Some technological advances have allowed clothing firms to reduce production times in the cutting out and pressing of garments, but not in sewing.[15] Only in the cases of relatively standard products, such as shirts and jeans, can significant economies of scale be realized. In other cases, changes in fashion dictate shorter production runs, which work to the advantage of smaller producers capable of flexible specialization. Recently some clothing manufacturers have been moved to close down sewing operations while letting out more final production to home workers. Normally, these workers are recent immigrants, usually women, who work in unhealthy conditions and are paid at piece rates that often fall well below the minimum wage. One estimate puts the number of home sewing workers in Ontario at about one-quarter the clothing labour force.[16] In short, concentration levels and capital intensity remain much lower in the clothing industry than in textiles, with over 2000 firms active in Canada in the mid 1980s.

While Canadian textiles and clothing firms have introduced new technologies to rationalize their production, they have not succeeded in stemming industrial decline. Beginning in the late 1950s, imports of primary textiles steadily increased their market share until the early 1970s.[17] The situation then stabilized with Canadian producers holding a 78 per cent share of the yarn market and a 47 per cent share of fabrics in 1978. As the recession began to have its effect in the early 1980s, imports made another surge and the share of Canadian producers dropped to 63 per cent in yarns and to 43 per cent in fabrics.[18]

Import penetration began later in the garment sector. In 1970, domestic man-ufacturers held a remarkable 89.5 per cent of the Canadian market.[19] Imports of clothing from low-cost sources then began to rise steadily with a surge coming in 1976 after the EC had concluded its restraint agreements with the low-cost countries.[20] By 1978, the market share of Canadian firms had fallen to 68 per cent and then slowly continued its decline, reaching 57 per cent by 1985. Not all sub-sectors have been equally penetrated by imports. The Ca-nadian industry remained strong in foundation garments, underwear, men's suits and sport coats, and winter outerwear but suffered competitive pressure in products better suited to mass production, such as men's tailored-collar shirts, sweaters, and swimwear.[21]

An additional difficulty faced by clothing firms has been the high tariff placed on imports of textile fabrics relative to finished garments. Clothing firms would prefer to import low-cost fabrics rather than purchase on the domestic market at a higher cost from protected firms.[22] Textile manufacturers are naturally opposed to such imports because the domestic clothing trade is critical to their industry. Unable to change the tariff on fabrics, Canadian clothing firms have responded by narrowing the number of products they manufacture and importing the remaining clothes they need to complete their product lines. This defensive strategy helps reduce their dependence on domestically produced fabric.[23]

These developments have meant that employment in textiles and clothing has fallen in absolute numbers over the past two decades. Politically, a decline in employment in primary textiles has more impact than in clothing. Textile mills tend to be concentrated in smaller towns and cities in Quebec and Ontario, such as Magog, Valleyfield, Cornwall, and Hawkesbury, where the impact of plant closures is immediate and wrenching for the community. Clothing firms tend to congregate in large cities, particularly Montreal, Toronto, and Win-nipeg. With literally hundreds of these establishments in each urban centre, the closing of a single firm is much less disruptive both economically and politically. Hence, pressure on governments to stave off decline has been more intense in the case of primary textiles than in clothing. Nevertheless, the overall decline in employment in such large industries has remained a serious policy problem over the past two decades in both these sectors.

Dairy Products

There are two principal types of milk products: fluid milk sold for direct consumption and industrial milk used in the preparation of other products, including butter, cheese, ice-cream, milk powder, and yoghurt. Fluid milk accounts for about 35 per cent of total milk sales and industrial milk for 65 per cent.[24] As in the case of primary textiles, technological advances have led to significant rationalization. Whereas fluid milk, butter, cheese, and ice-cream had traditionally been manufactured in separate plants by different companies, new equipment allows all products to be efficiently produced in integrated plants operated by a small number of companies. The number of dairy-processing establishments has fallen from 1413 in 1965 to 400 in 1983.[25] Concentration levels have also risen dramatically with one major producer accounting for over 50 per cent of sales in each of the provinces of Ontario, Quebec, and British Columbia. Technological advances have also brought significant changes to dairy farming. New breeding technologies and changes in feed composition have increased the output per cow from 2850 kg per year in 1961 to 4613 kg in 1981.[26] Herd sizes have been increasing, while the number of dairy farms has fallen from over 300,000 in 1960 to 46,859 in 1983.

Unlike the textiles and clothing industries, however, the dairy sector has not been forced to contend with the rise of new competitors. Rather, competition has intensified because advanced industrial countries have designed policies intended to support domestic dairy industries. The kinds of policy instruments used to attain this goal, combined with the technological advances in dairy farming, have tended to create surpluses in dairy products. International market prices have fallen drastically and most countries, including Canada, have responded by closing off their domestic markets to foreign competition. As a result, total milk production in Canada has been quite stable, with growth rates closely following increases in the population. Per capita consumption of cheese has risen steadily over the past fifteen years, consumption of fluid milk has remained constant, and butter has declined in popularity.[27] Imports are restricted completely in most product lines except cheese, where imports captured 9.8 per cent of the domestic market in 1983.[28] Canada does export a few milk products – evaporated and condensed milk, skim-milk powder – but at a financial loss and partly in conjunction with foreign-aid programs.

Under the pressure of international competition, both the dairy and the textiles/clothing industries have undergone considerable change during the last two decades. Yet the transformation of these industries has been much less dramatic than it would have been in the absence of significant state intervention. In both cases the Canadian state has devised a series of policy measures intended to cushion the impact of low-cost imports and to preserve the domestic market for Canadian-based firms. But that is where the similarity ends. With successive crises in the international market-place, the textiles and clothing sector has continued to demand protection and the state has responded ad hoc with a series of reactive policies. In the dairy industry, by contrast, a more comprehensive anticipatory policy framework has been devised in which a negotiated order based on an administrative rationality has replaced random political interventions.

Policy Networks and Policy Outcomes

Textiles and Clothing

When the first formal textiles policy was announced in 1971, it appeared to possess many of the qualities of anticipatory policy: special measures of protection were to shelter the industry for a limited time, while it restructured and rationalized to face international competition. But this image proved to be illusory. During the succeeding fifteen years, it became clear that the original objectives could not be accomplished with existing policy instruments. Although some restructuring has taken place, particularly in primary textiles, the industry appears no better prepared for international competition than before the policy was announced. Little systematic monitoring of firms' investment decisions had taken place; adjustment programs for displaced workers had barely been conceived at all. The evident lack of co-ordination marked the policy as primarily reactive in character and the inability of the state to implement the policies confirmed this impression. Responsibility for the sector had been diffused among numerous government agencies and bureaus, industry associations were poorly mobilized for policy discussions, and there was no well-developed pattern of collaboration between business and the bureaucracy. Such a combination of factors is, of course, associated with the dominance of a pressure pluralist policy network.

Let us begin with the organization of the state in this sector. State structure in the area of textiles and clothing is distinguished by the lack of co-ordination among a number of agencies. The most important bureaus in the sector have included the following:

1. Textiles, Clothing and Footwear Branch of the Department of Regional Industrial Expansion (DRIE), responsible for promoting the development of these sectors in Canada;

2. International Trade and Finance Branch of the Department of Finance, responsible for Canadian import policy, which advises the minister on questions related to quantitative restrictions on trade and administers the tariff;

3. Office of Special Trade Relations of the Department of External Affairs, which administers the Export and Import Permits Act as it relates to the sector, co-ordinates the implementation of border measures such as quotas, and negotiates bilateral trade agreements on the restriction of imports;

4. Textile and Clothing Board (TCB), set up as part of the 1971 textile policy,

which investigates complaints by industry about injury due to imports, advises the minister of Regional Industrial Expansion on a course of action to be taken, and monitors the steps taken by industry to restructure and rationalize production;

5. Canadian Industrial Renewal Board (CIRB), created as part of a renewed textiles, clothing, and footwear policy announced in 1981, which subsidized the revitalization of firms in these sectors, sought to diversify economic activity in regions heavily dependent on textiles and clothing, and tried to assist workers in the industry to adjust to the consequent changes. CIRB ceased operations in March 1986;

6. Ministry of State for Economic Development (MSED), which co-ordinated the activities of the Economic and Regional Development Committee of Cabinet and took a very active interest in the 1981 textile policy that created CIRB.

These have been the major players in the policy system, but the supporting cast has included the Department of Consumer and Corporate Affairs (CCA), a vociferous supporter of free trade and hence a strong opponent of existing textile policy; the Tariff Board; and the Anti-Dumping Tribunal. The provincial governments of Ontario and especially Quebec have taken an interest from time to time in the sector but neither province has been consistently involved or an important obstacle to policy.

In principle, the presence of a number of agencies and bureaus does not preclude co-ordinated and concentrated decision making for a sector. One agency may be clearly predominant, or informal, interdepartmental committees may take the lead in formulating policy. Such co-ordinating mechanisms existed in the textiles and clothing sector during the late 1950s and the 1960s, but they gradually declined in strength as more agencies became involved in the policy arena. Hence, Rianne Mahon has shown that when import competition became a serious problem in the late 1950s, the Department of Finance played a leading role, through an Interdepartmental Committee on Low Cost Imports, in developing a policy response.[29] With the creation of a Department of Industry in 1963 and the subsequent establishment of an Apparel and Textiles Branch staffed with experts drawn from the industry, the pre-eminence of Finance was gradually challenged. By 1969, when interdepartmental discussions had begun on the establishment of a textile policy, the Department of Industry, Trade and Commerce was given a key role, marking the end of Finance's dominant position. Although an interdepartmental committee was appointed to advise and assist in the development of the 1971 policy, it met only three times and its role was minimal.[30] Co-ordination had been replaced by bargaining among competing units.

By the early 1980s, interdepartmental committees were no longer a significant factor in policy formation. No single department dominated the policy system, bureaucratic authority was clearly diffused, and co-ordination had become a serious problem. An official in the Department of Finance summarized the situation in these fatalistic terms: 'You have all these different agencies floating off in this big netherland, going off in different directions without any sort of co-ordination. However, having said that, there is a *significant* problem in terms of linking all these agencies. It's really physically impossible. I don't think any government in the world has managed to do it. It's an impossibility. You have to operate a government in that fashion. The left hand doesn't know what the right hand is doing and I think it's a fait accompli. It really is difficult to do otherwise.' As we shall see, officials responsible for the dairy sector see matters differently.

Given their different, and in some cases contradictory, mandates, the relationship among these various bureaus often tends to be conflictual. Each agency assigns different weights to the concerns of textiles manufacturers, clothing manufacturers, distributors, and consumers of textiles products. The agency most supportive of the industry has been the Textiles and Clothing Board. It defines its objective as that of maintaining and protecting those parts of the industry with the potential to be internationally competitive upon completion of a modernization program.[31] The Office of Special Trade Relations defends the industry's interests in trade negotiations and as such engages in close consultation and co-ordination with the industry. It is not uncommon for industry representatives to accompany officials from Special Trade Relations to bilateral trade negotiations. Also relatively close to the industry is the sector branch in DRIE whose members are familiar with, and occasionally critical of, industry politics. Finally, during its brief bureaucratic history, CIRB was a hard-nosed industry advocate. Its officials boosted certain product lines, preached the gospel of specialization, and actively sought to promote sectoral winners.

More neutral in policy-making orientation has been the Department of Finance, which takes a macro-economic perspective. An official in the International Trade and Finance Branch described its objectives in the following terms. 'We try to minimize the impact of the controls on consumers. We try to be as liberal as possible in negotiations of trade agreements ... At the same time, we use whatever influence we have to put pressure on the industry to restructure.' Least supportive of the industry is the Department of Consumer and Corporate Affairs. The scourge of vested interests, officials in this department consider themselves the only serious critics of textile policy, which they construe as fundamentally protectionist.

The plurality of bureaus coupled with the gradual accretion of expertise and resources in the state prevent the development of the kind of dependency relationship associated with clientele pluralism. In these sectors, the key to the state's autonomy from business is, ironically, the mandate and operations of TCB. While this board has often been accused of parroting the demands of industry, pursuit of its mandate has led to the accumulation of a wide variety of detailed information that it publishes in clear and comprehensive reports. Officials in all bureaus have access to this information and hence no need to extract it from the industry.

In short, the state structure overseeing textiles and clothing has the twin characteristics of a low level of concentration in decision-making authority and a relatively high degree of autonomy from the industry. When these properties are coupled with a low mobilization of business interests, the result is the growth of pressure pluralist policy networks.

The key to the weak mobilization of business interests is the division within the associational system between textiles on the one hand and clothing on the other. Speaking for the primary textiles firms is the Canadian Textiles Institute (CTI), which has a mixed structure: either firms belong to it directly or they are members of an affiliated association such as the Knitters' Association of Canada or the Canadian Carpet Institute. The four major textiles firms – Dominion Textiles, Du Pont, Celanese, and Consoltex – all belong to the institute and sit on its board of directors. Although the association represents over 80 per cent of the productive capacity in primary textiles, only 150 of the 900 or so textiles firms actually belong to the association.

The clothing industry with its lower concentration levels and large numbers of firms has had difficulties defining a common interest. There are many associations in the industry, usually provincially if not locally based, each representing a sub-sector – shirts, dresses, rainwear, children's clothing, and so on. In the early 1960s, at the instigation of CTI, many of these associations were drawn into a formal alliance with the primary textiles firms through the formation of the Canadian Apparel and Textile Manufacturers Association.[32] This alliance proved to be short-lived, however, dissolving in 1964 when the apparel industry formed another association to lobby for a lowering of tariffs on textile fabrics. But organizational problems continued to prevent the formation of a strong association for the garment industry, and CTI, with fewer obstacles to collective action, continued to dominate consultation. This situation only began to change when, in 1976, a former Department of Finance official, Peter Clark, created a new peak association for the clothing sector, the Canadian Apparel Manufacturers' Institute (CAMI). CAMI has been more successful than its predecessors in securing regular consultation between the clothing industry and the state, a process that has led to a growing policy rift between primary textiles and clothing firms.

Both CAMI and CTI operate primarily as policy advocates and are not well

organized for a more intensive policy role. An official in the Department of
Finance described them in the following terms. 'They've got a very effective
lobby there ... I think they spend a lot of money on lobbying, money that
perhaps could be spent in more productive areas in terms of long-term viability.
They have taken a management position that money spent on lobbying is money
well spent. But I guess that's been confirmed ... They tend to perpetuate the
status quo, which has been quite profitable for them in recent years.' CTI has
been a particularly effective lobbyist, forming a Labour Relations Committee
with the trade unions in the sector and thereby enlisting labour's support in its
lobbying efforts. It also established a Textile Caucus Committee composed of
members of Parliament from Ontario and Quebec representing ridings with
important textile mills.[33] It drew on both of these alliances in the 1970s in
lobbying campaigns that took advantage of growing fears of Quebec independence. The association and its allies argued that if the federal government
permitted the textiles industry to decline, it would be interpreted as a lack of
interest in Quebec's economy and, as such, might trigger further support for
separation.

Confined to a policy advocacy role, the energies of CTI began to dwindle in
the early 1980s. The founding of CAMI, coupled with a decline in the effectiveness of CTI staff, helped to give clothing a greater voice in policy in the
1980s. Officials in the textiles branch of DRIE require a strong lobby from CTI
to command the attention of senior officials and politicians, but that strong
lobby had disappeared. A DRIE official illustrated the pivotal role of CTI as an
advocacy association by invoking the case of a particular company that was
being hurt badly by imports. In order to do something for this firm, he argued:
'What we need is some pressure from the industry so we can write a brief to
the minister and to the Special Trade guys who recommend on restrictions.
But if the minister says, "Well, what does the industry say?" and you say "I
don't know," you're nowhere. CTI used to go after these sorts of situations,
but now it doesn't. If the government doesn't act quickly, this company will
go under and there will be some embarrassing questions.'

CTI and CAMI, as traditional lobbies struggling to maintain a presence in
Ottawa, lack the organizational characteristics necessary for the intensive collaboration required for a concertation network. The associations have relatively
small professional staffs and tend to rely for expertise on committees staffed
with personnel from member firms. In the case of CTI, some of these industry
volunteers spend up to one-third of their time on association-related work.
These properties of the industry associations, when joined to the diffused but
autonomous set of state agencies responsible for the sector, make pressure
pluralism the pre-eminent policy network in the sector.

Emerging from this pressure pluralist policy network over the past fifteen years has been a mélange of anticipatory rhetoric and reactive policy. In 1971, when the first formal textiles policy was announced, CTI was at its zenith in terms of influence, while the state's administrative structure had become fragmented with the rise of the sector branch in the then Department of Industry, Trade and Commerce (ITC). Vinod Aggarwal, in his study of the world textile industry, has suggested that the combination of a divided state and an effective industry lobby will favour the emergence of a highly protectionist policy.[34] At first glance, the 1971 policy refutes this claim in that the policy involved a significant tightening on imports over the short term so that industry could rationalize to increase its competitiveness. In practice, protection has been a constant in textiles policy since 1971 and the state did not follow through on modernization. Officials from TCB confirm that the board, which was supposed to encourage and monitor industry rationalization, did virtually nothing related to this part of its mandate in the first decade of its existence. It was only in 1981, at which point a revised policy was outlined, that the board initiated a survey of equipment that would provide it with information required in the pursuit of modernization.

A second attempt at anticipatory policy seemed reasonable in 1981. First, in 1973, soon after the original textiles policy had been announced, Canada signed the Multi-fibres Arrangement (MFA) allowing for quantitative restrictions on trade in cotton, wool, and synthetic textiles and clothing under the GATT. Renewed in 1977, 1981, and 1986, this agreement has steadily increased the power of signatory states to restrict imports of textile products. The comprehensive character of this power enables the state to raise a more effective umbrella of protection to shelter industry while it restructures.

Second, during the 1971–81 period, the influence of CTI began to wane and, slowly, a more influential, autonomous industry voice for clothing emerged. Such divisions freed the hands of the state to redesign textiles and clothing policy. Third, changes within the state structure facilitated an attempt at policy change. The Progressive Conservative government of Joe Clark had upgraded the Board of Economic Development (created by the Liberals) to a Ministry of State responsible for bringing some co-ordination to economic policy. While this new Ministry of State for Economic Development (MSED) spent most of its time preparing briefing notes for ministers in response to policy initiatives, it was able, from time to time, to exercise an independent influence on policy. It did precisely this in late 1980 when presented with a policy recommendation from ITC for a continuation of high levels of protection for textile products. After considerable internal debate, and in the face of a divided industry, MSED was able to prevail and secure approval by Cabinet for a policy that departed from the 1971 version by including a more elaborate component for industry restructuring and labour adjustment.

The 1981 announcement contained the usual highly restrictive controls on imports, but it also provided for a marshalling of funds to support a concerted drive toward industry modernization. The promise of 1971 was to become a reality. Anticipating the need to cushion the shock of retrenchment, it drew funds from the departments of Regional Economic Expansion (DREE) and Manpower and Immigration to assist in the economic diversification of communities highly dependent on textiles and clothing and in the retraining of displaced workers. These three policy objectives – modernization, community adjustment, worker retraining – became the responsibility of a new agency, the Canadian Industrial Renewal Board. CIRB was given $250 million and a five-year life, after which highly protective trade policies would presumably be phased out.

The CIRB itself was an innovative structure. Building on the experience of ITC in using private-sector boards to implement subsidy programs, CIRB took the logic one step further. The leadership consisted of a president, Paul Desmarais, and a board of directors composed of seven businessmen, two representatives of trade unions active in textiles and clothing, a representative of consumers, and four senior public servants. Unlike the trade-union directors, the business directors were deliberately selected from industries other than textiles and clothing, ostensibly to avoid a 'conflict of interest.'

Such a structural arrangement should not be confused with a concertation or even a clientele pluralist network. It did not allow for any systematic collaboration with the textiles and clothing industries per se. Rather it served two quite different purposes. First, it was symbolically important because it could be portrayed as an attempt by government to bring hard-nosed business thinking to its decision making. In fact, however, the board acted as a 'rubber stamp,' meeting once a month to approve proposals prepared by CIRB's permanent staff. The government's policy was implemented essentially by bureaucrats alone. Second, the CIRB structure was to provide a shield against the type of political interference, based on short-term criteria, to which the Westminster model gives rise. An MSED official, closely involved with the policy, explained the origins of the Board structure in these terms: 'Osbaldeston [a former deputy minister of ITC] had seen how private-sector input into the decision-making end of the Enterprise Development Program – which he also invented – was useful: one, in bringing a cold-blooded, objective, unbiased, private-sector investor view to the decisions and, to a degree, in taking ministers off the hook. Unpopular decisions must be made. It's helpful when they are not made by people who are directly accountable to somebody who has to stand up in Question Period.'

This attempt to avoid what officials saw as one of the less appealing features of the doctrine of ministerial responsibility succeeded, at least in the eyes of bureaucrats at CIRB. One of its senior officers described how it worked: 'I think it was the most creative part of the creation of CIRB, putting a private-sector board of eminently respectable businessmen in between the government and the decision as a buffer. So that if somebody pleads a very special interest about a level of unemployment that may be created by a decision we have made in Three Rivers or Sherbrooke, the minister can stand up and say "This has been tested by people whose track record in the private sector is such that we have got to accept that commercially this was not a viable proposition." '

The CIRB's policy decisions met with mixed results. Through its Business and Industrial Development Program (BIDP), it claimed credit for creating 7185 new jobs in seven selected highly textiles-dependent areas, more than compensating for the loss of 6263 jobs in textiles and clothing during the 1981–5 period.[35] Subsequent evaluation of this program by the Economic Council of Canada indicates that BIDP led to the establishment of permanent production activities and were not simply make-work projects.[36] In its Sector Firms program, CIRB subsidies spurred investments for modernization totalling over $1 billion over the same period. In effect, the program hastened the speed and timing of investment, leading to an increase in capital intensity and to further industry lay-offs.[37] CIRB's Labour Adjustment Program was simply insufficient to cope with the increased labour-market congestion.[38] Most of the monies went to the payment of pre-retirement benefits, not retraining, and the majority of new jobs created under the Business and Industrial Development Program did not go to displaced textiles and clothing workers.[39]

The question remains whether the CIRB experiment broke with the established reactive pattern in the sector. We think not. No real planning involving concertation between state and industry took place. CIRB behaved in the classic reactive manner, accepting and processing applications for grants from individual firms and hoping that the cumulative effect of its decisions would result in sufficient industry restructuring to meet international competition. As time passed, CIRB allocated more money to the subsidy-based Sector Firms Program and less to the more proactive Business and Industrial Development Program.[40] When its mandate ended in 1986, the new policy unveiled in June of that year was as protectionist as ever. The government announced its intention to pursue still more restrictive bilateral trade agreements with over twenty-five low-cost countries in order to provide a 'more stable and secure environment' in which the industries could 'plan their future.' It added a special duty-remission program for tailored-collar shirts, long opposed by the primary textiles firms, and cemented the divorce settlement between these two sectors by announcing *separate* Sectoral Advisory Groups, each of which would be consulted during the negotiation of the bilaterals. In short, the policy strongly resembled its reactive predecessors of the 1970s.

The reactive character of policy in the 1980s is also evident from the mutually contradictory objectives pursued.[41] The use of quantitative restrictions on trade remained throughout the period of CIRB's existence, providing an incentive to low-cost countries to shift their business from lower- to higher-quality goods.[42] Consequently, domestic producers faced *increased* competition from imports and an incentive to restructure downward to the manufacture of low-quality goods that had previously been imported. A trade policy such as this one, which protects less-efficient labour-intensive operations, when combined with an industrial policy that seeks to provide incentives to more efficient ones, is a formula for frustration. CIRB's industrial-structure policies were designed to induce the substitution of capital for labour in the production process; its labour-adjustment policies were expected to ease the exit of older workers from industry. Yet trade policy has worked to protect the less-efficient firms, to reduce value added in the manufacturing process, and to reduce incentives for industrial renewal in dependent communities.[43]

Effective co-ordination of such policies requires either more extensive control over investment decisions through the banking system, the creation of public corporations, or the development of a concertation network in which industry assumes greater responsibility for planning. The Canadian textiles policies of 1981 and 1971 provided for none of these options. Thus, what was to have been an anticipatory approach ended up being generally reactive. State officials were simply too suspicious about the industry's capacity for longer-term planning; their suspicions were grounded in the cynicism that comes from decades of short-term lobbying on the part of the industry. The state remained seriously divided within itself: divisions increased with each subsequent policy announcement. Industry, for its part, showed no willingness or capacity to change its approach. It had developed a political formula, with the Quebec caucus as the centre-piece, which, notwithstanding CIRB, allowed it to deflect those interests seeking to strip it of its privileged position. The availability of these kinds of political short-cuts is, of course, endemic to pressure pluralism.

Dairy Products

The viability of the dairy industry in Canada has been a long-standing public-policy issue, dating at least from the 1930s. Various avenues have been followed and approaches attempted in the journey toward the present-day national supply-management system and its five-year planning horizon. Serving the domestic market is the primary objective of this system, in part because of the perishability of fresh milk and the short shelf life of products such as cottage cheese and yoghurt. The policy equilibrium that has emerged rests on the operation of a corporatist policy network. As suggested in chapter four, corporatism becomes more likely when state structures are autonomous, decision-making responsibility is diffused, and the industry is highly mobilized.

The mobilization of dairy farmers and processors into integrated, policy-capable associational systems occurred over a thirty-year period. In the 1950s both systems possessed a single dominant association on the national plane – the Dairy Farmers of Canada (DFC) and the National Dairy Council of Canada (NDC) – and highly differentiated associations on the provincial plane. Hence, farmers had separate provincial associations for each major dairy product: butter, fluid milk, cheese, and so on. Among processors, separate groups existed for ice-cream, butter, cheese, concentrated milk, and fluid milk. Beginning in the early 1960s, associations representing these commodities gradually merged into comprehensive marketing boards (in the case of farmers) and commodity-inclusive associations (in the case of processors). As a consequence, there now exist highly concentrated associational systems for both producers and processors.

In the case of dairy farmers, the integration of interests has progressed to the point that DFC is a peak association, that is, an association whose members are other associations with more narrowly defined domains of representation. DFC's members include the nine provincial marketing boards plus several groups representing different breeds of dairy cows.[44] Because all dairy producers are compelled by law to belong to a marketing board, DFC represents, in effect, every dairy farmer in Canada. Together with well-funded and highly professional marketing boards, DFC provides farmers with an associational system that plays a leading role in the dairy policy system.

NDC does not have a peak structure. Rather, individual dairy firms belong directly and do so in sufficient numbers that the council can claim to represent 90 per cent of the productive capacity of the industry. All major firms are active members of the association. The NDC does not have a particularly large professional staff (under ten employees in 1983) and tends to draw on information gathered by the Department of Agriculture and the Canadian Dairy Commission in its work. However, the NDC does possess that property critical to a highly mobilized association, a capacity to promote self-governance in the industry. For example, the industry has implemented its own system for monitoring cheese prices, a system that is accepted by the Food Production and Inspection Branch of the Department of Agriculture. In behavioural terms, NDC has managed to induce a considerable degree of policy compliance from its members. In 1983, when the province of British Columbia pulled out for a year from the national supply-management system, individual firms, working through the association, agreed to refrain from changing production patterns to take advantage of the disappearance of controls over milk supply. This self-discipline continued until an agreement was reached that brought British Columbia back into the program. Provincial processor associations have much the same characteristics as NDC and are intensely involved with the milk marketing boards in implementing dairy policy at the provincial level. In short, NDC and related provincial associations provide processors with an associational system highly adapted for participation in the policy-making system.

The state organization facing the industry is complex in that there are a number of agencies administering policy in the sector. But it is also rationalized and there is a minimum of inter-agency conflict. This applies to the federal/provincial dimension as well. Provincial governments play an important role in the system because they have assumed primary responsibility for fluid milk. The federal government has responsibility for industrial milk and hence serves as our focal point in this discussion. None the less, it is useful to note that co-ordination between the two levels of government in this sector is highly developed. Conflict occurs rarely, if at all. Similar to TCB and CIRB in the textiles and clothing sector, the dairy industry at the federal level possesses an independent agency specifically dedicated to the sector: the Canadian Dairy Commission (CDC). CDC plays the lead role in developing policy for the industry, administers the system of price supports, and manages the export of dairy products. The regulatory side of policy is shared by a variety of agencies: the Food Production and Inspection Branch of the Department of Agriculture regulates product quality; the Health Protection Branch (HPB) of the Department of Health and Welfare defines and enforces compositional standards; and the Department of Consumer and Corporate Affairs (CCA) regulates packaging and labelling.

The latter three agencies have co-ordinated some of their activities. The Department of Agriculture normally incorporates the standards developed by the other two agencies directly into its own regulations under the Canada Agricultural Products Standards Act. In addition, Agriculture has an agreement with CCA that allows it to regulate packaging and labelling at the point of manufacture. CCA exercises its responsibilities only at the retail level. Such understandings have not eliminated all conflict but it has become a much smaller problem than is the case in textiles and clothing. An official in the Department of Agriculture, when asked about inter-agency conflict, replied: 'I wouldn't be fooling anybody if I said it [co-ordination] wasn't a problem, and I think it's got to be treated as if it's a problem. But I would put it, on a scale of one to ten, on the low end of the scale. We've certainly got more important problems than this.'

Among the other problems is the relationship between CDC and the Department of Agriculture. CDC is a crown corporation, independent of the department, and hence a competitor for funds. The commission's one and only concern is the dairy industry, while the department necessarily takes a broader perspective and often feels the need for a reallocation of funds away from dairy to other farm sectors. Even this conflict, however, has become less frequent since dairy policy has moved to a five-year planning period.

These agencies vary in their autonomy from the industry. CDC, HPB, and CCA do not depend heavily on the industry for information and support. CDC believes such independence is essential if it is to discharge its responsibilities properly. This view is consistent with its central role in a corporatist, rather than a clientele pluralist, network. When asked whether the commission relied on industry for its information, an official replied as follows: 'No, we tend to rely on our own, we generate our own. If we do anything, sometimes, for example, when we want something from somebody else, we will cost share, so that we retain some control. But for example, processor margins – the processing industry goes out and they employ an accounting firm, Coopers Lybrand, to go and figure out processors's margins. And we say, "heck, unless we can get in there and look at them too, we're not taking your data." We develop our own data. You get caught too often.'

The Food Production and Inspection Branch, in contrast, has a much closer relationship with the industry. It prefers to administer quality-control regulations in close consultation with NDC. Officials in this branch clearly rely heavily on information supplied to them by the association: 'We are very reliant on them. We would ask them for input. They would generally give us the information through a questionnaire that they would send out to the industry, because we would be asking them "What kind of impact would it have to do this type of thing?" And they would come back and say, "Look, we've got 16 of the 18 manufacturers of this commodity who are against it and here is the reason that we as a council are against it." ... They would supply us that type of information all the time. We need that kind of justification.'

In fact, the branch is sufficiently confident about working with the council that it complied with NDC's request not to deal directly with individual firms or even with provincial associations. These firms and associations were to be asked to go through NDC. Another, more senior, official justified such a practice in the following terms: 'The association on the dairy side has requested that, in a decision-making process, they be the one voice of industry. It seems to work quite well, because the industry is so well organized and their communication patterns are quite good, and we feel reasonably comfortable that they can, on behalf of industry, give an unbiased, very objective, and very representative opinion of the industry.' Even with statements such as these, the same officials always add that *they* take the decision on what will be recommended to the minister and that they are not simply a mouthpiece for the industry.

Such autonomous state structures, when combined with highly mobilized associations, are conducive to the emergence of corporatist policy networks for defining and implementing policy. Dairy policy, as it emerged in the early 1970s, has been designed to achieve three objectives:[45]

1 Domestic requirements for milk and dairy products are to be met as far as possible from Canadian sources.
2 There should be price stability and a 'fair' level of return for 'efficient' dairy producers.
3 Canadian consumers should have an assured supply of 'high-quality' dairy products.

Broadly interpreted, these three objectives suggest governments have been concerned to remain self-sufficient in dairy products and to prevent a wholesale depopulation of the countryside. The government seeks to realize these objectives by employing four sets of policy instruments: quality-control regulation, price supports, quotas for supply, and trade measures. We have referred to the first of these in our previous discussion and will now concentrate on the latter three.

The most important set of instruments in the dairy sector involve controls on the supply of milk. The amount of industrial milk to be produced in a given year is decided upon by an organization called the Canadian Milk Supply Management Committee. Typical of corporatist bodies, the committee does not possess a formally defined constitution or operating rules, nor is it a body defined by statute.[46] CDC provides the secretariat for the committee, which is composed of the Dairy Farmers of Canada, provincial milk marketing boards, and representatives of provincial departments of agriculture. NDC sits as an ex officio member with the right to participate in discussion and the dairy-processing associations from Ontario and Quebec attend as observers. After agreeing on a national figure for milk production for a given year, the committee then allocates this amount among the provinces. The provincial marketing boards, in turn, divide this quota among the various producers and allocate supplies to individual processing plants. The entire system is planned and regulated, with heavy fines being the main disciplinary tool.

The process is more formally structured in the case of price and trade policies where the lead is taken by CDC. Prices are controlled by the use of support purchases of butter and skim-milk powder. The support price for these products is defined by CDC based on its estimate of the farmer's 'fair' market return and the assumption that the farmer is 'efficient.' Any volumes of butter or skim-milk powder that are not sold in the market-place are purchased by CDC, stored, and resold at a later date or disposed of in export markets. Based on these support prices, and following tripartite discussions of costs with processors and government officials, provincial marketing boards fix the price of milk sold to processors. In addition to the support prices, CDC administers a subsidy to all dairy producers. This procedure has had the effect of subsidizing the consumption of dairy products because retail prices are lower than they would be if based solely on producers' receipts.[47]

Complementing these price supports are quantitative restrictions on trade in the following products: cheese, casein and caseinates, animal feed containing more than 50 per cent non-fat milk solids, whole-milk powder, skim-milk powder, buttermilk powder, and evaporated and condensed milk.[48] CDC also exports such products as whole-milk powder, evaporated, and condensed milk. These products are sold at world prices, hence well below domestic prices, with dairy producers themselves paying a levy to support this trade.

No free market for dairy products exists in Canada. In its place is a tightly administered system where prices and supply are planning tools used to achieve the objectives noted above. Such a system requires regular and constructive consultation between CDC and the industry. CDC officials are blunt about the significance of industry associations for the operation of the milk supply system: 'The national supply management system wouldn't exist without them, that's it.' In this corporatist arrangement, both partners need one another to help them explain and justify a production and distribution system that does not rely on markets. They are driven to answer questions that simply never arise for officials in other policy networks. A CDC official explained the problem this way: 'You know, for example, what is an efficient producer? What is a fair return? You know ... right now, we use the industrial wage index. A dairy farmer would love to have the wage of postal workers you know. What is a fair return? There are substantial benefits on a farm in terms of roll-over provisions – you can hand down from father to son. All these sorts of things.' Resolving such problems requires systematic use by the commission of its advisory committee, which includes associations representing both farmers and processors. This committee is much more than a symbolic vehicle used to acquaint the state with the problems of producers. It is integral to the management of the policy system according to corporatist principles.

The Canadian dairy policy meets most of the criteria used for defining anticipatory policy. It has a broad range, taking account of price, supply, international trade, and quality; it operates on a five-year planning track; it has involved the extensive rationalization of dairy processing plants and of dairy farms. Policy is well co-ordinated: each agency has a distinct role, thereby keeping bureaucratic conflict to a minimum. Unlike the textiles and clothing case, each of the four sets of policy instruments complements rather than contradicts the other. For a sector threatened with serious decline for the past half-century, the Canadian dairy policy would appear to be a success in terms of industrial adjustment.

Evaluation and Conclusions

This chapter has examined two industries in relatively similar positions; both have required heavy protection in order to avoid serious decline. The analysis reveals that policies for the textiles and clothing sector have been reactive, poorly co-ordinated, and not particularly successful in achieving the declared goals of stabilizing the sector and preparing it for competition. In contrast, dairy policy has been anticipatory in character, has brought economic stability to the industry, and has encouraged more efficient farming and processing. Differences in the policy networks involved in both sectors account for these different outcomes. Other explanations are less convincing.

A first alternative explanation would suggest that the threat to textiles and clothing from low-cost producers is greater than that posed by advanced states to the Canadian dairy industry. Hence the policy problems in textiles and clothing are less tractable. Such an argument is difficult to sustain. The over-supplied, equally efficient, dairy industries in upper New York State and in Wisconsin could seriously damage the Canadian industry. Production in the State of Wisconsin alone already exceeds that in Ontario and Quebec combined. Imports of less perishable products such as butter and cheese have threatened Canadian producers since the 1930s. In short, there is convincing evidence of an international threat to dairy products and it is more than likely that the failure of anticipatory policy would be a prelude to the collapse of the dairy industry.

A second alternative argument might be based on the dairy industry's political salience, particularly in Quebec. Again circumstances suggest otherwise. In Quebec, three times as many voters work in textiles and clothing mills than run dairy farms. The Quebec caucus of the governing party, whether Liberal or Conservative, has acted as a conduit for inside pressure on behalf of both industries. Both sectors tend to have considerable strength in constituencies outside metropolitan centres where discontent can be intensely focused. It is unlikely that MPs will be more sensitive to the votes of dairy farmers than to the more numerous textiles and clothing workers. If anything, the political stakes in the industrial decline of textiles and clothing are higher than in the dairy industry.

More striking in comparing the two sectors are several differences in the policy process itself. First, policy objectives are more clearly specified in dairy: self-sufficiency in dairy products, fair stable returns to farmers, quality products. Objectives have not been well defined in the case of textiles and clothing. Does Canada wish to be self-sufficient? What wages and working conditions are 'fair' to workers? Should Canadian firms be guaranteed a certain proportion of the domestic market? No one really knows. A senior official described the problem that arises from such obscurity. 'If you asked me the question today if we are clear about what the aim of the policy is, I would say ... that the Cabinet never decided in any sense what the target is. What should it be? Should it be 50 per cent of the domestic consumption? Should it be less? Should it be more? Nobody ever decided anything. And when you don't decide about your aims, the real trouble is that you cave into whatever political pressure exists at the moment.'

Second, and related to these differences in the clarity of objectives, are important variations in state arrangements. Although conflict is not totally absent from the dairy policy system, it is confined to issues of minor importance. The allocation of decision-making responsibilities is sufficiently concentrated in the case of each policy instrument that 'bureaucratic turf' battles are infrequent. In the case of textiles and clothing, each policy decision has involved a protracted battle among several agencies. These struggles consume significant amounts of time and political energy. Officials at CIRB claimed to have spent between 50 and 75 per cent of their first nine months negotiating the terms of the agency's relationship with DRIE, Finance, and External Affairs.

Third, industry associations in the dairy sector are better prepared for participation in the policy process. The National Dairy Council of Canada heads a system of associations that has become both more concentrated and more representative over the past two decades. Its strategy has centred on collaboration rather than heavy-handed lobbying and confrontation. Gradually, using this strategy, the association has gained the confidence of the bureaucracy and politicians and with this confidence a role inside the policy-making system itself. Members of the council have played the game well by exercising a certain amount of self-discipline in times of crisis, thereby preserving their insider status. The Canadian Textiles Institute followed a different strategy and sought to maximize political pressures at crucial times by forging alliances with clothing firms and labour. In selected instances, the strategy paid off yielding short-term gains and generous subsidies. By the early 1980s, however, the association appeared to have undermined the confidence of both officials and politicians. It was excluded from the CIRB experiment, and watched as clothing firms improved their access to imported low-cost garments at the expense of domestic textile producers. An attempt at anticipatory policy, without an association designed for policy collaboration, yielded disappointing results.

In drawing this contrast between the dairy and textiles and clothing industries, we are certainly not implying that dairy policy is necessarily in the best interests of the Canadian political community writ large. That is a matter of political debate and many have attacked the policy on efficiency and equity grounds.[49] If the policy has any virtue, it lies in its transparency. It is clear that the policy requires the Canadian public to pay a premium for dairy products. Political decisions have been made and they are open for debate. The policy system for textiles and clothing, in contrast, is shrouded in pious statements and indecision. Millions of dollars are involved and yet it is difficult to debate the merits of these allocations and, therefore, to hold politicians to account. In a country like Canada, where industrial policy is made on a sector-by-sector basis, such obscurity is unfortunate for the economy and for the political system.

Conclusion:
The State and
Policy Options

In reviewing the theory and practice of industrial policy in Canada, two fundamental features of policy outcomes have become evident. First, industrial policy is riddled with inconsistencies; there are very few readily identifiable patterns to policy making. The state can intervene heavily in one sector such as space satellites while assuming a nineteenth-century laissez-faire stance in the contiguous sector of telecommunications equipment. The same state can initiate a process of concertation to assess problems in the manufacture of petrochemicals while simultaneously introducing a wide-ranging program of energy development involving significant intervention into the sector and the promotion of a public corporation. In some cases, the state relies heavily on the co-operation of business, in others its actions invite determined and vociferous business opposition. At first blush, it appears that the only pattern is no pattern.

Second, despite the occasional expression of interest in broadly-based, anticipatory industrial policy, Canada has been unable to drive toward it since the early 1970s. Canada, of course, is not alone in this respect. Obtaining the compliance and co-operation of business for state-led projects aimed at improving productive capacity is bound to be a difficult task in all market societies. And yet, in countries like Japan and France, the state has regularly negotiated with business the introduction of policies designed to shape market structures. On some of these occasions, the state has reorganized industrial sectors and pioneered successful strategic adjustment; on others it has presided over industrial disasters. In either case, the state has shown a taste for heroic intervention that is rarely found in Canada. Even Britain, with its National Economic Development Council and the various spin-off efforts from this venture, has shown greater capability for the marshalling of resources and the co-ordination of industrial effort. Moreover Canada, unlike many of the smaller European democracies, has also been unwilling or unable to arrange for programs of compensation to aid workers and employers in adjusting to the effects of global competition.

In this concluding chapter, we seek to improve our understanding of why Canadian industrial policy is characterized by hesitancy and inconsistency. The chapter begins by reviewing two possible explanations for these patterns that focus on the nature of the Canadian state. The strengths and weaknesses of these perspectives point us toward a third, rather disaggregated, view of the state as a means of understanding the industrial policy process in Canada. In the final section of the chapter, we return to the question of the advisability of industrial policy in light of our assessment of the Canadian state.

State Theory and Industrial Policy

Alan Cairns has described the Canadian state as 'embedded' in Canadian society.[1] In his view, the boundary between state and society is rapidly dissolving as each order deeply penetrates the other. The state has become ubiquitous and activist, with the result that most aspects of daily life have become politicized. According to Cairns, this politicization has been costly. By developing programs and assuming ongoing responsibility for administering past decisions, the state has become tied down to, or embedded in, society. As such, the state has gradually lost much of its autonomy and, with it, the ability to articulate and pursue a distinct set of public goals. This is how Cairns describes the situation:

The relationship between state and society is not one in which an active vanguard state moulds the responsive clay of an inert society willing to be fashioned according to state dictates. Neither is the state a neutral executor mechanically implementing societal choices and choosing among competing demands by some agreed calculus. It has some autonomy, and its lenders have goals for their people, but goals and autonomy operate primarily at the margin, skirmishing around the edges of the existing network of established policies linking state and society.[2]

It is the peculiar feature of this embedding process that it further fragments state and society alike. Cairns writes: 'The result is a fragmented state with a fragmenting impact on society. Social actors are pulled in multiple directions by the scattering of state structures and policies.'[3] These social actors react, in Cairn's view, by abandoning any residual affection they may have for the larger political community and immersing themselves in the politics of self-interest. In so doing, they give organizational expression to societal divisions, force them on the state, and demand an indulgent response. The state, then, becomes a myriad of departments, bureaus, agencies, and crown corporations reproduced across two levels of government and active in all aspects of social relations. It can offer nothing more than a 'species of bureaucratized pluralism that reinforces and reflects societal fragmentation.'[4]

In some respects, the Cairnsian perspective fits well with the one developed in this volume. Cairns has described, and we have documented, a highly diffused and fragmented federal state that is poorly equipped to conduct anything more than reactive industrial policy. As well, we have emphasized that it is Canada's representative institutions, unfortified by a strong state tradition, that have reduced the capacity for a concerted, broadly based approach to industrial policy. And yet the very fact that the Canadian state is disaggregated reminds us that there will always be important exceptions. For Cairns, these exceptions usually take the form of unilateral declarations: 'the *fait accompli* takes its place in the arsenal of democratic statecraft.' Launched from the highest political levels, such unilateral strikes destroy civility and invite retaliation.[5] They are the antithesis of consensus building.

We have discussed state intervention in rather different terms. Concentrating on the meso or sectoral level, we have identified critical differences in business/ state relations and tied these to long-term policy developments. The concept of policy network has been crucial in this regard. It has allowed us to identify departures from the pressure pluralist paradigm and show that these new networks are often accompanied by an integration of public and private objectives. There is no point in denying the unilateralism on which Cairns focuses. Given the rudimentary character of business/state relations at the macro level, it is not surprising that the state will occasionally undertake short-term initiatives that are not justified in broad developmental terms. But there is much more to economic policy making than spasmodic outbursts of state actions that inflame regional and class antagonisms. At the meso level, sustained patterns of business/state relations provide numerous opportunities for the exercise of political influence and the development of policy innovations.[6]

Rianne Mahon offers a second, rather different, image of the Canadian state.[7] Her analysis begins with an assumption borrowed from Poulantzas: in the absence of a crisis, one particular fraction of the capitalist class will gain a determining influence over the direction of the national economy and become the dominant political force.[8] Termed the hegemonic fraction, this group of capitalists achieves this pre-eminent position by securing the consent of other fractions of the capitalist class, and of subordinate classes, to a particular strategy of economic development. But the hegemonic fraction can neither secure consent nor pursue an economic strategy entirely on its own. Rather, the state must become involved as the organizer of hegemony, forging coalitions and lending legitimacy to the preferred economic vision. The state's role is indispensable: its action allows the interests of subordinate classes and other capitalist fractions to be taken into account while the core interests of the hegemonic fraction are realized.

In Mahon's view, the state in Canada, is neither ineffective nor, strictly speaking, fragmented. It pursues a particular strategy, that of the hegemonic fraction, and is hierarchically organized to ensure that this strategy prevails. 'Embedded in the apparatus of the state is a structure that normally permits it to translate particular demands into policy compromises compatible with the maintenance of a particular pattern of hegemonic class domination.'[9] This state structure is 'representative' in that the various organs and branches of the state 'represent' the interests of classes and class fractions present in society. But because of that representation, there are profound bureaucratic inequalities. The unequal distribution of power in society is mirrored in relations among departments and agencies. The pre-eminent departments represent the interests of the hegemonic class fraction; subordinate departments represent other class interests.[10]

In Canada, Mahon writes, the hegemonic fraction of capital is composed of resource or staples firms. This staples fraction has promoted a vision of economic development based on the export of natural resources and the establishment of a liberalized trading environment. It is naturally hostile to anticipatory industrial policy because it could easily strengthen the hand of a competing fraction of capital, namely firms engaged in secondary manufacturing. For this reason, its 'representative' in the state – the Department of Finance – has consistently opposed interventionist industrial policy making. For Mahon, the absence of anticipatory industrial policy and the presence of a patchwork of meliorative policy initiatives simply reflect the dominance of resource-producing firms in the determination of state policy.

Mahon's version of the state is a good deal more orderly than the one provided by Alan Cairns. There are precise and persistent patterns of state activity, rather than a general and diffuse politicization of society. Of course, the order she observes is supplied by the character of class relations. From Mahon's perspective, the state organizes a policy compromise in keeping with the 'correspondence' that apparently exists between state structures and the distribution of power among classes in society. Evidence for this correspondence is rather difficult to adduce however. It is undeniable that particular business interests successfully prevail upon state officials, but it is much harder to believe that an unequal structure of representation pre-ordains their success or that the state's own internal rules and administrative culture are irrelevant. As Margaret Levi observes of their explanations for state behaviour, 'Marxists still suffer from a serious functionalist tendency. The state is understood to be acting in order to save capitalism, and no other explanation seems necessary.'[11]

Disaggregating the State

The perspective on the state developed and employed in this volume shares much with both the Mahon and Cairns versions. In particular, we have stressed that it is impossible to assess state capacity without some consideration of the organization of society. In doing so, we have concentrated heavily on describing institutional arrangements at the sectoral level. We introduced the concept of policy network to draw the institutions of state and society together and account for variation in strategies and outcomes.

There are two advantages to an approach that is institutional in focus and deliberately disaggregative. First, emphasis on institutions provides some scope for systematically accounting for the immense variation in state/society relations. The image of a state embedded in society is attractive conceptually, but it does not indicate how this embeddedness is mediated. In fact, it suggests that there is no mediation because the boundaries of the state are indeterminate. An institutional analysis recovers those boundaries and provides a means whereby they can be described and explored. More generally, an institutional approach reminds us that state structure is relevant not merely because it is reflective of society. The state is more than a mirror. The state possesses legitimacy and exercises authority unlike any other social or political institution. For this reason, it is necessary to appreciate the state's capacity for autonomous action. An institutional approach will always consider state structure itself, in addition to societal arrangements, in fashioning an explanation for the successes and failures of policy.

None the less, it is also clear that our own analysis of structure has drawn extensively upon interviews with state officials and industry representatives. As we noted in the introduction to this book, we hold that a careful analysis of the ideals and values of individuals is crucial to clarifying the nature of institutions. In this respect, we join those theorists who look to the micro level and to the actions of human beings, as well as to the meso and macro levels, when seeking to understand political institutions.[12] The norms, values, beliefs, and rules articulated by our respondents are the product of a transcendent institutional framework. Yet, in the words of Robert Grafstein, 'there cannot be a change in institutions without some change in the associated group of people.'[13]

If the first advantage of our disaggregated approach lies in the importance it accords state structure in its own right, the second pertains to the study of public policy. Because relations between state and society are established at different levels, monistic views of the state are not particularly helpful in the realm of public policy. The capabilities of the state differ from sector to sector and these capabilities, in turn, produce variations in the formulation and implementation of public policy. For this reason, it is necessary to disaggregate levels of the state and to consider separately different structures within each level. In the words of Cawson, Holmes, and Stevens, the state is 'a set of institutions in which individual and collective actors interact within a set of opportunities and constraints afforded by the relationship between the state system and the wider society. It is important to recognize that this relationship obtains at different levels, and the extent to which it is possible to establish and implement coherent policy objectives at one level may be constrained by the type of relationship that obtains at other levels.'[14]

Such a perspective is especially useful in the Canadian case. Canada has a weak state tradition with occasional instances of strong state direction of economic policy. The concept of a state tradition operates at the macro-political level and is based on an assessment of constitutional arrangements and the administrative practices prevalent in state institutions.[15] One of the rules of the game that emerges from these arrangements and practices concerns the legitimacy of state intervention: the willingness of business generally, or particular sections of business, to negotiate terms allowing for intrusive state intervention. We argued in chapter two that business in Canada shares in a firm-centred industry culture that discourages the formation of effective, encompassing interest associations and that reflects a decided unwillingness to tolerate anything more than a minimum of state intervention at the macro level. We showed in chapter three that this firm-centred view also enjoys widespread support within the federal bureaucracy.

Although the general orientation of the Canadian state favours a reactive approach to industrial policy at the macro-political level, the impact of this orientation at the sectoral level varies. The presence of a weak state tradition means that policy making at the meso level is often relatively autonomous from macro orientations. Thus, while the general policy strategy at the meso level remains reactive, particular combinations of state structures, industry organization, interest associations, and experiences of co-operation create the potential for alternative policy strategies. We have argued in part two of this book that these alternatives vary widely along the anticipatory/reactive continuum with decidedly mixed results. A disaggregated view of the state, a view that respects the different levels of policy development and the variation in institutional arrangements within the state system, offers an avenue for explaining the very mixed pattern of industrial policy making in Canada. It is to this pattern of policy making, and the available alternatives, that we turn in closing.

Policy Options: Trade and Industrial Policy

Given the presence of institutional obstacles to industrial policy, trade policy – that is, policy designed to facilitate advantageous international exchange – takes on increased importance. Trade policy is closely connected to industrial policy.[16] Political leaders will normally combine attempts to alter the structure of industrial organization with measures to raise or lower barriers to trade. The critical question is which type of policy, trade or industrial, takes pride of place. If governments stress industrial policy as the primary means to economic growth and stability, then an anticipatory approach is ordinarily employed with trade measures applied on a case-by-case basis at the sectoral level. If, however, a liberal trade policy is emphasized, then industrial policy becomes a supplementary tool, normally reactive in character and often applied primarily at the level of the firm.

For some, the absence of state capacity and the primacy of a liberal trade policy are welcome developments. These observers maintain that state interventions of the type embodied in anticipatory industrial policy will produce nothing other than a system of politically orchestrated subsidies and protection. They argue that countries like Canada would be well advised to employ enlightened trade policy as a surer menas of generating higher per capita incomes. This seems a particularly compelling line of reasoning given the number of tradable-goods sectors in the Canadian economy and the supposedly inefficient industrial structure that lingers in the few sectors still protected by trade barriers. Smaller European countries with economies more open than Canada's have pursued trade liberalization as a prologue to acquiring market niches and engaging in 'flexible adjustment.'[17] Perhaps Canada should be following the same path.

A liberal trade policy has a number of attractive features from a political point of view. Beyond the inevitable problems that accompany the negotiation of trade agreements, the state is not expected to undertake detailed interventions into the economy. Even policies of labour-market adjustment can be resisted on the grounds that the victims of trade policy are no more entitled to compensation than those who fare badly by virtue of tax policy or any other policy with redistributive effects. In addition, it is difficult to identify in advance the winners and losers of trade policy changes, or to estimate the magnitude of their losses or gains. For those opposed to an activist state, part of the charm of trade policy is that it is hard to know what kind of entrepreneuiral activity will be promoted by a liberalization of trading rules.[18]

Although Canadian governments have, on numerous occasions, sought to liberalize trade with the United States, it was not until the Second World War that a concerted effort was made to spread the gospel of freer trade on a multilateral basis. Canada promoted liberalization as part of the Bretton Woods agreement, offered strong support for GATT, and lowered most of its tariffs following the Kennedy and Tokyo Rounds. However, the movement toward further liberalization, embodied in a bilateral free-trade agreement with the United States, constituted a much deeper commitment to the trade-policy instrument. Why did this additional step toward trade liberalization occur in the 1980s? Economically, it would have made more sense to take the step decades earlier, when tariffs were much higher. It seems unlikely that politicians and bureaucrats were drawn to trade policy because they believed that the gains at that moment were too great to be missed or even that a new electoral coalition could be organized around beneficiaries, because it remained unclear just who these would be.[19]

In the face of the economic problems of the 1980s, state officials in Canada were inclined to rely on the trade policy solution because there was no other ideologically palatable choice on offer in the face of increasing United States protectionism.[20] The recent record of industrial policy initiatives in Canada had not inspired much faith in the state as a source of guidance in matters of industrial development. The long-established firm-centred industry culture, the lack of state influence over investment, and the mix of macro-political institutions rendered trade policy the 'logical' option for dealing with difficult economic circumstances. Alternatives to the neo-classical paradigm of economic growth, such as that offered by broad state/society concertation and an anticipatory industrial policy, seemed impossible in Canada.

Yet the obstacles to industrial policy do not relieve the state of the obligation to pursue it. Industrial policy is required in every sector of the Canadian economy, not as a competitor to trade policy, but as an equal partner. The issue is not industrial policy per se, but one of devising policies appropriate to the economic circumstances and the institutional configuration of policy networks in place at the sectoral level.

In some cases, industrial policy will be necessary to cope with market failures and situations in which the by-products of competition, such as entry barriers, work to the disadvantage of firms in small, open economies. This is particularly the case in the volatile technologies where Schumpeterian competition is the norm and states in the world economy engage in a considerable degree of R&D

subsidization. Firms in these sectors may have to contend with higher capital costs arising from capital market imperfections and, in the post-innovation phase, with the problem of scale economies. Moreover, the risks associated with Schumpeterian competition are much higher for small countries than for large ones. The latter are normally able to spread the investment risks across a number of multinational firms located in R&D-intensive industries; the former are typically denied this luxury.

At the same time, the potential benefits of Schumpterian firms are substantial. Richard Harris argues that all governments have an incentive to foster domestic Schumpeterian monopolists because the long-term quasi-rents earned by such firms are likely to be high.[21] But the correction of capital market imperfections, and the attainment of a high level of R&D investment, normally require some form of state intervention. The state can respond in a variety of ways: reorganizing markets through forced mergers, relaxing competition policy, engaging in export subsidies, underwriting R&D, or using public ownership to launch joint ventures. A pre-emptive strike is required in these sectors. The precise strategy will depend on a realistic assessment of the strengths of the firms involved and the capacity of the state and industry to engage in either anticipatory or reactive industrial policy. In any event, a liberal trading environment will be a necessity because both firms and the state will require some means of earning quasi-rents and of spreading R&D costs over a large market.

In sectors in which firms are undergoing rapid transition or retrenchment, industrial policy cannot be based on narrow notions of market failure. Indeed, it is market success that is the problem. Markets are very successful at responding to price signals. As the cost of capital and labour rise in sectors such as knitting, leather, footwear and furniture, the impetus toward disinvestment is strong. Here, industrial policy must slow the process of destruction and facilitate transformation. Once again the precise instruments chosen will depend, above all, on political factors. The response of large countries has been to devise new and ingenious ways of protecting their industries and hence exporting their problems. Some of the small states of Europe have maintained a liberal trade policy and then relied on a country-wide system of domestic compensation fashioned around incomes policies, wage restraint, and a large public sector.[22] Other small states have favoured an increased emphasis on global trading, support for multinational corporations, and private mechanisms of compensation.[23] In either case, compensation is accepted as a sine qua non on both sides of the class divide.

It has become increasingly clear that Canada cannot afford further protectionism yet lacks a commitment to systematic compensation to cope with changes ushered in by liberalized trade. For these reasons, adjustment in the Canadian case will have to take the form of political intervention in industrial sectors. Trade policy may be one of the instruments employed, but emphasizing trade policy alone is tantamount to an abdication of political responsibility. The cold-shower approach to adjustment undervalues the status quo and invites political retaliation. It is not at all surprising that on almost every occasion in which trade liberalization has been suggested as an answer to collapsing markets, the idea has prompted organized resistance. When industrial policy becomes a mere afterthought, the human cost is high.

Canada requires a means of coping with change in a manner that ensures the retention and development of human resources. Either existing industries must be afforded the opportunity to change their product mix, or workers must be retrained and moved to new jobs, or some direct form of compensation, perhaps in the form of cash settlements, must be made to those who cannot readily adjust. Policies like these will require the establishment and targeting of labour-adjustment programs. And because the typical response of firms in these sectors is to engage in a general lowering of output, it may also involve forced mergers and restructuring.

Where change is rapid and outcomes uncertain, the role of the state will necessarily be pronounced. But state intervention will not be confined to these circumstances. As trade negotiations remind us, industrial policy can be thought of quite broadly to include almost any interference in the functioning of markets. Since the nineteenth century, societies, including Canada, have struggled to contain the market and to protect individuals from the worst consequences of the decision to treat land, labour, and capital as commodities.[24] Industrial policy is, in some respects, the latest in a long history of such efforts. It seeks to use the state's capacity for long-range detection to articulate public objectives that reach beyond the goal of an efficient market-place.

An excessive reliance on trade policy to achieve economic growth at the expense of industrial policy is an invitation to exchange our own understanding of what constitutes civilization for a further burst of market energy. If markets were capable of producing social solidarity by drawing buyers and sellers together in long-term affectionate arrangements, a good deal of industrial policy would not be necessary.[25] Unfortunately, the market society that economists celebrate is an ideal type. The real economy is one in which production is rationalized over huge distances and crucial decisions are made in private corporate bureaucracies. This type of market society has the capacity to corrode not only the industrial communities affected by specific changes but also the entire sense of community in society at large. This sense of community is nourished by the exercise of public authority and by a host of institutions that provide a measure of societal integration. The expansion and redeployment of market forces often seriously undermines these social relationships, some of which will have taken decades to build.[26] This process of destruction is inevitable, but if it is not guided in some fashion, obstacles to efficient production, including the social programs around which class compromises are constructed, will be removed in the service of competitive prices.

Industrial policy efforts need to concentrate on harnessing the best features of markets and protecting citizens against the worst. Protection, in this sense, is not simply the protection of profits or wages, but of social relationships and class compromises. Of course, too much protection means greater pressure to preserve the industrial past and less chance of securing an inflation-free future. For countries that cannot transfer their problems to their economic neighbours, the task of managing market forces seems to work best when change is negotiated and participants are assured that the gain and pain of adjustment will not be borne too heavily by one class of workers, by one region, or by one industry.[27] This pattern of bargained change has been pioneered in small European democracies where the capacity to absorb economic change by forging nation-wide bargains has been impressive.

Canada, in contrast, currently lacks the institutional prerequisites for such negotiations. Of course, overcoming these obstacles is far from easy. The Westminster model makes electoral support the critical variable. Not only would a party committed to anticipatory industrial policy require a majority in the House of Commons but probably a significant representative voice in each region of the country. It would need to design a policy that was perceived to benefit all regions or, at a minimum, was regionally neutral.[28] Even with such a policy, and a political mandate, a party may not be free to proceed. It would require, in addition, support in provincial legislatures or at least an absence of concerted opposition. In short, the electoral system reinforces regional divisions while closing off the representation of a broader range of economic and class interests.

As a consequence of these electoral and interest-intermediation systems, bargained change takes place almost exclusively at the sectoral level, where organizational factors occasionally combine to favour a limited form of consensus. Elsewhere, Canada partakes heavily of the Anglo-American solution of company-led adjustment. Business enjoys an unassailable advantage in negotiating the terms of economic change, distributional issues are never explicitly resolved, and there is an ever-present danger that the entire subject of economic adjustment will be overwhelmed by ideological battles of the market-versus-state variety.

The company-led solution, with its stress on trade policy as a panacea, suggests that all the difficult political issues can be avoided by treating economic growth as if it were not a political problem. The evidence for this view diminishes daily. Canada needs to reconsider its political institutions with an eye to elevating to the national political level some of the flexibility and imagination that has occasionally characterized particular industrial sectors. It needs institutions that can provide greater opportunities for participation in the process of industrial change. Some of the practices nourished by the parliamentary and federal character of the Canadian state need to be reconsidered, especially those that give pride of place to territorial divisions. These too often fail to provide adequate representation of the emerging cleavage lines in advanced capitalist systems. Without some attention to these institutions, the Canadian state will not only remain a reluctant and ineffective partner in the process of industrial change, but its actions, when they occur, will lack the legitimacy necessary to assure orderly transition.

General Format of Interviews with Public Officials

1 *Job Description*
   a. Could you give us a description of your own job in this branch?
   b. In terms of the SIC code, exactly what part of the economy are you directly concerned with? What are the programs run by this branch that you are directly involved with?
2 *Bureau's Policy Mandate (Optional)*
   a. Under what legislative or regulatory authority do you do your work? What are the main acts of Parliament that impinge on your activities?
   b. Besides these grants of authority, are there any policy statements that add to the bureau's policy mandate?
3 *Policy Goals, Instruments, and Formation*
   a. Thinking of that part of the industry with which you have been directly involved, what do you believe has been the *overall policy goal* of the federal government?
   b. Does this policy goal represent a recent change of direction or is it a long-standing policy orientation?
   c. Who is responsible for establishing this policy direction? [Probe for role of politicians.]
   d. In what ways has the government tried to achieve this (these) policy goals? What have been the chosen means?
   e. What have been the main *obstacles* to the achievement of this policy goal?
   f. Is the presence of other federal agencies and departments in this policy field an obstacle to the achievement of this policy goal?
   g. Do the policies of provincial governments constitute an obstacle?
   h. Could you describe for us the process by which this (these) policy goal(s) and policy instrument(s) was (were) developed?
      (i) How would you rate the importance of *your own branch* in establishing the present policy direction?

(ii) How important have *senior civil servants* been?

(iii) *Politicians*?

(iv) The *industry* itself?

[Probe here for specific replies.]

4 *Industry Problems*

a. From your perspective as an official, what do you believe are the *main problems* faced by that part of the industry that you are concerned with?

b. Do you think industry representatives would agree with your assessment of the problems?

c. In your view, do these problems exist because of failures in government policy, failure of the industry to act wisely or because of other, external, factors?

d. (Given answers to 'a') Would you consider *foreign ownership* to be a serious problem for the industry? *International competition* for the domestic market? A *lack of rationalization* within the industry? A low rate of *technological innovation*?

(Probe: What are the reasons given for these evaluations?)

5 *Government/Industry Relations*

Transition: We would like to turn now to your relations with the industry and industry spokesmen.

a. How frequently would you say that you are in *contact* with *individual firms* in your industry? What are the types of issues that dominate your discussions?

b. When you deal with individual firms, what position in the firm do your contacts usually have?

c. How frequently would you say you are *in contact* with *interest associations* in your industry? What are the types of *issues* that dominate your discussions?

d. When you deal with associations, would you say that you deal primarily with the permanent staff of the association or with member firms in the industry through a committee of the association?

e. What has been the reception of *individual firms* to the goals and instruments of government policy? What has been the reception of *interest associations*? Have they been cooperative?

f. (i) In your experience, are there any areas in your job where you rely on information provided by industry associations? What associations are you thinking of here? What areas are you speaking of?

(ii) Are there any areas in your job where you rely on information provided by individual firms? What are these areas?

(iii) Could the government itself generate the information you have noted here? Why or why not?

g. Given a choice would you prefer to deal with associations or individual firms? Why?

h. Do you believe that the government could initiate a major policy change without the support of *individual firms*? Without the support of *interest associations*? Are there any firms or associations more important than others here?

i. (i) Thinking of your own industrial sector, how would you rate the capacity

of the government to *resist industry pressure* (whether from associations or individual firms?) Example?
(ii) To *change the behaviour* of existing firms? Example?
(iii) To change the *industrial structure*: number of firms, competition, etc.? Example?

6 *Future Directions*
Transition: We would like to talk a little about the future of the industry?
a. What do you think the ———— industry will look like 20 years from now? What kind of changes can we expect?
b. Will the industry be exporting more in 20 years?
c. Will there be more domestic competition?
(If respondent answers 'Don't Know' to question 'a,' ask)
d. What would you like the industry to look like in 20 years?
e. Will this require a stong effort to:
(i) secure the domestic market for firms operating in Canada?
(ii) develop export markets for Candian products?
(iii) take measures to ensure that Canadian-owned firms are given preferential treatment?
(Ask *all* respondents)
g. How important will the government be in creating this future?

7 *Intervention*
a. In general, what is your attitude toward government intervention in the economy?
b. How effective are *loans, subsidies*, and *tax incentives* in securing objectives?
c. As you know, several countries have adopted a policy of favouring particular *industrial sectors*.
(i) How would you feel if the federal government were to implement the logic of this approach across the entire economy?
(ii) Would it be important to select sectors in which Canadian-owned firms are dominant?
(iii) Do you think your sector would be selected for preferential treatment?
d. Another approach would be to concentrate attention on promising firms in a variety of sectors.
(i) How would you respond to this type of initiative?
(ii) Would it work in your sector?
(iii) How important would it be that the firms selected be Canadian-owned?
e. How would you react if cabinet proposed to establish a *tripartite industrial board* in your sector which would have the power to take binding decisions on the problems you have outlined for us?
f. Can you think of any circumstances in which the introduction of a *public enterprise* in your sector would be warranted?

8 *Close*
In closing, we would like to ask you about other people we should talk to. They may already be on our list, but it would be very helpful if you could identify for

us three or four of the most important people in the development of policy in your sector.

Thinking about industrial policy in general, who, in your opinion, are the three or four public servants in Canada who now exercise the most influence over the direction of industrial policy?

Thank you.

Notes

Introduction

1 James G. March and Johan P. Olsen 'The New Institutionalism: Organizational Factors in Political Life' *American Political Science Review* 78 (1984) 735. For a review of various 'organizational' approaches to the study of public policy, see B. Guy Peters 'Review article: The Structure and Organization of Government: Concepts and Issues' *Journal of Public Policy* 5 no. 1 (1985) 107–20.

2 Peter Hall *Governing the Economy: The Politics of State Intervention in Britain and France* (New York: Oxford University Press 1986) 10

3 James G. March and Johan P. Olsen 'Popular Sovereignty and the Search for Appropriate Institutions' *Journal of Public Policy* 6 no. 4 (1986) 362

4 Ibid. 346–7

5 Stephen D. Krasner 'Sovereignty: An Institutional Perspective' *Comparative Political Studies* 21 no. 1 (1988) 67

6 March and Olsen 'Popular Sovereignty' 349–53

7 Ibid. 362–5 and Hall *Governing the Economy* 277

8 Aaron Wildavsky 'Choosing Preferences by Constructing Institutions: A Cultural Theory of Preference Formation' *American Political Science Review* 81 no. 1 (1987) 5

9 John Zysman *Governments, Markets, and Growth: Financial Systems and the Politics of Industrial Change* (Ithaca, NY: Cornell University Press 1983) 78–9

10 Krasner 'Sovereignty' 74

11 Richard Cyert and James G. March *A Behavioral Theory of the Firm* (Englewood Cliffs, NJ: Prentice-Hall 1963)

12 For a fuller discussion of the need for such comprehensiveness, see Hall *Governing the Economy* chapter 9.

13 The inspiration for the use of the concept of policy network comes from the work of Peter Katzenstein, who originally developed it for the comparison of national political systems. As chapter four indicates, we use this concept

exclusively at the sectoral level. See Katzenstein *Between Power and Plenty: The Foreign Economic Policies of Advanced Industrial States* (Madison: University of Wisconsin Press 1978), especially the conclusion.

14 We draw this term from Paul Whiteley *Political Control of the Macro-Economy: The Political Economy of Public Policy Making* (London: Sage 1986) chapter one.

15 Kenneth Dyson 'The Cultural, Ideological and Structural Context' in Dyson and Stephen Wilks eds *Industrial Crisis: A Comparative Study of the State and Industry* (Oxford: Oxford University Press 1983) 33

16 Ibid. 33ff.

17 Michael Atkinson and Richard Powers 'Inside the Industrial Policy Garbage Can: Selective Subsidies to Business in Canada' *Canadian Public Policy* 13 no. 2 (1987) 208–17

18 This comparative study of the activities and structures of business-interest associations covered nine European countries besides Canada: Austria, Denmark, Federal Republic of Germany, Italy, the Netherlands, Spain, Sweden, Switzerland, and the United Kingdom. Each country had its own research team and research funds. Schmitter and Streeck provided the co-ordination of the research teams and played a central role in defining the theoretical and empirical objectives of the project.

Chapter 1

1 Robert M. Campbell *Grand Illusions: The Politics of the Keynesian Experience in Canada 1945–1975* (Peterborough, ON: Broadview Press 1987) 49

2 Ibid. 35ff. See also Ronald Manzer *Public Policies and Political Development in Canada* (Toronto: University of Toronto Press 1985) 41–2.

3 Campbell *Grand Illusions* 113–14

4 John Williamson *The Open Economy and the World Economy* (New York: Basic Books 1983) 14

5 Raymond Vernon 'The Product Cycle Hypothesis in a New International Environment' *Oxford Bulletin of Economics and Statistics* 41 (November 1979) 261–2

6 Michael J. Piore and Charles F. Sabel, *The Second Industrial Divide* (New York: Basic Books 1984) 173–4

7 Lester Thurow *The Zero-Sum Society: Distribution and the Possibilities for Economic Change* (Harmondsworth, UK: Penguin 1981)

8 Barry Bluestone and Bennett Harrison *The Deindustrialization of America* (New York: Basic Books 1982)

9 In Canada, see William Watson *A Primer on the Economics of Industrial Policy* (Toronto: Ontario Economic Council 1983), and in the United States, Bruce Bartlett 'Trade Policy and the Dangers of Protectionism' in Chalmers Johnson ed. *The Industrial Policy Debate* (San Francisco: Institute for Contemporary Studies 1984) 159–72.

10 Donald Wright ' "The Japanese Model" and the Canadian Debate over Freer Trade' *Queen's Quarterly* 93 (Spring 1986) 107–21

11 For a similar assessment of the United States with predictable conclusions drawn for Canada, see Donald J. Lecraw 'Industrial Policy in the United States: A Survey' in Donald McFetridge ed. *Economics of Industrial Policy and Strategy*, The Collected Research Studies Royal / Royal Commission on the Economic Union and Development Prospects of Canada vol. 5 (Toronto: University of Toronto Press 1986) 1–46.

12 Roy A. Matthews *Structural Change and Industrial Policy: The Redeployment of Canadian Manufacturing, 1960–1980* (Ottawa: Economic Council of Canada 1985) 19

13 See, for example, Patricia Marchak *Green Gold: The Forest Industry in British Columbia* (Vancouver: UBC Press 1983) and Marchak, Neil Guppy, and John McMullan eds *Uncommon Property: The Fish and Fish-Processing Industries in British Columbia* (Toronto: Methuen 1987).

14 Hugh Thorburn *Planning and the Economy: Building Federal-Provincial Consensus* (Toronto: Canadian Institute for Economic Policy 1984) 22–4

15 John N.H. Britton and James M. Gilmour *The Weakest Link: A Technological Perspective on Canadian Industrial Underdevelopment* (Ottawa: Science Council of Canada 1979)

16 Robert M. Laxer ed. *(Canada) Ltd.: The Political Economy of Dependency* (Toronto: McClelland and Stewart 1973)

17 Roy George, *Targeting High-Growth Industry* (Montreal: The Institute for Research on Public Policy 1983) 57

18 Richard Harris *Trade, Industrial Policy and International Competition* The Collected Research Studies / Royal Commission on the Economic Union and Development Prospects for Canada vol. 13 (Toronto: University of Toronto Press 1985) chapter 6, esp. 99–103

19 Monetarists are by no means the only ones who have made this observation. For a radical political-economy perspective, see Claus Offe 'Competitive Party Democracy and the Keynesian Welfare State' in Offe *Contradictions of the Welfare State* (Cambridge: MIT Press 1984) 198–9.

20 Roger Bacon and W. Eltis *Britain's Economic Problem: Too Few Producers* 2nd ed. (London: Macmillan 1978)

21 Paul Whiteley *Political Control of the Macro-economy: The Political Economy of Public Policy-making* (London: Sage 1986) 177

22 John Zysman *Governments, Markets, and Growth* (Ithaca, NY: Cornell University Press 1983) 34

23 Chalmers Johnson *MITI and the Japanese Miracle* (Stanford, CA: Stanford University Press 1982)

24 For an argument that casts the net very widely indeed for these requirements, see David Friedman *The Misunderstood Miracle: Industrial Development and Political Change in Japan* (Ithaca, NY: Cornell University Press 1988).

25 See Charles Lindblom *Politics and Markets* (New York: Basic Books 1977);

David Marsh 'The Politics of Private Investment' in André Blais ed. *Industrial Policy* The Collected Research Studies / Royal Commission on the Economic Union and Development Prospects for Canada vol. 44 (Toronto: University of Toronto Press 1986) 83–117. Marsh makes the important point that it is critical to understand the complexity of the processes through which this structural power is translated into particular political decisions. We return to this point in chapter two.

26 Peter Hall *Governing the Economy: The Politics of State Intervention in Britain and France* (New York: Oxford University Press 1986) 262

27 On the conditions favouring class collaboration in this process, see Adam Przeworski and Michael Wallenstein 'The Structure of Class Conflict in Democratic Societies' *American Political Science Review* 76 (June 1982) 215–38

28 Jeanne Kirk Laux and Maureen Appel Molot *State Enterprise: Public Enterprise in Canada* (Ithaca: Cornell University Press 1988) 126

29 Chalmers Johnson writes: 'Protectionism does not work, industrial policy is the specific antidote for it – the only way to maintain both competitive domestic industries and free trade' (Chalmers Johnson 'Introduction: The Idea of Industrial Policy' in Johnson ed. *The Industrial Policy Debate* 23). But in the same volume another opinion is offered: 'Although it is downplayed by industrial policy advocates, trade protectionism is a major element of their program' (Bartlett 'Trade Policy' 161).

30 See Hall *Governing* chapter 1.

31 We have drawn the names and some of the content of these two approaches from Geoffrey Shepherd and François Duchêne 'Introduction: Industrial Change and Intervention in Western Europe' in G. Shepherd, F. Duchêne, and C. Saunders eds *Europe's Industries* (London: Frances Pinter 1983) 21.

32 R.M. Grant 'Appraising Selective Financial Assistance to Industry: A Review of Institutions and Methodologies in the United Kingdom, Sweden and West Germany' *Journal of Public Policy* 3 (October 1983) 373

33 Michael Trebilcock *The Political Economy of Economic Adjustment* The Collected Research Studies / Royal Commission on the Economic Union and Development Prospects for Canada vol. 8 (Toronto: University of Toronto Press 1986) 33

34 Zysman *Governments, Markets, and Growth* 91ff.

35 Alan Cawson 'Introduction: Varieties of Corporatism' in Cawson ed. *Organized Interests and the State: Studies in Meso-Corporatism* (Beverly Hills, CA: Sage 1985) 16 and Diane Green 'Strategic Management and the State: France' in K. Dyson and S. Wilks *Industrial Crisis: A Comparative Study of the State and Industry* (Oxford: Martin Robertson 1983) 161–92

36 See Cawson 'Introduction' 11 and also *Corporatism and Political Theory* (Oxford: Oxford University Press 1986).

37 Arthur F.P. Wassenberg 'Neo-corporatism and the Quest for Control: The Cuckoo Game' in G. Lehmbruch and P.C. Schmitter eds *Patterns of Corporatist Policy-Making* (London: Sage 1982) 83–108

38 G. Lehmbruch 'Comparative Political Economy of Neo-corporatism: Inter-organizational and Institutional Logics' paper presented to the ECPR Workshop on Meso-corporatism Amsterdam 10–15 April 1987
39 François Duchêne 'Policies for a Wider World' in Duchêne and Geoffrey Shepherd eds *Managing Industrial Change in Western Europe* (London: Frances Pinter 1987) 223
40 Richard J. Samuels *The Business of the Japanese State: Energy Markets in Comparative and Historical Perspective* (Ithaca, NY: Cornell University Press 1987)
41 Michael Bliss 'The Evolution of Industrial Policies in Canada: An Historical Survey' Economic Council of Canada, Discussion Paper no. 218 (Ottawa 1982) 4
42 H.G.J. Aitken 'Defensive Expansionism: The State and Economic Growth in Canada' in W.T. Easterbrook and M.H. Watkins eds *Approaches to Canadian Economic History* (Toronto: McClelland and Stewart 1967) 183–221
43 Glen Williams, *Not for Export: Towards a Political Economy of Canada's Arrested Industrialization* (Toronto: McClelland and Stewart 1983) 40 and passim
44 Michael Bliss, *A Living Profit: Studies in the Social History of Canadian Business, 1883–1911* (Toronto: McClelland and Stewart 1974)
45 These included policies to promote cartelization and permit collusion. See Bliss 'Evolution' 23–6.
46 Richard Pomfret, *The Economic Development of Canada* (Toronto: Methuen 1981) 188
47 K.S. Palda and B. Pazderka *Approaches to International Comparison of R&D Expenditures* (Ottawa: Supply and Services 1982)
48 See Sanford F. Borins with Lee Brown *Investments in Failure: Five Government Corporations That Cost the Canadian Taxpayer Billions* (Toronto: Methuen 1986) and Economic Council of Canada, *Minding the Public's Business* (Ottawa: Supply and Services 1986) 76
49 Richard D. French *How Ottawa Decides: Planning and Industrial Policy Making 1968–1984*, 2nd ed. (Toronto: Lorimer 1984) chapter 6
50 Michael J. Trebilcock *The Political Economy of Economic Adjustment* The Collected Research Studies / Royal Commission on the Economic Union and Development Prospects for Canada vol. 8 (Toronto: University of Toronto Press 1986) chapter one
51 See Laux and Molot *State Capitalism* 140–50. They note that the governments of Quebec and Alberta, for example, have created significant pools of investment capital and sought, albeit indirectly, to use these as instruments of economic development. See also Stephen Brooks 'The State as Financier: A Comparison of the Caisse de dépôt et placement du Québec and Alberta Heritage Savings Trust Fund' *Canadian Public Policy* 13 (September 1987) 318–29.
52 Marsha Chandler and Michael Trebilcock 'Comparative Survey of Industrial Policies in Selected OECD Countries' in Donald G. McFetridge ed *Economics of Industrial Policy and Strategy* The Collected Research Studies / Royal Commission on the Economic Union and Development Prospects for Canada vol. 5 (Toronto: University of Toronto Press 1986) 193–4

53 Energy Options Advisory Committee *Energy and Canadians into the 21st Century: A Report on the Energy Options Process* (Ottawa: Supply and Services 1988)

Chapter 2

1 This definition is adapted from two sources. Kenneth Dyson introduces the concept of industry culture in his essay entitled 'The Cultural, Ideological and Structural Context' in Dyson and Stephen Wilks, eds *Industrial Crisis: A Comparative Study of the State and Industry* (Oxford: Martin Robertson 1983) 26–66. David Friedman makes reference to a similar phenomenon in his very broad definition of 'politics'. See *The Misunderstood Miracle: Industrial Development and Political Change in Japan* (Ithaca, NY: Cornell University Press 1988) 17–19.
2 One of the earliest, and certainly the most important, of these models was offered by Harold A. Innis in a variety of publications including the famous conclusion to his book *The Fur Trade in Canada* rev. ed. (Toronto: University of Toronto Press 1956).
3 Alexander Gerschenkron *Economic Backwardness in Historical Perspective* (Cambridge, MA: Harvard University Press 1962) esp. 5–30 and 353–64
4 See John Zysman *Governments, Markets, and Growth: Financial Systems and the Politics of Industrial Change* (Ithaca, NY: Cornell University Press 1983) chapter six.
5 Simon Kuznets, *Modern Economic Growth: Rate, Structure and Spread* (New Haven, CT: Yale University Press 1966) 106–7
6 Data are calculated from the excellent table provided by Daniel Drache in appendix A of his article 'The Formation and Fragmentation of the Canadian Working Class: 1820–1920' *Studies in Political Economy* no. 15 (Fall 1984) 43–90.
7 G. Laxer 'Foreign Ownership and Myths about Canadian Development' *Canadian Review of Sociology and Anthropology* 22 no. 3 (1985) 329
8 Ibid. 330
9 Pentland sees the labour market evolving on the basis of immigration and surplus workers from the agricultural sector. Yet, his interpretation of how that process actually worked has been strongly questioned by others. See H.C. Pentland *Labour and Capital in Canada, 1650–1860* (Toronto: Lorimer 1981) and Allan Greer 'Wage Labour and the Transition to Capitalism: A Critique of Pentland' *Labour/Le Travail* no. 15 (1985) 7–24.
10 Leo Panitch 'Dependency and Class in Canadian Political Economy' *Studies in Political Economy* no. 6 (Autumn 1981) 14
11 Ibid. 18
12 R.C. McIvor *Canadian Monetary, Banking and Fiscal Development* (Toronto: Macmillan 1958) 55
13 V. Ross, *A History of the Canadian Bank of Commerce* vol. II (Toronto 1920) 129–30 and cited in ibid. 55
14 Ian M. Drummond 'Capital Markets in Australia and Canada 1895–1914: A

Study in Colonial Economic History' unpublished PhD dissertation, Yale University 1959 4

15 Drummond 'Capital Markets' 19

16 E.P. Neufeld *The Financial System of Canada: Its Growth and Development* (New York: St Martin's Press 1972) 482

17 For more information on the German system, see Zysman, *Governments, Markets, and Growth* 261ff.

18 Ian M. Drummond *Progress without Planning: The Economic History of Ontario* (Toronto: University of Toronto Press 1987) 15–16

19 McIvor *Canadian Monetary* 77

20 G. Laxer 'Class, Nationality and the Roots of the Branch Plant Economy' *Studies in Political Economy* no. 21 (Autumn 1986) 43–4

21 Neufeld *The Financial System* 482

22 Drummond 'Capital Markets' 15

23 Ibid. 57

24 In observing the presence of a significant bond market in Canada, Ian Drummond thus rejects the view that there was no real bond market in Canada until after the war (see Drummond 'Capital Markets' 184). The contrary position is expressed in Kenneth Buckley *Capital Formation in Canada, 1896–1930* (Toronto: University of Toronto Press 1955).

25 Drummond 'Capital Markets' 179

26 Neufeld *The Financial System* 494

27 For a discussion, see Glen Williams *Not for Export: Toward a Political Economy of Canada's Arrested Industrialization* (Toronto: McClelland and Stewart 1983).

28 William K. Carroll *Corporate Power and Canadian Capitalism* (Vancouver: University of British Columbia Press 1986) 50

29 Neufeld *The Financial System* 494

30 Zysman *Governments, Markets, and Growth* 70

31 Beginning 30 June 1987, the federal and provincial governments have changed the rules on financial intermediation by, among other things, permitting the banks to create their own securities and merchant banking subsidiaries.

32 H.H. Binhammer, *Money, Banking and the Canadian Financial System*, 4th ed. (Toronto: Methuen 1982) 98ff. Under legislation proposed in the late 1980s, the federal government plans to change this policy by introducing a new category of banks that could be 'closely held' by non-financial firms.

33 Zysman *Governments, Markets, and Growth* 80ff.

34 For a brief discussion of how this is done, see Ronald Manzer *Public Policies and Political Development* (Toronto: University of Toronto Press 1985) 39–40.

35 See David Vogel 'Why Businessmen Distrust Their State' *British Journal of Political Science* 8 no. 1 (1978) 45–78.

36 As we noted in chapter 1, state intervention was always extensive. But when it occurred, in the words of Armstrong and Nelles, it 'was not so much the result of any clearly stated ideological preference on the part of Canadians but rather the complex sum of many separate interactions of technologies in a distinctive

economic and political setting' (Christopher Armstrong and H.V. Nelles *Monopoly's Moment: The Organization and Regulation of Canadian Utilities, 1830–1930* [Toronto: University of Toronto Press 1988] 322).

37 Paul Craven and Tom Traves 'The Class Politics of the National Policy, 1872–1933' *Journal of Canadian Studies* 14 no. 3 (1979) 14

38 Ben Forster *A Conjunction of Interests: Business, Politics, and Tariffs, 1825–1879* (Toronto: University of Toronto Press 1986) 73

39 Ibid. 81

40 Ibid. 115

41 Ibid. 125ff.

42 Michael Bliss *A Living Profit: Studies in the Social History of Canadian Business, 1883–1911* (Toronto: McClelland and Stewart 1974) 96

43 Ibid. 95

44 Craven and Traves 'Class Politics' 15

45 Paul Craven *'An Impartial Umpire': Industrial Relations and the Canadian State 1900–1911* (Toronto: University of Toronto Press 1980) 122ff.

46 See Bliss *Living Profit* 93 and Craven *'Impartial Umpire'* 127–9

47 Craven *'Impartial Umpire'* 174ff.

48 Ibid. 178

49 Ibid. 188

50 Gordon Laxer 'The Social Origins of Canada's Branch Plant Economy, 1837–1914' Unpublished PhD dissertation, University of Toronto 1981

51 Gordon Laxer 'Class, Nationality and the Roots of the Branch Plant Economy' *Studies in Political Economy* no. 21 (1986) 32

52 Laxer 'Social Origins' 388

53 Craven and Traves 'Class Politics' 34

54 See S.D. Clark *The Canadian Manufacturers Association* (Toronto: University of Toronto Press 1939) for elaboration on this point.

55 Bliss *Living Profit* 112

56 The CRA is discussed at length in Tom Traves *The State and Enterprise: Canadian Manufacturers and the Federal Government, 1917–1931* (Toronto: University of Toronto Press 1979).

57 Janine Brodie and Jane Jenson *Crisis, Challenge and Change: Party and Class in Canada* (Toronto: Methuen 1980) 1

58 Ibid. 2

59 See William Stanbury *Business-Government Relations in Canada* (Toronto: Methuen 1986) chapter ten.

60 See Gérard Boismenu *Le Duplessisme* (Montreal: Les Presses de l'Université de Montréal 1981) and 'L'Etat fédératif et l'hétérogenéité de l'espace' in Gérard Boismenu, Gilles Bourque, Roch Denis, Jules Duchastel, Lizette Jalbert, and Daniel Salée *Espace régional et nation: Pour un nouveau débat sur le Québec* (Montreal: Boréal Express 1983); Lizette Jalbert 'Régionalisme et crise de l'Etat' *Sociologie et société* 12 no. 2 (1980) 65–72; and 'La question régionale comme enjeu politique' in Boismenu et al. *Espace régional.*

61 Jalbert 'La question régionale' 98
62 James R. Mallory *Social Credit and the Federal Power in Canada* (Toronto: University of Toronto Press 1954)
63 Reginald Whitaker *The Government Party: Organizing and Financing the Liberal Party of Canada, 1930–58* (Toronto: University of Toronto Press 1977) 49, 62
64 William Stanbury 'The Mother's Milk of Politics: Political Contributions to Federal Parties in Canada' *Canadian Journal of Political Science* 19 no. 4 (1986) 795–821
65 Ibid. 817–18
66 Carroll *Corporate Power* 176
67 Analysis taken from W.D. Coleman *Business and Politics: A Study of Collective Action* (Montreal and Kingston: McGill-Queen's University Press 1988) chapter 5.
68 Carroll *Corporate Power* 160
69 Jorge Niosi 'Continental Nationalism: The Strategy of the Canadian Bourgeoisie' in Robert J. Brym ed. *The Structure of the Canadian Capitalist Class* (Toronto: Garamond Press 1985) 53–65
70 Stephen Clarkson *Canada and the Reagan Challenge: Crisis and Adjustment, 1981–1985* (Toronto: Lorimer 1985) 18
71 These developments are not confined to Canada. For a treatment of the US case, see Jack L. Walker 'The Origins and Maintenance of Interest Groups in America' *American Political Science Review* 77 no. 2 (1983) 390–406 and David Vogel 'The Power of Business in America: A Reappraisal' *British Journal of Political Science* 13 no. 1 (1983) 19–43.

Chapter 3

1 Dietrich Reuschemeyer and Peter B. Evans 'The State and Economic Transformation: Toward an Analysis of the Conditions Underlying Effective Intervention' in P.B. Evans et al. eds *Bringing the State Back In* (New York: Cambridge University Press 1985) 53. As Armstrong has observed of state-directed projects of industrial development in Europe: 'A large measure of organizational unity and homogeneity in socialization among élite administrators has been crucial for development interventionist role definitions' (John A. Armstrong *The European Administrative Elite* [Princeton: Princeton University Press 1973] 305).
2 Nicos Poulantzas *Political Power and Social Classes* (London: New Left Books 1973)
3 'The state is ready-to-wear; it is tailored before class conflicts, as if in anticipation of those conflicts, appearing fully clothed whenever these conflicts threaten the reproduction of capitalist relations' (Adam Przeworski and Michael Wallerstein 'The Structure of Class Conflict in Democratic Societies' *American Political Science Review* 76 [June 1982] 235).
4 The best example is Eric Nordlinger *On the Autonomy of the Democratic State* (Cambridge, MA: Harvard University Press 1983).

5 Ibid. chapter 6
6 See Stephen Krasner *Defending the National Interest: Raw Materials Investments and US Foreign Policy* (Princeton: Princeton University Press 1978) part 1.
7 John Zysman *Governments, Markets, and Growth: Financial Systems and the Politics of Industrial Change* (Ithaca, NY: Cornell University Press 1983) 309
8 See Robert R. Alford and Roger Friedland *Powers of Theory: Capitalism, the State and Democracy* (Cambridge, UK: Cambridge University Press 1985) 209–18
9 Stephen Wilks and Maurice Wright 'Conclusion: Comparing Government-Industry Relations: States, Sectors, and Networks' in Wilks and Wright *Comparative Government-Industry Relations: Western Europe, the Unites States, and Japan* (Oxford: Clarendon Press 1987) 274–313; Ezra N. Sulieman *Private Power and Centralization in France* (Princeton: Princeton University Press 1987)
10 Kenneth Dyson *The State Tradition in Western Europe* (New York: Oxford University Press 1980)
11 Ibid. 232
12 Ibid. 232–3; Armstrong *European Administrative Elite* chapters 8–10
13 Peter Hall 'Policy Innovation and the Structure of the State: The Politics-Administration Nexus in France and Britain' *The Annals of the American Academy of Political and Social Science* no. 466 (March 1983) 47, 57
14 Bertrand Badie and Pierre Birnbaum *The Sociology of the State* (Chicago: University of Chicago Press 1983) 111
15 Ibid. 111–12
16 Keith Thomas 'United Kingdom' in Raymond Grew ed *Crisis of Political Development in Europe and the United States* (Princeton: Princeton University Press 1978) 82
17 Dyson *State Tradition* 36–44; Badie and Birnbaum *Sociology of the State* 121–5
18 J.P. Nettl 'The State as a Conceptual Variable' *World Politics* (July 1968) 580
19 Dyson *State Tradition* 41
20 For an excellent treatment of parliamentary government in Canada that is fundamentally sympathetic to an executive-dominated system, see C.E.S. Franks *The Parliament of Canada* (Toronto: University of Toronto Press 1987).
21 Nevil Johnson *In Search of the Constitution* (Oxford: Pergamon Press 1977) 51
22 The strengths and deficiencies of the adversarial system, especially as it applies to policy making, are discussed at length in Franks *The Parliament of Canada*. On balance, Franks makes a strong case for the adversarial system. Despite its elements of gamesmanship and its tendency to trivialize issues, Franks argues that the virtues of this system, particularly its capacity to make governments behave and to mobilize consent in society, are often underestimated. See ibid. 15, 221, 260.
23 Johnson *In Search* 70
24 Among the many who have documented changes in the organization of cabinet, note Richard French with Richard Van Loon *How Ottawa Decides: Planning and Industrial Policy-Making 1968–1984* 2nd ed. (Toronto: James Lorimer 1984) and

Peter Aucoin 'Organizational Change in the Machinery of Canadian Government: From Rational Management to Brokerage Politics' *Canadian Journal of Political Science* 19 (March 1986) 3–27.

25 See David E. Smith 'The Federal Cabinet in Canadian Politics' in Michael Whittington and Glen Williams, eds *Canadian Politics in the 1980s* 2nd ed. (Toronto: Methuen 1984) 351–70. On the persistence of the idea of regional ministers with politically sensitive tasks, see Herman Bakvis 'Whither Regional Ministers: Regional Politics and Policy in the Mulroney Cabinet, 1984–88' paper presented to the Annual Meeting of the Canadian Political Science Association University of Windsor 1988.

26 Hall 'Policy Innovation' 43–59

27 R.M. Dawson *The Civil Service of Canada* (London: Oxford University Press 1929) 252

28 Taylor Cole *The Canadian Bureaucracy* (Durham, NC: Duke University Press 1949) 277

29 See Colin Campbell *Governments under Stress: Political Executives and Key Bureaucrats in Washington, London, and Ottawa* (Toronto: University of Toronto Press 1983) chapter 12 passim.

30 Michael M. Atkinson and William D. Coleman 'Bureaucrats and Politicians in Canada: An Examination of the Political Administration Model' *Comparative Political Studies* 18 (April 1985) 58–80

31 Zysman *Governments, Markets, and Growth* 311; Chalmers Johnson, *MITI and the Japanese Miracle* (Stanford, CA: Stanford University Press 1982) chapter 1 passim

32 Reuschemeyer and Evans 'State and Economic Transformation' 56

33 Armstrong *European Administrative Elite* chapter 13

34 Theda Skocpol 'Political Responses to Capitalist Crisis: Neo-Marxist Theories of the State and the Case of the New Deal' *Politics and Society* 10 (1980) 175

35 Jonathan Bendor and Terry Moe 'An Adaptive Model of Bureaucratic Politics' *American Political Science Review* 79 (September 1985) 755–74

36 Leon Lindberg 'Energy Policy and the Politics of Economic Development' *Comparative Political Studies* 10 (October 1977) 355–82

37 B. Guy Peters 'The Problem of Bureaucratic Government' *Journal of Politics* 43 (1981) 82; also, Theodore Lowi *The End of Liberalism* 2nd ed. (New York: Norton 1979) 83

38 Zysman *Governments, Markets, and Growth* 311

39 Campbell *Governments under Stress* 77–99

40 French *How Ottawa Decides* 27–35

41 A. Paul Pross 'Parliamentary Influence and the Diffusion of Power' *Canadian Political Science Review* 18 (June 1985) 247

42 For a full discussion of these changes, see G. Bruce Doern 'The Political Administration of Government Reorganization: The Merger of DREE and ITC' *Canadian Public Administration* 30 no. 1 (1987) 34–56.

43 Richard van Loon 'Stop the Music: The Current Policy and Expenditure Manage-

ment System in Ottawa' *Canadian Public Administration* 24 (Summer 1981) 175–99; A.W. Johnson 'Public Policy: Creativity and Bureaucracy' *Canadian Public Administration* 21 (Spring 1978), 1–15

44 Pross 'Parliamentary Influence' 251. For the view that the executive-centred conception is still the most appropriate, see Franks *Parliament of Canada* 257. He notes, however (260), that parliamentary reform intended to strengthen committees could easily accentuate the problem that Pross has identified.

45 The term 'state manager' denotes officials in the following departments: the Economic Programs Division of the Department of Finance, the Ministry of State for Science and Technology, the former Ministry of State for Regional and Economic Development, and the Privy Council Office.

46 A.V. Dicey *Introduction to the Study of the Law of the Constitution* 7th ed. (London: Macmillan 1908)

47 Garth Stevenson *Unfulfilled Union* 2nd rev. ed. (Toronto: Gage 1982)

48 Judith Maxwell and Caroline Pestieau *Economic Realities of Contemporary Confederation* (Montreal: C.D. Howe Research Institute 1980); Alan Cairns 'The Other Crisis of Canadian Federalism' *Canadian Public Administration* 22 no. 2 (1979) 175–95

49 *The Federal Condition in Canada* (Toronto: McGraw-Hill Ryerson 1987) 22

50 Alan Tupper *Public Money in the Private Sector* (Kingston, ON: Institute of Intergovernmental Relations 1982) chapter 3

51 Nettl 'State as a Conceptual Variable' 568

52 Douglas V. Verney 'The ''Reconciliation'' of Parliamentary Supremacy and Federalism' in Verney *Three Civilizations, Two Cultures, One State* (Durham, NC: Duke University Press 1986) 149–71

53 Roger Gibbins 'Federal Societies, Institutions, and Politics' in H. Bakvis and W.M. Chandler eds *Federalism and the Role of the State* (Toronto: University of Toronto Press 1987) 15–31

54 Leo Panitch and Donald Swartz *From Consent to Coercion*, rev. ed. (Toronto: Garamond Press 1988)

55 Michael M. Atkinson and Richard D. Powers 'Inside the Industrial Policy Garbage Can: Selective Subsidies to Business in Canada' *Canadian Public Policy* 13 (June 1987) 208–17

56 Michael Jenkin *The Challenge of Diversity: Industrial Policy in the Canadian Federation* (Hull: Supply and Services Canada 1983) 87–9; Michael M. Atkinson 'On the Prospects for Industrial Policy in Canada' *Canadian Public Administration* 27 (Fall 1984) 454–67; R.A. Young, Phillipe Faucher, and André Blais 'The Concept of Province-Building: A Critique' *Canadian Journal of Political Science* 17 (December 1984) 808–13

57 Canada, Royal Comission on the Economic Union and Development Prospects for Canada *Report* vol. 3 (Ottawa: Supply and Services Canada 1985) 116–20

58 John Whalley 'Induced Distortions of Interprovincial Activity: An Overview of Issues' in M.J. Trebilcock, J.R.S. Prichard, T.J. Courchene, and J. Whalley eds

Federalism and the Economic Union (Toronto: Ontario Economic Council 1983) 161–200; Jenkin *Challenge of Diversity* 95–6

59 Royal Commission *Report*, vol. 3 133–4

60 Tupper *Public Money* 82

61 Franks *The Parliament of Canada* passim

62 Jenkin *Challenge of Diversity* 157–8

63 D.J. Savoie *Regional Economic Development: Canada's Search for Solutions* (Toronto: University of Toronto Press 1986); Peter Aucoin and Herman Bakvis 'Organizational Differentiation and Integration: the Case of Regional Economic Development Policy in Canada' *Canadian Public Administration* 27 (Fall 1984) 348–71; and Atkinson and Powers 'Inside the Industrial Policy Garbage Can' 208–17

64 Peter Leslie *Federal State, National Economy* (Toronto: University of Toronto Press 1987) 178

65 See, for example, D.J. Savoie *Federal-Provincial Collaboration: The Canada-New Brunswick General Development Agreement* (Montreal: McGill-Queen's University Press 1981).

66 On the importance of the link between corporatist institutions and those of party government, see Gerhard Lehmbruch 'Concertation and the Structure of Corporatist Networks' in John H. Goldthorpe ed. *Order and Conflict in Contemporary Capitalism* (Oxford: Clarendon Press 1984) 72–8.

67 For example, the tendency in Canada to resort to interdepartmental committees as an attempt to offer flexible policy responses has been pioneered in statist France where inter-ministerial committees have restored a much needed measure of co-ordination to industrial policy. See Diana Green 'Strategic Management and the State: France' in Kenneth Dyson and Stephen Wilks eds *Industrial Crisis: A Comparative Study of the State and Industry* (Oxford: Martin Robertson 1983) 173–81.

68 I.A. Litvak 'The Ottawa Syndrome: Improving Business/Government Relations' *Business Quarterly* 44 (1979) 25

69 Johnson *MITI* chapter 1. However, some analysts point to France, where they argue that the bureaucracy succeeded in master-minding the collapse of the French electronics industry in the 1960s by employing measures better suited to technologically stable, production-oriented, sectors (See John Zysman *Political Strategies for Industrial Order: State, Market, and Industry in France* [Berkeley: University of California Press 1977] 202).

70 Based on their responses, we created an intervention 'scale' that, although it masks differences in attitudes toward these two instruments, is none the less a useful starting point from which to assess the acceptability of a larger role for the state. Almost all these interviews were tape-recorded and the reliability of the coding procedures was tested by comparing the judgments of two independent coders.

71 M.M. Atkinson and W.D. Coleman 'Is There a Crisis in Business-Government

Relations? *Canadian Journal of Administrative Sciences* 4 (December 1987) 321–40

72 Robert Presthus *Elite Accommodation in Canadian Politics* (Toronto: Macmillan 1973) 21–4

73 Jenkin *Challenge of Diversity* 22

74 Gordon Stewart *The Origins of Canadian Politics: A Comparative Approach* (Vancouver: University of British Columbia Press 1986) chapter 1

75 Tom Traves *The State and Enterprise: Canadian Manfacturers and the Federal Government, 1917–1931* (Toronto: University of Toronto 1979) 158

76 In this respect we have tried to heed the advice of Peter Leslie, who has argued that federalism is best understood when it is treated as embedded in other variables to which it 'bears a reciprocal and evolving relation' (Leslie *Federal State, National Economy* 47).

Chapter 4

1 One of the messages contained in Ezra N. Sulieman *Private Power and Centralization in France* (Princeton: Princeton University Press 1987) is that 'state power or autonomy varies across sectors' and one cannot approach this problem in a formalistic manner without 'the necessary empirical investigations' (303).

2 The classic statement of 'partisan mutual adjustment' is provided in Charles Lindblom *The Intelligence of Democracy* (New York: Free Press 1965). On the relationship between group theory, disjointed incrementalism, and public policy, see J.J. Richardson and A.G. Jordan *Governing under Pressure* (Oxford: Martin Robertson 1979), chapter 1; and, in Canada, A.P. Pross *Group Politics and Public Policy* (Toronto: Oxford University Press 1986).

3 Peter J. Katzenstein *Between Power and Plenty: The Foreign Economic Policies of Advanced Industrial States* (Madison: University of Wisconsin Press 1978) 311

4 Ibid. 316

5 Pross begins to give us some idea of this greater complexity when he introduces the concept of a 'policy community' with its attendent notions of sub-governments and attentive publics (see Pross *Group Politics* 96–107).

6 Michael M. Atkinson 'The Bureaucracy and Industrial Policy' in André Blais ed. *Industrial Policy* The Collected Research Studies / Royal Commission on the Economic Union and Development Prospects for Canada vol. 44 (Hull: Supply and Services 1986) 262

7 Peter Hall 'Policy Innovation and the Structure of the State: The Politics-Administration Nexus in France and Britain' *The Annals of the American Academy of Political and Social Science* no. 466 (March 1983) 46–7

8 Ibid. and Diana Green 'Strategic Management and the State: France' in Kenneth Dyson and Stephen Wilks, eds *Industrial Crisis: A Comparative Study of the State and Industry* (Oxford: Martin Robertson 1983) 161–92

9 John Zysman, *Governments, Markets, and Growth: Financial Systems and the Politics of Industrial Change* (Ithaca, NY: Cornell University Press 1983) 300

10 Hall 'Policy Innovation' 46–7

11 Ezra N. Sulieman 'State Structures and Clientelism: The French State versus the "Notaires" ' *British Journal of Political Science* 17 (1987) 257–79

12 An initial statement of these conditions can be found in M.M. Atkinson and W.D. Coleman 'Corporatism and Industrial Policy' in Alan Cawson ed. *Organized Interests and the State: Studies in Meso-Corporatism* (London: Sage 1985) 30

13 This distinction among types of agencies is made by Theodore Lowi *The End of Liberalism* 2nd ed. (New York: Norton 1979) 79–91

14 Hall 'Policy Innovation' 46–7

15 These attributes are taken, in large part, from William D. Coleman 'Canadian Business and the State' in Keith Banting ed. *The State and Economic Interests* The Collected Research Studies / Royal Commission on the Economic Union and Development Prospects for Canada vol. 32 (Hull: Supply and Services Canada 1986) 261–72.

16 W.D. Coleman 'Analysing the Associative Action of Business: Policy Advocacy and Policy Participation' *Canadian Public Administration* 28 no. 3 (1985) 413–33

17 See J.J. Richardson and A.G. Jordan *Governing under Pressure* (Oxford: Martin Robertson 1979).

18 Graham T. Allison *Essence of Decision: Explaining the Cuban Missile Crisis* (Boston: Little, Brown and Co. 1971) and Kim Richard Nossal 'Allison through the (Ottawa) Looking Glass: Bureaucratic Politics and Foreign Policy in a Parliamentary System' *Canadian Public Administration* 22 (Winter 1979) 610–26. For a specific Canadian application, see M.M. Atkinson and Nossal 'Bureaucratic Politics and the New Fighter Aircraft Decisions' ibid. 24 (Winter 1981) 531–62.

19 Stephen Krasner *Defending the National Interest: Raw Materials Investments and U.S. Foreign Policy* (Princeton: Princeton University Press 1978) 27

20 W. Streeck and P.C. Schmitter eds *Private Interest Government: Beyond Market and State* (London: Sage 1985)

21 Lowi *End of Liberalism* 60. His notion of 'sponsored pluralism' is closely related to the phenomenon we are describing here.

22 Alan Cawson *Corporatism and Political Theory* (Oxford: Basil Blackwell 1986) 38

23 J. Lapalombara *Interest Groups in the Italian System* (Princeton: Princeton University Press 1964)

24 See Atkinson and Coleman 'Corporatism and Industrial Policy' for an example drawn from the dairy industry.

25 Cawson makes a similar point. Because meso-corporatist networks examine a restricted range of issues, 'there is no presumption that meso-corporatist arrangements are tripartite in form, or that the interests they embrace are restricted to capital and labour' (Alan Cawson 'Varieties of Corporatism: The Importance of the Meso-level of Interest Intermediation' in Cawson ed. *Organized Interests* 11).

26 P.C. Schmitter 'Neo-Corporatism and the State' in Wyn Grant ed. *The Political Economy of Corporatism* (London: MacMillan 1985) 32–62

27 For further discussion of this point, see Klaus von Beyme 'Neo-corporatism: A New Nut in an Old Shell?' *International Political Science Review* 4 no. 2 (1983) 173–96

28 See, in particular, P.C. Schmitter 'Modes of Interest Intermediation and Models of Social Change in Western Europe' *Comparative Political Studies* 10 No. 1 (1978) 7–38.

29 See Lehmbruch's discussion of this point in 'Concertation and the Structure of Corporatism Networks' 60–80 in J.H. Goldthrope ed. *Order and Conflict in Contemporary Capitalism* (Oxford: Clarendon 1984) 72–4.

30 B. Marin 'Austria: The Paradigm Case of Liberal Corporatism' in Grant ed. *Corporatism* 89–125

31 Schmitter 'Neo-corporatism and the State' 36

32 Lehmbruch makes a distinction similar to ours between corporatism and concertation. See his article 'Concertation' in Goldthorpe *Order and Conflict* 60–80.

33 See, in particular, Eric Nordlinger *On the Autonomy of the Democratic State* (Cambridge, MA: Harvard University Press 1983).

34 M.A. Chandler 'The State and Industrial Decline: A Survey' in A. Blais ed. *Industrial Policy* The Collected Research Studies / Royal Commission on the Economic Union and Development Prospects for Canada vol. 44 (Toronto: University of Toronto Press 1986) 171–218

35 Yehuda Kotowitz *Positive Industrial Policy: The Implications for R&D* (Toronto: Ontario Economic Council 1986) 34

36 For some discussion of this chosen-firm approach, see John Zysman *Political Strategies for Industrial Order: State, Market, and Industry in France* (Berkeley: University of California Press 1977).

37 Organization for Economic Cooperation and Development (OECD) *The Semi-conductor Industry: Trade Related Issues* (Paris: OECD 1985) 67–9

38 For a discussion of such a policy in British Columbia, see P. Marchak *Green Gold* (Vancouver: University of British Columbia Press 1983).

39 Some controversy exists over whether the Pulp and Paper Modernization Program actually achieved its objectives. The Economic Council of Canada has criticized the program on several counts, one of which being that it subsidized the pulp-and-paper machinery industry (see Economic Council of Canada *Adjustment Policies for Trade-Sensitive Industries* [Ottawa: Minister of Supply and Services 1988] 84–5). The background study for these conclusions is by K.E.A. de Silva 'Pulp and Paper Modernization Grants Program – An Assessment' Discussion Paper no. 350 (Ottawa: Economic Council of Canada 1988).

40 Jon Pierre, 'Industrial Policy and Meso-corporatism: The Policy and Implementation of Terminating Three Shipyards in Sweden' paper presented to the ECPR Joint Sessions Workshop on Meso-corporatism Amsterdam 10–15 April 1987

41 We illustrate such circumstances in chapter 8 in our discussions of the textiles and dairy industries.

42 The observation that industry associations accumulate over time is made most
   forcefully in Mancur Olson *The Rise and Decline of Nations: Economic
   Growth, Stagflation, and Social Rigidities* (New Haven: Yale University Press
   1982).

43 As Ikenberry has pointed out, 'a minimalist state strategy that involves enforcing
   market processes may be as efficacious as the juggernaut of extensive and systematic direct intervention' (G. John Ikenberry 'The Irony of State Strength:
   Comparative Responses to the Oil Shocks in the 1970s' *International Organization* 40 [1986] 137).

44 Pross captures this process well in his discussion of sub-governments in policy
   communities (see *Group Politics* 99–102).

45 P.C. Schmitter and Luca Lanzalaco 'Regions and the Organization of Business
   Interests' Florence 1987 (mimeo) 47

46 Arthur F.P. Wassenberg 'Neo-corporatism and the Quest for Control: The
   Cuckoo Game' in Gerhard Lehmbruch and P.C. Schmitter eds *Patterns of
   Corporatist Policy-Making* (London: Sage 1982) 83–108

47 Stephen Wilks and Maurice Wright 'Conclusion: Comparing Government-Industry Relations: States, Sectors, and Networks' in Wilks and Wright eds *Comparative Government-Industry Relations: Western Europe, the United States, and
   Japan* (Oxford: Clarendon Press 1987) 291–3

Chapter 5

1 Restrictive Trade Practices Commission (RTPC) *Telecommunications in Canada,
   Part 1: Interconnection* (Ottawa: Supply and Services 1981)

2 Organization for Economic Cooperation and Development (OECD) *Telecommunications: Processes and Policies for Change* (Paris: OECD 1983) 20

3 Department of Communications (DOC) *The Supply of Communications Equipment
   in Canada* (Ottawa: DOC 1984) 25

4 RTPC *Telecommunications in Canada* 10; and M. Prentis 'Monopoly, Competition
   and Regulation: Developments in the Canadian Telecommunications Industry' in
   OECD *Microelectronics, Productivity and Employment* (Paris: OECD 1981) 146–7

5 RTPC *Telecommunications in Canada* 10

6 OECD *Telecommunications* 54

7 Ibid. 56

8 OECD *Telecommunications* 57; see also OECD *The Semi-conductor Industry: Trade
   Related Issues* (Paris: OECD 1985) 13–14

9 Ibid. 65

10 For a brief discussion of these changes, see Richard Schultz and Alan Alexandroff *Economic Regulation and the Federal System* The Collected Research Studies / Royal Commission on the Economic Union and Development Prospects for
   Canada vol. 42 (Toronto: University of Toronto Press 1985) 87–8.

11 R. Brian Woodrow and Kenneth B. Woodside 'Policy Instruments and Industrial

Policy in Canada: The Case of the Telecommunications and Informatics Sector in Canada' paper presented to the Annual Meeting of the Canadian Political Science Association Hamilton, ON, June 1987 12

12 Ibid. 5–6. See also Schultz and Alexandroff *Economic Regulation* 95–9.

13 DOC *Supply* 6

14 Department of Regional Industrial Expansion (DRIE) *The Electronics Industry in Canada: An Overview* (Ottawa: DRIE 1986) 9

15 Statistics Canada *Exports* catalogue 65–202, varying years

16 Ibid. 8

17 RTPC *Telecommunications in Canada* 105

18 Peter F. Cowhey 'Trade Talks and the Informatics Sector' *International Journal* 42 no. 1 (1986–7) 123–4

19 Northern Telecom *Annual Report 1985* (Toronto: Northern Telecom 1986) 1

20 DOC *Supply* 37

21 Northern Telecom *Annual Report, 1985* 5

22 Cowhey 'Informatics Sector' 120. Cowhey also notes that the major equipment firms in the United States have argued that the preferential buying arrangement between Northern and Bell Canada allows Northern to subsidize its exports to the United States. This issue was brought up in the free-trade talks in 1986–7 (ibid. 122–3).

23 OECD *Telecommunications* 130. The firm trails, in order, Western Electric, ITT, Siemens (Germany), L.M. Ericsson, and GTE.

24 For further discussion, see I. Litvak *The Canadian Multinationals* (Toronto: Butterworths 1981) and J. Niosi *Canadian Multinationals* (Toronto: Between the Lines 1985).

25 DOC *Supply* 52

26 Theodore Hartz and Irvine Paghis *Spacebound* (Ottawa: Supply and Services 1982) 15–17

27 OECD *The Space Industry* (Paris: OECD 1985) 16

28 Ibid. 14

29 Ibid. 17

30 Ibid. 17

31 Ibid. 38 and DOC *Supply* 82–3

32 John Kirton 'An Uncertain Takeoff: The North American Space Industry in the 1980s' *International Journal* 42 (Winter 1986–7) 162–3

33 Ibid. 167

34 See James Eberle and Helen Wallace *British Space Policy and International Collaboration* Chatham House Papers 42 (London: Routledge & Kegan Paul for the Royal Institute of International Affairs 1988).

35 Hartz and Paghis *Spacebound* 15

36 For elaboration, see G. Bruce Doern and James A.R. Brothers 'Telesat Canada' in Allan Tupper and Doern eds *Public Corporations and Public Policy in Canada* (Montreal: IRPP 1981).

37 Larry Clark 'Industry-Government Co-operation: A Canadian Perspective' in

John Kirton ed. *Canada, the United States, and Space* (Toronto: Canadian Institute of International Affairs 1986) 47

38 Department of Communications *The Canadian Space Program; Five-Year Plan (80/81–84/85)* Discussion Paper (Ottawa: DOC 1980) 17

39 Ibid. 17

40 Ibid. 17

41 Clark 'Industry-Government Co-operation' 49

42 DOC *Annual Report, 1983–84*

43 For further information on this program, see Economic Council of Canada *The Bottom Line: Technology, Trade, and Income Growth* (Ottawa: Supply and Services 1983) 73–4.

44 Kirton 'An Uncertain Takeoff' 164

45 DOC *A Discussion Paper on the Industrial Strategy for the MSAT Ground Segment* (Ottawa: DOC 1985)

46 Cowhey 'Informatics Sector' 120–1

47 Jon S. Cohen, Jeffrey Rubin, and Ronald S. Saunders 'Chasing the Bandwagon: Government Policy for the Electronics Industry' *Canadian Public Policy* 10 (March 1984) 25–34

48 Stephen Cohen and John Zysman *Manufacturing Matters* (New York: Basic Books 1987) 191–2

49 Information on these field trials and on other aspects of the program is available in the following sources: DOC *The Electronic Office in Canada* (Ottawa: DOC 1982); *Trying Out the Future: Office Systems in the Federal Government* (Ottawa: DOC n.d.); and *Annual Report, 1983–84* (Ottawa: DOC 1985).

50 DOC *The Electronic Office*

51 Alex Curran 'The State of Canada's Industry' in Kirton ed. *Canada, the United States, and Space* 43

52 Kirton 'An Uncertain Takeoff' 168

53 J.J. Richardson 'Policy, Politics and the Communications Revolution in Sweden' 9 *West European Politics* (October 1986) 80–97

54 DRIE *The Electronics Industry* 11

55 These include Epitek, Garrett, Linear Technology, Microtel, Mitel, Mosaid, Silonex, and Siltronics (see ibid.).

56 OECD *The Semi-conductor Industry* 13

57 Ibid. 47

58 Ibid. 81ff. See also Cohen and Zysman *Manufacturing Matters* 192–3.

59 Richardson 'Communications Revolution in Sweden'

Chapter 6

1 W. Duncan Reekie *The Economics of the Pharmaceutical Industry* (London: MacMillan 1975) chapter 1

2 A policy review paper tabled by the minister of Consumer and Corporate Affairs in 1983 stated: 'The government is seeking ways to stimulate growth in the Ca-

aceutical industry while maintaining its policy objective of moderat-
' (Canada, Consumer and Corporate Affairs *Compulsory Licensing
ticals: A Review of Section 41 of the Patent Act* [Ottawa: Supply
983] ix).

or Economic Cooperation and Development (OECD) *Pharmaceutical
...uustry: Trade Related Issues* (Paris: OECD 1985) appendix 8

4 Reekie *Pharmaceutical Industry* 45
5 Ibid. 13
6 For more on the success of generic companies, especially in the United States, see the article 'Pharmaceuticals' *The Economist* 7 February 1987.
7 Much of this trade was intra-European, suggesting that a high level of interdependence based on an elaborate division of labour has developed among EC member countries (OECD *Pharmaceutical Industry* 18–19).
8 Canada, Commission of Inquiry on the Pharmaceutical Industry *Report* (Ottawa: Supply and Services 1985) 62. Cited hereafter as Eastman commission.
9 Myron J. Gordon and David J. Fowler 'Performance of the Multinational Drug Industry in Home and Host Countries: A Canadian Case Study' in C.P. Kindleberger and D.B. Audretsch eds *The Multinational Corporation in the 1980s* (Cambridge, MA: MIT Press 1983) 149
10 Eastman commission 422; Douglas Hartle 'Federal Proposals to Restrict Competition in the Canadian Pharmaceutical Industry' *Canadian Public Policy* 10 (March 1984) 82 and Paul K. Gorecki 'Changing Canada's Drug Patent Law: The Minister's Proposals' 78–9
11 Eastman commission 259
12 Yehuda Kotowitz *Positive Industrial Policy: The Implications for R&D* (Toronto: Ontario Economic Council 1985) 26–7
13 Eastman commission, 318, 344
14 There is almost no doubt that compulsory licensing has effected an overall reduction in drug prices. See David J. Fowler and Myron J. Gordon 'The Effect of Public Policy Initiatives on Drug Prices in Canada' *Canadian Public Policy* 10 (March 1984) 64–73.
15 For a discussion of the British case, see Keith MacMillan and Ian Turner 'The Cost-Containment Issue: A Study of Government-Industry Relations in the Pharmaceutical Sectors of the United Kingdom and West Germany' in Stephen Wilks and Maurice Wright eds. *Comparative Government-Industry Relations: Western Europe, the United States, and Japan* (Oxford: Clarendon Press 1987) 117–47.
16 The description contained in this paragraph is taken largely from Eastman commission 372–7, augmented by information gathered during interviews.
17 Ibid. 386
18 Ibid. 387
19 A clientele pluralism network can be found in both the prescription and the proprietary drug industries. We confine our discussion here to the former.
20 Mario Iacobacci *Pressure Groups and the Federal Government: The Case of*

Pharmaceutical Lobbies Regarding Compulsory Licensing, unpublished manuscript Ottawa May 1985 13

21 Thomas L. Ilgen 'Between Europe and America, Ottawa and the Provinces: Regulating Toxic Substances in Canada' *Canadian Public Policy* 11 (September 1985) 578–90

22 Joel Lexchin 'Pharmaceutical Promotion in Canada: Convince Them or Confuse Them' *International Journal of Health Services* 17 (1987) 79. In the case of proprietary or over-the-counter drugs, the state has retained responsibility in part because the relevant association (the Proprietary Association of Canada) is in no position to assume it.

23 On the matter of co-responsibility, see Philippe C. Schmitter 'Reflections on Where the Theory of Neo-corporatism Has Gone and Where the Praxis of Neo-corporatism May Be Going' in G. Lehmbruch and P.C. Schmitter eds *Patterns of Corporatist Policy-Making* (Beverly Hills, CA: Sage 1982).

24 Eastman commission 390–1

25 Opren, an arthritis drug, resulted in several deaths when it was introduced in Britain. The company involved, Eli Lilly, failed to report these results when it was seeking approval for the drug under the name Oraflex in the United States (see Christopher Joyce and Frank Lesser 'Opren Deaths Kept Secret, Admits Lilly' *New Scientist* 29 August 1985 15–16).

26 Yehuta Kotowitz *Issues in Patent Policy with Respect to the Pharmaceutical Industry* Background Study Commission of Inquiry on the Pharmaceutical Industry (Ottawa: Supply and Services 1986) 5

27 Eastman commission 398

28 Kenneth Arrow 'Economic Welfare and the Allocation of Resources for Invention' Universities National Bureau Committee for Economic Research *The Rate and Direction of Inventive Activity* (Princeton: Princeton University Press 1962)

29 Joseph D. Williams 'Investment in Canada as Viewed from the US Boardroom' *Business Quarterly* 50 (Autumn 1985) 77

30 See the remarks of David Bond cited in Joel Lexchin *The Real Pushers: A Critical Analysis of the Canadian Drug Industry* (Vancouver: New Star Books 1984) 98.

31 Paul K. Gorecki and Ida Henderson 'Compulsory Patent Licensing of Drugs in Canada: A Comment on the Debate' *Canadian Public Policy* 4 (Autumn 1981) 565. This line of reasoning is also found in Eastman commission 62.

32 Gordon and Fowler 'Multinational Drug Industry' 155

33 *Federal Government Response* (June 1984) 8–9

34 These three bureaus are the primary actors in this policy area. They are not May 1987. This figure represents a tripling of sales since 1978. See also Paul K. Gorecki *Regulating the Price of Prescription Drugs in Canada: Compulsory Licensing, Product Selection and Government Reimbursement Programmes* Technical Report no. 8 (Ottawa: Economic Council of Canada 1981).

35 Iacobacci *Pressure Groups* 19–51. The categorization is developed in A. Paul

Pross *Group Politics and Public Policy* (Toronto: Oxford University Press 1986) chapter 5.

36 Quoted in Ronald W. Lang *The Politics of Drugs* (Westmead, UK: D.C. Heath 1974) 57

37 Graham Allison *Essence of Decision* (Boston: Little, Brown 1971)

38 Canada, Department of Industry, Trade, and Commerce *A Sector Analysis of the Health Care Products Industry in Canada* (Ottawa: Chemicals Branch ITC 1980)

39 CCA, *Compulsory Licensing of Pharmaceuticals*

40 Iacobacci 'Pressure Groups' 68

41 Ibid. 70–5

42 Eastman commission 362–5

43 Peter Temin *Taking Your Medicine* (Cambridge, MA: Harvard University Press 1982)

Chapter 7

1 See Melissa H. Clark *A Staple State: Canadian Industrial Resources in Cold War* (Toronto: University of Toronto Press 1987).

2 Oliver Bertin 'Meat Packers Face Competitive Hurdles' *The Globe and Mail* 7 January 1985

3 M. Zafiriou 'Changing Meat Consumption Patterns in Canada' *Food Market Commentary* 7 no. 4 (1985) 21–3

4 Organization for Economic Cooperation and Development (OECD) *Petrochemical Industry: Energy Aspects of Structural Change* (Paris: OECD 1985) 15–18

5 Ibid. 72

6 Federal Interdepartmental Task Force on the Canadian Petrochemical Industry *Report and Discussion Paper* edited version (Ottawa: 27 August 1983) 31

7 Petrochemical Industry Task Force *Report* (Ottawa: Department of Regional Industrial Expansion 1984) 10

8 On the impact of this oil shock on industry, see Michael J. Piore and Charles F. Sabel *The Second Industrial Divide* (New York: Basic Books 1984), especially chapter 7.

9 OECD *Petrochemical Industry* 98

10 Some companies get by with little or no R&D. Licensing of technology occurs frequently in the industry and companies can get access to the latest process improvements through licensing agreements.

11 M. Fayad and H. Motamen *The Economics of the Petrochemical Industry* (London: Frances Pinter 1986) 9–11

12 The chemical companies, accordingly, have faced increased competition from the oil majors that they have sought to counter by integrating backward into the petroleum sector, by seeking to conclude long-term contracts directly with oil-producing countries, and by increasing research into alternative feedstocks (ibid. 55ff.).

13 OECD *Petrochemical Industry* 82–3

14 Ibid. 21. Ethylene consumption breaks down as follows: 53 per cent into poly-
ethylenes, 17.7 per cent into ethylene dichloride, which leads to polyvinyl
chloride (PVC), 7.5 per cent into ethylbenzene, which leads to styrene and
polystyrene; 12.4 per cent into ethylene oxide, which leads to ethylene glycol;
and 9.7 per cent into other uses (ibid. 20).

15 For details of the take-over and the resulting size of NOVA, see Deirdre McMurdy
'Chemistry Right in Polysar deal' and Colin Languedoc 'New Nova Ready to
Take on the World' *Financial Post* 26 June 1988.

16 For more details on these changes, see Polysar's Annual Report for 1985 titled
'Changing for the Future.'

17 NOVA expects to construct a third ethylene plant in Alberta if conditions remain
favourable (see NOVA, An Alberta Corporation *Annual Report* 1986 12).

18 Interdepartmental Task Force *Report* 21

19 OECD *Petrochemical Industry* 90–1

20 Fayad and Motamen *The Economics* 65–6

21 D. McClatchy and M. Cluff 'Developments in the Canadian Beef and Cattle
Market during 1984' *Canadian Farm Economics* 20 no. 1 (1986) 19–20

22 W.A. Kerr and S.M. Ulmer 'The Importance of the Livestock and Meat Processing Industries to Western Growth' Discussion Paper no. 255 (Ottawa: Economic
Council of Canada 1984) 12

23 Ibid. 15–16. For a useful discussion of the whole debate and controversy over
rates for transporting grain, see Grace Skogstad *The Politics of Agricultural
Policy-making in Canada* (Toronto: University of Toronto Press 1987) chapter 6.

24 See J.C. Gilson 'Evolution of the Hog Marketing System in Canada' (Ottawa:
Economic Council of Canada 1982) and Larry Martin 'Economic Intervention
and Regulation in the Beef and Pork Sectors' (Ottawa: Economic Council of
Canada 1980).

25 Kerr and Ulmer 'The Importance' 49–50

26 Interview with the president of the SPI 1982

27 See Thomas L. Ilgen 'Between Europe and America, Ottawa and the Provinces:
Regulating Toxic Substances in Canada' *Canadian Public Policy* 11 no. 3 (1985)
586.

28 See W. Streeck and P.C. Schmitter *Private Interest Government: Beyond Market
and State* (London: Sage 1985) for a discussion of this concept.

29 Statistics Canada uses the following classification: inorganic industrial chemicals,
organic industrial chemicals, and plastics and synthetic resins. The organic category includes some petrochemicals but also some non-petroleum-based chemicals. In addition, the industry normally includes plastics resins and synthetic
resins in its definition.

30 Department of Industry, Trade and Commerce *The Canadian Petrochemical
Industry, Sector Profile* (Ottawa: ITC 1978) 6

31 John Richards and Larry Pratt *Prairie Capitalism: Power and Influence in the
New West* (Toronto: McClelland and Stewart 1979) 244

32 Ibid. 245

33 *Federal Government Response* (June 1984) 8–9
34 These three bureaus are the primary actors in this policy area. They are not alone, however. For a more comprehensive discussion of the various bureaus and acts of legislation involved in food regulation, see Lloyd Brown-John 'Comprehensive Regulatory Consultation in Canada's Food Processing Industry' *Canadian Public Administration* 28 no. 1 (1985) 70–98.
35 This problem was noted in the report of the Neilsen task force. Following its suggestion, a co-ordinating committee of deputy ministers from Agriculture, Health and Welfare, Consumer and Corporate Affairs, and Fisheries and Oceans has been formed. It was working, at the time of writing, on devising 'memoranda of understanding' that would define which department was responsible for which task. It was also seeking to make standards in regulations and inspection methods more uniform (letter, Department of Agriculture official, 20 November 1987). Because the same problems existed in the early 1980s (at the time of our interviews) and such efforts were under way then, the problem of co-ordination remains an enduring one.
36 For elaboration on the role of these technical committees, see W.D. Coleman and H.J. Jacek 'The Roles and Activities of Business Interest Associations in Canada' *Canadian Journal of Political Science* 16 no. 2 (1983) 257–280.
37 These density figures are calculated in W. Coleman 'The Political Organization of Business Interests in the Canadian Food Processing Industry' Discussion Paper IIM/LMP 84–6 (Berlin: Wissenschaftszentrum Berlin 1984) 47–9.
38 'Agricultural Export Assistance Programs' Report of the Study Group to the Export Trade Promotion Committee, Working Paper for Discussion between Federal and Provincial Governments on the Development of Canadian Agricultural Exports, October 1980, 30
39 Although this is the view of the OECD and of the industry, it is not necessarily shared by DRIE officials. They argue that the deregulation of natural gas and the elimination of any minimum price on gas exports to the United States will eliminate the feedstock cost advantage that Alberta has enjoyed. Accordingly, with capital costs higher in Alberta than on the US Gulf Coast, and with the Alberta industry landlocked, there is unlikely to be any further expansion in Alberta.
40 OECD *Petrochemical Industry* 121–2

Chapter 8

1 Statistics Canada *Dairy Products Industries*, Catalogue 32–209 (Ottawa: Supply and Services Canada 1986) 10
2 Textiles and Clothing Board (TCB) *Textile and Clothing Inquiry* Report to the Minister of Regional Industrial Expansion (Ottawa: Textile and Clothing Board 1985) 11
3 Canadian Industrial Renewal Board (CIRB) *Final Annual Report, 1984–85* (Montreal: CIRB 1986) 2. This figure includes workers in the footwear industry.

4 Statistics Canada *Dairy Products* 10; Canadian Dairy Commission *Annual Report, 1983–84* (Ottawa: CDC 1985).

5 For a discussion of the evolution of the various textiles arrangements, see Vinod K. Aggarwal *Liberal Protectionism: The International Politics of Organized Textile Trade* (Berkeley: University of California Press 1985) and Ying-Pik Choi, Hwa Soo Chung, and Nicolas Marian *The Multi-fibre Arrangement in Theory and Practice* (London: Frances Pinter 1985).

6 United Nations *General Agreement on Tariffs and Trade* vol. 1 (New York: UN 1947) 22–3

7 Organization for Economic Cooperation and Development (OECD) *Textile and Clothing Industries: Structural Problems and Policies in OECD Countries* (Paris: OECD 1983) 20–1

8 See ibid. 21 for a discussion of why knitting has tended to displace weaving in some instances.

9 Taken from Government of Canada News Release 'New Textile and Clothing Import Policy' no. 137 30 July 1986 11. We do not include the footwear sector, which has its main backward linkages to the leather and tanning industry rather than to primary textiles.

10 Ibid. 84

11 See F. Frobel, J. Heinrichs, and O. Kreye *The New International Division of Labour* (Cambridge: Cambridge University Press 1980).

12 Aggarwal *Liberal Protectionism* 31

13 For a useful discussion of such rationalization, see Rianne Mahon *The Politics of Industrial Restructuring: Canadian Textiles* (Toronto: University of Toronto Press 1984) 114ff.

14 See Textile and Clothing Board *Inquiry* 53.

15 OECD *Textile and Clothing Industries* 25–6

16 Laura C. Johnson with Robert E. Johnson *The Seam Allowance: Industrial Home Sewing in Canada* (Toronto: Women's Educational Press 1982) 104

17 See Mahon *The Politics* chapter three.

18 Textile and Clothing Board *Inquiry* 22

19 Department of Industry, Trade, and Commerce *Sector Profile: Canadian Clothing Industry* (Ottawa: ITC 1978) 12

20 For a brief discussion, see Mahon *The Politics* 99–100.

21 Textile and Clothing Board *Inquiry* 20

22 Canadian primary textiles firms do not fare well in international competition; only Norway among the OECD countries has a poorer export performance (see OECD *Textile and Clothing Industries* 48ff).

23 Textile and Clothing Board *Inquiry* 65

24 Dairy Farmers of Canada (DFC) *Facts and Figures at a Glance* 1982 (Ottawa: DFC 1982) table 9

25 Statistics Canada *Dairy Products Industries* Catalogue 32–209, various years

26 DFC *Facts and Figures* table 35

27 *Food Market Commentary* 'Statistical Appendix' 7 no. 2 (1985) table 9

28 Canadian Dairy Commission *Annual Report* 1983–84
29 Mahon *The Politics* 60 ff.
30 Ibid. 81ff.
31 Interview, TCB official, October 1982
32 Mahon *The Politics* 68–9
33 Ibid. 74
34 Aggarwal *Liberal Protectionism* 34–5
35 CIRB 'Update of the Fourth and Final Annual Report, Cumulative Results November 1 1981 – March 31, 1986' (Montreal: CIRB 1986)
36 See Economic Council of Canada (ECC) *Adjustment Policies for Trade-Sensitive Industries* (Ottawa: Supply and Services Canada 1988) and Jaleel Ahmad 'Trade-Related, Sector-Specific Industrial Adjustment Policies in Canada: An Analysis of Textile, Clothing, and Footwear Industries' Discussion Paper no. 345 (Ottawa: Economic Council of Canada 1988).
37 Ahmad 'Industrial Adjustment Policies' 69–70
38 Ibid. 70
39 ECC *Adjustment Policies* 110–11; Ahmad 'Industrial Adjustment Policies' 71
40 ECC *Adjustment Policies* 95–6
41 OECD *Textile and Clothing Industries* 125
42 For the development of this argument, see Glenn P. Jenkins *Costs and Consequences of the New Protectionism: The Case of Canada's Clothing Sector* (Ottawa: North-South Institute 1980) 13–14; and OECD *Textile and Clothing Industries* 121ff.
43 In this respect, trade policies are analogous to some of the policies for regional development that sought to increase employment in depressed regions but, in fact, subsidized the cost of capital (see Robert S. Woodward 'The Capital Bias of DREE Incentives' *Canadian Journal of Economics* 7 no. 2 (1974) 161–73).
44 There is no provincial marketing board in Newfoundland where dairy production is minimal.
45 D. Peter Stonehouse 'Government Policies for the Canadian Dairy Industry' *Canadian Farm Economics* 14 nos 1–2 (1979) 1–11
46 For a discussion of this property of corporatism, see Bernd Marin 'Austria: The Paradigm Case of Liberal Corporatism' in W. Grant ed. *The Political Economy of Corporatism* (London: MacMillan 1985).
47 OECD *Positive Adjustment Policies in the Dairy Sector* (Paris: OECD 1983) 58
48 Canadian Dairy Commission (CDC) *Annual Report* 1983–84
49 For example, see J.D. Forbes, R.D. Hughes, and T.K. Warley *Economic Intervention and Regulation in Canadian Agriculture* (Ottawa: Economic Council of Canada 1982).

Conclusion

1 Alan Cairns 'The Embedded State: State-Society Relations in Canada' in Keith Banting ed. *State and Society: Canada in Comparative Perspective* The Collected

Research Studies / Royal Commission on the Economic Union and Development Prospects for Canada vol. 31 (Toronto: University of Toronto Press 1986) 53–87

2 Ibid. 58

3 Ibid. 56

4 Ibid. 76

5 Ibid. 81–2

6 Michael M. Atkinson and W.D. Coleman 'Is There a Crisis in Business-Government Relations?' *Canadian Journal of Administrative Sciences* 4 no. 4 (1987) 321–40

7 Rianne Mahon *The Politics of Industrial Restructuring: Canadian Textiles* (Toronto: University of Toronto Press 1984)

8 Ibid. 9

9 Ibid. 38

10 See Mahon 'Canadian Public Policy: The Unequal Structure of Representation' in Leo Panitch ed. *The Canadian State: Political Economy and Political Power* (Toronto: University of Toronto Press 1977) 165–98.

11 Margaret Levi *Of Rule and Revenue* (Berkeley: University of California Press 1988) 192

12 Robert Grafstein, for example, writes that institutions aggregate 'spatio-temporal segments' or 'time-slices' of human beings. 'The pertinent segments would be those extending over the times in which people do whatever is relevant to the particular institution, be it obeying, commanding, or signing a contract' (see 'The Problem of Institutional Constraint' *Journal of Politics* 50 no. 3 [1988] 590).

13 Ibid. 588. This simultaneous interest in individual action and political structure also characterizes the rational-choice approach to institutions (Levi *Of Rule and Revenue* 202–4). This approach, however, is essentially reductionist in character. It begins at the micro level and seeks to build to the macro-institutional level of society. We prefer to give neither level priority and to seek explanations that appreciate the interplay among several levels of analysis.

14 Alan Cawson, Peter Holmes, and Anne Stevens 'The Interaction between Firms and the State in France: The Telecommunications and Consumer Electronics Sectors' in Stephen Wilks and Maurice Wright eds *Comparative Government-Industry Relations: Western Europe, the United States, and Japan* (Oxford: Clarendon Press 1987) 29

15 We follow here the views of Stephen Wilks and Maurice Wright in their concluding essay to ibid. entitled 'Conclusion: Comparing Government-Industry Relations: States, Sectors and Networks,' 274–313.

16 André Blais with Claude Desranleau and Yves Vanier *A Political Sociology of Public Aid to Industry* The Collected Research Studies / Royal Commission on the Economic Union and Development Prospects for Canada vol. 45 (Toronto: University of Toronto Press 1986)

17 Peter J. Katzenstein, *Small States in World Markets: Industrial Policy in Europe* (Ithaca, NY: Cornell University Press 1985)

18 William Niskanen, 'The Hard Choices' in Edward R. Fried et al. eds *Building a Canadian-American Free Trade Area* (Washington, DC: The Brookings Institution 1987) 155–9

19 For a critical consideration of some of these interpretations, see William Watson Canada-US Free Trade: Why Now?' *Canadian Public Policy* 8 (September 1987) 337–49.

20 On this point, see the discussion between Richard Simeon and Duncan Cameron and Daniel Drache: Richard Simeon 'Inside the Macdonald Commission' *Studies in Political Economy* no. 22 (1987) 173–6; Duncan Cameron and Daniel Drache 'Outside the Macdonald Commission: Reply to Richard Simeon' ibid. no. 26 (1988) 173–81.

21 Richard G. Harris, *Trade, Industrial Policy and International Competition* The Collected Research Studies / Royal Commission on the Economic Union and Development Prospects for Canada vol. 13 (Toronto: University of Toronto Press 1985) 102–3, 139

22 Katzenstein, *Small States* 47–57

23 Peter Katzenstein *Corporatism and Change: Austria, Switzerland and the Politics of Industry* (Ithaca, NY: Cornell University Press 1984). The best example of this approach is Switzerland.

24 Karl Polanyi *The Great Transformation* (Boston: Beacon Press 1944)

25 For a useful discussion of the effects of markets, see Albert O. Hirschman 'Rival Interpretations of Market Society: Civilizing, Destructive or Feeble?' *Journal of Economic Literature* 20 no. 4 (1982) 1463–84.

26 See Robert Gilpin *The Political Economy of International Relations* (Princeton: Princeton University Press 1987) chapter one for some elaboration on this point.

27 For further discussion of the advantages and disadvantages of this negotiated approach, see John Zysman *Governments, Markets, and Growth: Financial Systems and the Politics of Industrial Change* (Ithaca, NY: Cornell University Press 1983) chapter six.

28 Peter Leslie *Federal State, National Economy* (Toronto: University of Toronto Press 1987) chapter 9

Index

THE STATE AND ECONOMIC LIFE

Editors: Mel Watkins, University of Toronto; Leo Panitch, York University

This series, begun in 1978, includes original studies in the general area of Canadian political economy and economic history, with particular emphasis on the part played by the government in shaping the economy. Collections of shorter studies, as well as theoretical or internationally comparative works, may also be included.